"*The Drama of Discipleship* is Greg Perry's lon
resource for making disciples committed to go
eryday settings. Drawn from multiple local contexts and from listening
to learned global voices, Greg's work accessibly combines the metaphor
of dramatic performance with a missional hermeneutic and a medley
of image-bearing roles. Bravo! Here are contextually wise and biblically
faithful directions for gospel performances I'm excited to see creatively
staged by innumerable congregations."

—MARK P. RYAN
Director, Francis A. Schaeffer Institute, Covenant Theological Seminary

"Christian discipleship is broken, and this brokenness is global. Fortunate-
ly, Perry has written a timely volume to help the church course correct. *The
Drama of Discipleship* is appropriately titled, because Christian discipleship
is not only grounded in the grand drama of Scripture but is riddled with
suspense . . . The reader will be hospitably treated to in-depth exegesis and
much-needed 'rubber-meets-the-road' application that can be used in the
here and now."

—LUKE BRAD BOBO
Vice President of Networks, Made to Flourish

"*The Drama of Discipleship* explains the narrative of Scripture and invites
us to enter into this story in the company of others in ways that will bless
our communities. Depth of theological insight is conveyed in a simple and
artistic manner that results in a book that is accessible to all. It bridges the
gap from knowledge to application. I highly recommend it."

—IAN SMITH
Principal, Christ College

"Western spirituality often takes an individualistic approach to discipleship, but this book presents a holistic perspective of discipleship with an
emphasis on forming communities who live out the biblical story in all
domains of life. This is a book I want to read with our entire church family,
as I believe the application of this book will allow us to more faithfully love
our neighbors and each other."

—DENNAE PIERRE
Codirector, Crete Collective, City to City
North America, and Surge Network

"Greg has been training our students with this paradigm-shifting content for years. Finally, it is published, so more of the church can be challenged to take up our roles in the biblical story!"

—CHRIS GONZALEZ
President, Missional Training Center

"What a gift! Greg has provided us a biblically rich, theologically informed, humanly hospitable, globally envisioned, hands-on manual for helping everyday followers of Jesus fulfill their daily purpose. Ready-made for use in Bible studies and small groups, I'm eager to utilize this book for our local congregation and when equipping leaders in ministry."

—ZACK ESWINE
Lead Pastor, Riverside Church, Missouri

"We don't get a word-for-word script for life, though we might wish that we did. In this book, Greg helps us understand how the Bible informs who we are and how we can redemptively engage in a constantly changing world in a way that's genuinely profound, yet understandable and practical. I trust that the wisdom and insights in the book will be foundational for the church's ongoing work of making and training disciples of Jesus."

—RYAN BROWN
Pastor of Discipleship, Perimeter Church, Georgia

"Perry has provided a good gift to all who desire to be . . . sustained in the pursuit of God's purposes of shalom in Christ for the flourishing of our world! The conceptual frameworks, practical tools, scriptural engagement, and community-based processes embedded within *The Drama of Discipleship* make it a strategic resource for equipping ministry leaders to equip all of God's people for all of God's mission."

—JEREMY W. MAIN
Director, City Ministry Initiative, Covenant Theological Seminary

"Combining a theologian's insight, pastor's heart, friend's love, and the wisdom of life, Dr. Perry provides a generational work on discipleship. *The Drama of Discipleship* addresses one of the most critical issues facing Christian leaders today—how to teach disciples to *act* as disciples in the roles in which they have been cast. Eschewing the role of critic, Perry opts for the role of director to offer needed guidance."

—**MICHAEL LANGER**

Founder and Executive Director, Faithful Presence

"Practical. Scriptural. Missional. Challenging. Inspirational . . . Communities of Jesus's followers will find guidance here for growth in all areas of our lives. Many thanks to Greg Perry for *The Drama of Discipleship*, a facilitating tool for God's transforming communication with his people—that pointed, divine exhortation which spurs us to serve as kingdom outposts in our local communities."

—**J. NELSON JENNINGS**

Mission Pastor, Consultant, and International
Liaison, Onnuri Church, Seoul

The Drama of Discipleship

The Drama of Discipleship

Gregory R. Perry

Foreword by Michael W. Goheen

CASCADE *Books* · Eugene, Oregon

THE DRAMA OF DISCIPLESHIP

Cascade Books
An Imprint of Wipf and Stock Publishers
199 W. 8th Ave., Suite 3
Eugene, OR 97401

www.wipfandstock.com

PAPERBACK ISBN: 978-1-6667-0415-0
HARDCOVER ISBN: 978-1-6667-0416-7
EBOOK ISBN: 978-1-6667-0417-4

Cataloguing-in-Publication data:

Names: Perry, Gregory R., author. | Goheen, Michael, foreword.

Title: The drama of discipleship / Gregory R. Perry; foreword by Michael Goheen.

Description: Eugene, OR: Cascade Books, 2022 | Includes bibliographical references.

Identifiers: ISBN 978-1-6667-0415-0 (paperback) | ISBN 978-1-6667-0416-7 (hardcover) | ISBN 978-1-6667-0417-4 (ebook)

Subjects: LCSH: Christian life. | Spiritual life—Christianity.

Classification: BV4501.2 P430 2022 (print) | BV4501.2 (ebook)

04/18/22

For Robert and Dixie Perry
Disciples, Parents, and Disciple-Makers

All the ends of the earth shall remember
and turn to the LORD,
and all the families of the nations
shall worship before you.
For kingship belongs to the LORD,
And he rules over the nations . . .

Posterity shall serve him;
it shall be told of the LORD
to the coming generation;
they shall come and proclaim his righteousness
to a people yet unborn that he has done it.

PSALM 22:27–28, 30–31

Contents

List of Figures

Foreword

I met Greg Perry in 2013 in Grand Rapids at a conference I organized on "A Missional Reading of Scripture." Little did I know then that I would come to know and appreciate him as one who shared many of the same passions and common experiences I did, and that this would lead me to invite him to become a faculty colleague at the Missional Training Center in Phoenix. It is precisely those shared convictions that are embodied in this book that make me happy to introduce it to you. I recommend that you take it up, not just to read it, but work through it and learn its practices. For that is the kind of book it is. What were those shared convictions that impressed me then and are now expressed in this book?

First, Greg believes that we must employ a missional and narrative hermeneutic to renarrate our lives. Over the past half-decade, we have watched a church lose its way as its life has been increasingly captured by the idolatrous narrative of our culture. Rigorous discipleship has not been a priority and we are not equipped to withstand the powerful cultural narrative. We need to recover the difficult and intentional task of discipleship that renarrates the lives of God's people with the biblical story. But if the power of God's word is to be unleashed for that purpose, we must read it along its true grain. It tells a story of God's purpose to restore the whole creation with a people at the center of the story. God is working *in* them to form them to be the new humanity but also *through* them as a sign of the new creation for the sake of the world. This book is a fine example of using Scripture in this narrative and missional way to renarrate the lives of God's people.

Second, Greg appreciates the drama metaphor to clarify how Scripture functions. N. T. Wright has introduced the powerful metaphor of drama to understand scriptural authority. It is not just an illuminating metaphor but illustrates in a vivid way how the Bible is to be read today. It is an image that brings alive a sophisticated and nuanced hermeneutic. Greg creatively employs this imagery to good effect, speaking of the biblical story as the script of the play, our local contextual setting as the stage, and the church as the ensemble called to play its role. This book opens up this imagery to imprint a vivid image on our hearts to equip us for faithfulness.

Third, Greg is passionate to see churches live out their missionary identity in their particular neighborhoods. The script of Scripture does not invite us to participate in the drama as solo performers but as an ensemble or troupe. A witnessing community is at the center of the biblical drama. While many existing discipleship curriculums focus on the individual, this book opens up concrete congregational practices of outreach and communal involvement. But it also attends to the stage—the local setting where we play our part. This book is born of a desire to see churches live out their true biblical identity for God's glory and for human flourishing in particular locations.

Fourth, Greg desires to use his scholarship as a tool to nurture the church in its missionary vocation. For many, scholarship is about professional success driven by personal ambition. But for Greg it is a gift God can use to build up the church in its true identity. He is a fine biblical scholar who knows how New Testament authors used the Old Testament to disciple the early Christian congregations. And he is able to follow that pattern to disciple us. But Greg does not simply employ biblical scholarship but systematic, missional, cultural, and practical theology to bring a unique blend of interdisciplinary insights to equip local church and ministry leaders for their missionary vocation. This book is the work of a well-trained scholar who puts that knowledge to practical use for the sake of local churches and ministries who need insight for their complex cultural environments.

Fifth, Greg is committed to practice what he teaches and trains others to do. While teaching in a seminary setting, he remained deeply involved in inner-city ministry as a high priority. And so, he is able to offer a unique blend of careful exegesis (as a scholar) and tried and tested congregational practices (as a practitioner) to guide his readers to connect their worship to their witness. The story of redemption we reenact together on Sunday is meant also to produce a gospel show-and-tell the other six days of the week. And this book helps us to see how. So, what you are about to read is not simply the fruit of scholarly study but of concrete involvement in real ministry, in the worship and witness about which the book speaks.

Sixth, Greg has a global vision for theological education in other parts of the world and is committed to learning from them. He trains leaders in many Southern and Eastern Hemisphere countries, both offering the gifts the Western church have to contribute but more importantly, receiving the gifts the non-Western church can give us. This book is not parochial; it is informed by a scholar-practitioner who has been shaped by the voices of global Christians who are able to critique our Western blind spots and enrich us where our insight is limited. The life of local congregations in many parts of the world inform this study.

I have been involved for almost ten years pioneering a creative way of doing missional theological education that equips men and women to lead missionary congregations in the urban setting of Phoenix. I invited Greg to participate as a faculty member because his missionary vision, scholarly gifts, ministry experience, and global experience is a boon to our leaders. This book can offer you the same gift.

Michael W. Goheen

Acknowledgments

THIS BOOK GREW IN the soil of communities of faith as part of the fieldwork of shared life and mission. So there are far more people to thank than I could fit within the expected length of opening acknowledgements.

The seeds for *The Drama* were sown and watered by my parents, Robert and Dixie Perry, to whom this work is dedicated. They are the ones who first discipled me in the script by their words and deeds. Though their teaching is most formative, God has given me many more teachers, whose influence is evident on every page.

The first ensemble performances of "gospel theater" took place after my ordination with the people of Intown Community Church in Atlanta. They taught me much about ministry and "attempting great things for God." They also helped support a partnership with the Presbyterian Church in Australia over three years.

But, the people of Christ College and Hurstville Presbyterian Church (Sydney) gave far more than they received. Learning with them taught me the importance of giving close attention to both the script and the local stage at a time of dramatic change in Sydney during "the Hong Kong handover," just before they hosted the Olympics.

Master teacher Dr. Richard L. Pratt Jr. challenged me with the opportunity to serve in Sydney and, later, invited me to serve Third Millennium Ministries both as a board member and, now, as part of its leadership team. His visionary leadership and innovative approach to theological education is changing the lives of thousands of leaders in Christ's global church.

As is clear from the foreword by Michael W. Goheen to the footnotes and bibliography, I owe much to those who have taught me to read the Bible missionally and approach discipleship holistically. I want to thank

Mike, along with Chris Gonzales, for giving me the opportunity to serve under their leadership on the faculty of the Missional Training Center. I always look forward to our time together in Phoenix. However, I would not know MTC were it not for my dear friends and former colleagues, Drs. Mike Williams and Mark Ryan of Covenant Seminary.

My readers will notice that many of the ensemble performances described in these pages are set in the neighborhoods of St. Louis. For fourteen years, I had the privilege of teaching and learning with the faculty and students of Covenant Seminary and its City Ministry Initiative. With strong support from the Schaeffer Institute, its Directors, Luke Bobo and Mark Ryan, Directors of Field Education, Drs. Brad Matthews and Jeremy Main, many urban pastors, and the people of New City Fellowship, we sought to "learn Christ" together in the classroom of the city.

My wife, Darlene, wisely encouraged me to recruit an editor, and together we wish to thank Dr. Rebecca Rine for bringing her expertise and professionalism to this work. Dr. Rine's training in rhetoric and religion, and her editorial experience on many projects, has made this book much better. Of course, I remain responsible for what remains in need of improvement on these pages.

I would like to express appreciation for my editors at Cascade Books, Matthew Wimer and Rodney Clapp, for their philosophy of publishing and how it serves both the church and the academy. Thank you for taking a chance on this new writer of books.

My wife, Darlene, has co-labored with me to bring this project to completion. Without her gift of time for writing on too many Saturday mornings, continual interest, encouragement, and practical help with formatting, this project would not be making its appearance at this time. Darlene, I simply cannot imagine walking on the stage of life without you beside me.

Abbreviations

BDB   Francis Brown, S. R. Driver, and Charles A. Briggs. *Hebrew and English Lexicon of the Old Testament.* Peabody: Hendrickson, 1994.

CD   Barth, Karl. *Church Dogmatics.* Edited by G. W. Bromley and T. F. Torrance. Edinburgh: T. & T. Clark, 1956.

ECNT   *Exegetical Commentary of the New Testament.* Edited by Clinton E. Arnold. Grand Rapids: Zondervan, 2011.

JETS   *Journal of the Evangelical Theological Society*

LNTS   *Library of New Testament Studies.* London: Bloomsbury, 2016.

NTS   New Testament Studies. Cambridge: Cambridge University Press, 1967–68.

PBS   Public Broadcasting System.

WBC   *Word Biblical Commentary.* Grand Rapids: Zondervan, 1982, 1990.

What This Book Is About

THE DRAMA OF DISCIPLESHIP is a training resource for followers of Jesus Christ who not only want to study with and pray for each other, but who want to roll up their sleeves to serve their communities together. In corporate worship, we rehearse the lines of the script as we sing the Psalms and reenact the gospel, first in confession and pardon, then with bread and wine. But, beyond the walls of the sanctuary in our public witness, Monday through Saturday, we are called to continue acting "in character" as God's people, dramatizing grace for our extended families, co-workers, and neighbors. But, how? How will we know what to say? And, where will we find the courage to do what needs to be done? Can we find a rhythm or pace we can sustain?

Let's face it: we often know what to do. Most of us have read the script, perhaps even memorized parts of it. The difficulty is in actually doing something as outrageous as loving our enemies (Matt 5:44) or as inconvenient as visiting orphans and widows in their distress (Jas 1:27). According to Jesus and his brother, James, however, these are not "add-on," "if-you-get-around-to-it" kinds of activities. Rather, they are actions that characterize Christ's followers. They are gestures that express the character of the gospel of grace. Jesus says, "Love your enemies and pray for those who persecute you, that you may be sons of your Father in heaven" (Matt 5:44–45). James writes, "Religion that God our Father accepts as pure and faultless is this: to look after orphans and widows in their distress and to keep oneself from being polluted by the world" (Jas 1:27). Of course, we don't become God's family by doing these things, but rather because we have been adopted as God's daughters and sons, we do these things to imitate him as his dear children (cf. John 8:39; Eph 5:1).

1

As the church, the body of Christ, we are being called to and equipped for every good work (cf. Eph 2:8–10; 2 Tim 3:16–17). We are called to be holy (cf. Lev 11:44; 1 Pet 2:15), to do justice (Mic 6:8; Matt 23:23), to love mercy (cf. Hos 6:6; Mic 6:8; Matt 9:13; 23:23), and to speak good news to the poor (cf. Isa 61:1; Luke 4:18). These imperatives of a sanctified, Christian life are made possible by the wondrous indicatives of God's salvation, accomplished by Christ, appropriated and energized by the Holy Spirit. We have been redeemed from darkness for our role as lights in the world (Phil 2:15). Having been rescued from the deforming power of sin, we are being restored as divine image-bearers in Christ's new humanity (Eph 4:20–24). Because we are answering the Holy Spirit's call to follow, we are learning to walk in his steps (cf. Gal 5:16; 1 Pet 2:21), to imitate Christ's ways. But, we cannot do so by mere recitation or mimicry. And we cannot do it alone. Rather, we are growing up in Christ together (Eph 4:7–16), learning to live as responsible citizens in his commonwealth as ambassadors of his kingdom.

How did you learn to ride a bicycle, play the guitar, or cook a meal? Did you learn merely by reading a book or a recipe? I am sure you learned, like me, by imitating others. We did it with the help of parents, older siblings or teachers, who were with us in it, coaching us through it. Moreover, by preparing a meal or practicing for a recital, we also learned to share our gifts and work with others. And, that is how we keep growing up in the one who is the very image of God.

We cultivate healthy, life-sustaining habits when we meet each other at the gym to train for the next race, when we let others see our failures, and when we approach one another with compassion. We grow in particular cultural and relational contexts as we engage our whole selves—head, heart, and hands—in practices that sustain the life, equity, and beauty of our communities. As adult learners, we are more likely to adopt changes in our lives when we see how using new information, habits, and skills not only benefits us, but also blesses the people and places that we love. This study offers a holistic approach to making and becoming disciples that cultivates Christ's ways of thinking, being, and acting together for God's glory and for the common good of a particular place. I call this approach the *Drama of Discipleship.*

Dustin Hoffman says, "As an actor you're trying to get one with the author."[1] Your job is to see the scene not just from your character's point of view, but to discern the author's purpose for the scene, for all the characters

---

1. Book, *Book on Acting*, 504.

in the scene. Once you know your place in the story, the nature of your relationships with these people in this place, you have what you need to act in character. Our role as the body of Christ in the world draws on two vital resources: the intention of the scriptwriter, that is to say, the way the Holy Spirit describes the identity and purposes of the people of God in the text of Scripture; and, the cultural dimensions and interpersonal dynamics of our local stage. Our gospel show-and-tell must respect the tenacious, covenantal bond between the scriptwriter and the stage. God's creative Word formed the world, and God's redemptive Word entered creation, even the constraints of creatureliness, to reclaim and renew it.[2] Good gospel show-and-tell not only requires a thorough knowledge of the story of Scripture and the various dimensions of our local stage, it also appreciates the roles of others who are on the stage of life with us.

Improvising the Script on Every Stage

Like the people of God who are depicted in Scripture, Christian congregations in each generation and every cultural context must imaginatively re-appropriate God's word. It is more like improv than repeating the script line by line, gesture by gesture. One brief, but poignant, example illustrates this interpretive challenge. To honor my father and mother as an adult child looks quite different than the honoring of my childhood. As a boy, I tried to obey their instructions. As a man, I stay in close communication, value their opinions, and, on occasion, seek their advice. Add to this difference in stage of life, differences between ancient Near Eastern traditional cultures and late modern, North American, nontraditional cultures—especially changes in communication technology, food storage and delivery, health care, forms of insurance, etc.—and you can understand why our current, separate living arrangement "honors" their desire for independence today.

Such separate arrangements in the ancient world would not only have dishonored my parents, it would have put them at great risk. But, what does "honor your parents" look like when a Christian is asked to speak at the funeral of a Buddhist friend's mother in Japan; and, how does Jesus, "our Ancestor" relate to the mediating spirits of fathers and mothers in the

2. The script and dramatic performance metaphors as a way to describe biblical interpretation for the Christian life have been suggested by Wright, "How Can the Bible Be Authoritative?"; Bartholomew and Goheen, *Drama of Scripture*; Wells, *Improvisation*; and Vanhoozer, *Drama of Doctrine*, to name only a few.

Akan spirit world of West Africa?[3] The gestures and speech of my honoring, as well as that of my Japanese and Ghanaian brothers and sisters, are articulated differently in each translation of the script's command into the modalities, practices, cultural frameworks, and technologies of each particular, local stage. The episodes that follow display many more examples.

How, then, can we evaluate whether or not our interpretive improvisations are any good? Are we just ad-libbing and shooting from the hip as we apply our lives to the script of Scripture? As any aspiring actor knows, improvisation is more about doing or saying what is obvious for your character in the story and in relation to your ensemble onstage than it is about coming up with something original.[4] Good gospel theater actualizes and develops our character as Christ's social body in ways that are consistent with the script's plotline through the Spirit's particular work in our congregations for local witness among our neighbors. To evaluate whether or not we are, in fact, acting in character as church for the world, we must always ask and answer these two questions simultaneously: 1) "Is our gospel theater faithful to God's script?" and 2) "Is it also fitting for our local stage?"

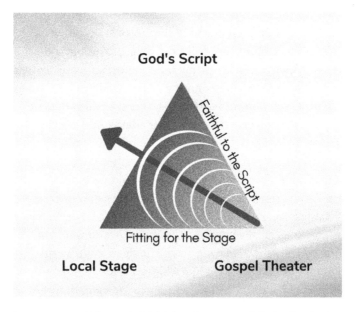

Figure 1—Gospel Theater Is Faithful to the Script and Fitting for the Stage

3. The issue of "honoring ancestors" is explored helpfully in Neely, "Funeral for Noriko-San," 51–65, and Bediako's description of Jesus as "our Ancestor" in *Jesus in African Culture*, 8–20.

4. Wells, *Improvisation*, 67.

As the Apostle Paul has shown, these two questions must be asked and answered together, because the gospel is God's revelation of himself in flesh to particular people in specific cultural locations:

> To those under the law I became like one under the law (though I myself am not under the law), so as to win those under the law. To those not having the law I became like one not having the law (though I am not free from God's law but am under Christ's law), so as to win those not having the law. To the weak I became weak, to win the weak. I have become all things to all people, so that by all possible means I might save some. I do all this for the sake of the gospel, that I may share in its blessings. (1 Cor 9:20b–23).

Paul ministered simultaneously "for the sake of the gospel" and as "all things to all people," mediating the relationship between God's script and God's stage in his interaction with others.

An Ensemble, Not Solo, Performance

Our gestures and speech as local churches play simultaneously *coram Deo* (before the face of God) and *coram mundo* (before the world). Our improvisational witness as Christ's ensembles either strengthens the covenantal bond between God's Word and God's world or strains it. As Kevin Vanhoozer describes,

> The church's fitting contemporary performance[s] . . . are creative extensions of the definitive form of communicative action embodied in the history of Jesus Christ, transposed into a different cultural key . . . We need to discover the cross-modal similarities that enable us to continue the same way, truth and life depicted in Scripture in terms that are fitting for today . . . [It's] all about transposition.[5]

"What would Jesus do?" is always a pertinent question for his followers to ask, but this study emphasizes the value of exploring and practicing answers together in community.

"What would the body of Christ say and do? What social practices display Christ's reign here and now?" Good answers will translate the redemptive drama of Scripture to address the specific opportunities and challenges on the local stage for God's glory and for the common good. This

---

5. These evaluative questions are consistent with the criteria of "canonical sense" and "catholic sensibility" articulated by Vanhoozer, "Drama of Redemption Model."

book, *The Drama of Discipleship*, describes ecclesial gestures, speech, and dispositions of being and making disciples. The real drama of discipleship is a local Christian community's socially embodied response in worship and witness to God's prior actions in Christ "to reconcile to himself all things" (Col 1:20).

The Drama of Discipleship is a lived ecclesiology, performing gospel theater by taking off the old ways of being human and "putting on Christ" (cf. Rom 6:1–11; 13:8–14; Eph 4:17–24) together in every arena of human vocation.[6] Because this "costume change" embodies daily repentance, and because it takes place in the dramatic conflicts of a world caught between the ages, our attempts to act in character as Christ's body form an operational, not an ideal ecclesiology.[7] Still, with the Holy Spirit's energy and breath, our gestures and speech anticipate the kingdom that has come and is coming still.

Group Expectations and How to Use This Book

The Drama of Discipleship is designed as a weekly or biweekly group experience that engages and appropriates the script of Scripture in and through the life of your group on your local stage. Ideally, these gestures for acting in character as Christ's body will be studied and practiced together. Instead of chapters, this book is divided into episodes that introduce your group to the primary roles of image-bearing and the gestures for being and making disciples. You are encouraged to arrive at each gathering having read the episode and studied examples of its corresponding gestures in worship and witness. Give prayerful thought to the Scripture cited. Write down one or two questions, notes, and suggested improvisations. I suggest you set aside sixty to ninety minutes of study to engage the next episode between gatherings.

The Drama of Discipleship is a training resource for being and making disciples of Jesus Christ in the everyday tasks of being human. In each gathering, you will explore patterns of covenantal life from a particular episode of the biblical narrative, along with gestures of worship and witness that

---

6. I first read the phrase "lived theology" in an unpublished paper written by Charles Marsh, "What is a Lived Theology?" See also Marsh, Slade, and Azaransky, eds., *Lived Theology*.

7. Vanhoozer uses the image of "putting on" a costume to describe Paul's metaphor of taking off the old ways of being human and putting on the practices of a renewed humanity (Eph 4:22–24). See Vanhoozer, *Faith Speaking Understanding*, 120–38.

embody them. Each episode will offer at least one group activity that is designed to engage your local stage and build your muscle memory in the gestures of the new humanity (Eph 4:17–32). The book concludes with stage notes and additional tools for those who co-direct these ensemble gospel performances in both worship and witness.[8] The group activities of each episode are bundled together and summarized in a neighborhood survey. The combination of demographic tools and ethnographic interviews in this survey helps a Christian congregation or other ministry build awareness of how our missionary God is orchestrating the drama of discipleship locally, and to assess their own role in that drama.

Christ has called us out onto the local stages of our homes, workplaces, campuses, and neighborhoods to act as his body in the drama of his redemptive mission. This is our moment to do good work that will glorify our Father, when others see it (cf. Matt 5:16; 1 Pet 2:12). No other part of God's family has the same network of relationships that you do. Your troupe of players has a unique set of challenges and opportunities, a unique group of audiences, and therefore a unique witness to Christ. God's worldwide mission is being worked out in every square inch of our lives "to bless all the families of the earth" (Gen 12:3). The Lord is calling us into "the theater of his glory" to act in character as his "peculiar people" (cf. Exod 19:4–6; 1 Pet 2:9–10).[9]

8. Vanhoozer describes the roles of theologians and pastors as providing stage direction for the church's local performance of the gospel. This is not dictation, but "helping people to understand the play and to grow into his or her part." See *Drama of Doctrine*, 246–47, 445–49.

9. Calvin described the created order as "a theater of God's glory." See *Institutes* 1:5:8; 1:14:20; 2:6:1.

Introducing the Drama
of Discipleship

Do you remember the first time a teacher asked you to bring something to class for "show-and-tell"? Some of us were excited; others of us terrified. I remember coming home from school and telling my parents about it. They asked, "What do you have, that others may not have, that you think your classmates might want to learn about?" Honestly, I hadn't been thinking about my classmates. My awareness was self-awareness. My interest was self-interest. But, all education, especially discipleship, is about relationships. More than the relationship between students and teachers, education is about learning to relate to a third thing—an object of study. From our teachers, we acquire new language for how to describe this object in detail. We learn what to feel in relation to it, and how to relate it to others.

I decided to take a lantern, one of a few things I still have from my great-grandparents. I brought it with oil, wick, and globe to share with the class. We had used the lantern at home only during blackouts, so I needed a refresher course on preparing the lantern for use. To transport all the materials with care, I needed my mom's oversight, time, and service as a driver. To draw my classmates into the benefit of my presentation, I needed my Pepa's story and his animating emphases about running to the storm cellar to escape an approaching tornado and finding a lantern ready to use. True learning is crowdfunded with multiple resources, interpretive texts, and perspectives.

What we choose to highlight or overlook in a story is affected not only by where we are, but also by where we have been, who is with us, and where they have been. Most of my classmates were raised in the city like me. Many had never seen, much less touched a real lantern. But, learning how to use it became all the more pertinent to them, when I put them in that scene from *The Wizard of Oz* when "the twister" approaches. Then, I told them my Pepa's story about running to the storm cellar in the rain, wind, and darkness. "When you close the door over a hole in the ground, where there is no electricity, you want a lantern that works," he said. At that time, I asked my teacher to close the blinds and turn out the lights as I lit the lantern. "Seeing" its use in the context of a storm cultivated desire in my classmates to learn more mundane details about the lantern, like what kind of oil to use and how to keep the wick trimmed. All good teachers keep us coming back for more. Jeff, my college pastor and discipler, is a good teacher.

On-Location Bible Study: Dramatizing the Story

For our first on-location Bible study, Jeff took us to a large, lit fountain beside our downtown arena. Shouting over the roar of the water, he read Jesus' words, "If anyone is thirsty, let him come to me and drink. Whoever believes in me, as the Scripture says, 'Out of his heart will flow rivers of living water'" (John 7:37–38). Jeff went on to explain the difference between the stagnant swamps and running streams of Louisiana, where he grew up. Directing our attention to John's commentary on Jesus' words in verse 39, Jeff asked whether our personal relationship with Christ was clogged with mud and algae or flowing with the Spirit's life. That evening, it seemed that the triangle Jeff drew between the clean, abundant flow of water from the fountain, the description of the Holy Spirit in John 7, and our personal disciplines of prayer and Bible reading adequately summarized the meaning of the text.

But, every time we read the Bible, we read on location, from a point of view shaped by cultural traditions, habits of thought, and embodied social practices. Jesus understood this very well. When he chose to enter the temple during the Feast of Booths and began teaching (7:14) about "living water" (7:37) and "light" (8:12), he knew his words would pluck and vibrate the prophetic lines of Isaiah (44:3), Ezekiel (47:1–12), Zechariah (14:8–9), and Joel (2:28; 3:18). Moreover, he anticipated how his metaphors would resonate with the practices of the feast in the temple.[1]

The priestly actions of pouring water and wine beside the altar, and lighting the giant menorah in the court of the women, recalled God's

---

1. See the discussion in Keener, *Gospel of John*, 724–27.

provision for Israel in the wilderness after the exodus, and his promise to return with them to the land after the exile.[2] Remarkably, Jesus claimed the same Holy Spirit who once traveled with Israel in the wilderness now dwelt in him. Moreover, this Spirit would dwell in and among Jesus' followers, even those who live amidst the nations. Jesus' words and actions translated the words of the prophets to his local stage to identify him, and all who believe in him, as the final temple representing God's presence in the world.[3]

Wherever and with whom we read is an on-location Bible study that opens and obscures different aspects of the text.[4] The Bhutanese refugee families of my local church are mentoring their majority-culture sisters and brothers in the emotional texture of Abram's call to "go from your country, your people and your father's household to a land that I will show you" (Gen 12:1). The eagerness of newly arrived Banyamulenge neighbors to find work and an education for their children embodies obedience to Jeremiah's exhortation: "seek the peace and prosperity of the city to which I have carried you into exile" (Jer 29:7). The readings and prayers of Ghanaian seminary students have challenged me to take the evangelists' accounts of Jesus' encounters with demons with deadly seriousness. As Ghanaian scholar Kwame Bediako summarizes,

> The application of Scripture to our cultures is not a matter of applying so-called "principles" from Scripture, on the one hand, to the issues of culture on the other. Rather, it is the process of the coming together, pulling together, of life with life, life touching life. Our cultural particularity and concreteness are brought into a meeting with the activity of God in history, the building up of a community of the people of God throughout history which now includes us and our particular tradition, history, [and] culture.[5]

Of course, not every Christian will have opportunity to read Scripture with their African or Asian kin, but the mission of Israel's God to the nations, and the migratory realities on our contemporary, world stage require interpreting with "others," if we are to align ourselves with Scripture's pattern of reconciliation between males and females, slaves and free people, Jews and Gentiles (cf. Gal 3:27–28; Col 3:9–11).

---

2. Keener, *Gospel of John*, 724–27. See also Perrin, *Jesus the Temple*, 54.

3. See also Beale, *Temple and the Church's Mission*, 197–98.

4. I owe this observation to Pratt, *He Gave Us Stories*, 383–402.

5. Bediako, "Scripture as the Hermeneutic of Culture and Tradition."

A Festival of Nations

In St. Louis's beautiful Tower Grove Park, a Festival of Nations is held annually on the last weekend in August. Over forty different ethnic foods are offered in booths alongside a bazaar of handcrafted clothing, jewelry, and accessories. Several sound stages come alive with traditional dances and music. Lessons are available for those who want to learn the gestures and instruments of their immigrant neighbors. Learning the ways of Jesus and his followers is like engaging a festival of nations, acquiring new cultural perspectives, even adopting different practices in order to deepen our new family relationships.

Not too long ago, no one used smartphones, understood the shorthand of texting (i.e., LOL, BTW, etc.), or used videoconferencing tools. Now, however, even late adopters from the boomer and builder generations are using the language and daily habits of these new technologies to stay in touch with their children and grandchildren. In order to keep communicating with and understanding each other well, we must adapt our intellectual and bodily habits.

That night in Baton Rouge, our on-location Bible study produced only a tangential connection between Jesus' metaphor and the fountain before us, because we mapped John's Gospel on to our group's relatively privileged and largely interior experience of faith. But what if we were to reverse the direction of application, and align our personal and cultural scripts with Jesus' performance of Israel's script? More than mere metaphor for the Spirit's refreshment of late modern Christians through personal Bible reading and prayer, Jesus' dramatic fulfillment of the Feast of Booths signaled God's presence, rule, and provision, despite the presence in his day of an occupying army and corrupt temple leadership. That night around the fountain in Baton Rouge, the flow of water was signifying that Christ's kingdom had extended far beyond Jerusalem into our potpourri of late modern, North American cultures. To bear witness to God's presence and rule amidst the nations, we not only need to read and pray privately as individual Christians, we must also read and dramatize Scripture together publicly as congregations of Christians who are animated with God's Spirit.

Two Kinds of Performance: Worship & Witness

N. T. Wright is one of the first theologians to suggest how the Bible authorizes the church for its improvisational role in the narrative of God's mission.[6] He describes the authority of Scripture in the life of the church as similar to that of improvisational performances of an unfinished Shakespearean play by local Shakespearean drama troupes. Though the script of Scripture records the theodrama of redemption from its beginning through the climactic, long-awaited entrance of Christ on to the world stage, there is a gap in the record.[7] Sandwiched in between the script's record of Christ's earthly ministry and its foreshadowing of his return to the world stage, local churches function like those local troupes of trained Shakespearean actors that Bishop Wright describes. Scattered throughout the cities and towns, cultures and countries of the world, these troupes bear witness to Christ's kingdom, providing Spirit-guided, Spirit-gifted, but far from perfect, improvisational performances of the Spirit's script.

Indeed, the script of Scripture depicts the covenant community in two types of performances that are necessary for maintaining its integrity and developing its vocation as divine image-bearers: 1) Worship—wherein the congregation gathers to rehearse the story of its redemption, and 2) Witness—wherein the congregation and its members enact living parables about God's reign in their homes, workplaces, schools, council meetings, etc. On the one hand, the worship of Israel remembered the exodus as prescribed in the liturgy of the Festival of Firstfruits:

> My father was a wandering Aramean. He went down into Egypt and sojourned there, few in number, and there he became a nation, great, mighty and populous. And, the Egyptians treated us harshly and humiliated us and laid on us hard labor. Then, we cried out to the LORD, the God of our fathers, and the LORD heard our voice and saw our affliction, our toil and our oppression. And the LORD brought us out of Egypt with a mighty hand

---

6. Wright was the first to suggest the metaphor of Scripture as a partial script providing the church with four of five acts in the biblical drama, wherein the church must improvise the final act in ways that are consistent with the previous acts and which culminate with its revealed conclusion. See Wright, "How Can the Bible Be Authoritative?"

7. Hans Urs von Balthasar, one of the most important Catholic theologians of the twentieth century, coined the term *theodrama* in his five-volume work, *Theodrama*. The third and central volume, "Dramatis Personae: Persons in Christ," articulates his views on the Christian life. Vanhoozer, a Reformed Protestant theologian, picks up and develops von Balthasar's metaphor in *Drama of Doctrine*, 37–56; 399–457.

and an outstretched arm, with great deeds of terror, with signs and wonders. (Deut 26:5–8)

On the other hand, the witness of Israel to its neighbors and visitors also drew attention to the character of God and to their identity as a redeemed people by providing protection and resources for those who were particularly vulnerable in their midst:

> When a stranger sojourns with you in your land, you shall not do him wrong. You shall treat the stranger who sojourns with you as the native among you, and you shall love him as you love yourself, for you were strangers in the land of Egypt: I am the LORD your God. (Lev 19:33–34)

The offering of firstfruits in worship not only resourced the priests and Levites who served God and Israel, it also supported "the sojourner, the fatherless and the widow" (Deut 26:12–13), bearing witness to Israel's God and the character of his reign. The prophet Isaiah's question underscores this vital connection between worship and witness in the covenant community: "Is not this the true fast [the true worship] that I choose: to loose the bonds of wickedness . . . to let the oppressed go free, and to break every yoke? Is it not to share your bread with the hungry?" (Isa 58:6–7).

Translating Performances of the Script to Local Stages

While N. T. Wright's metaphor of an unfinished play helpfully explains biblical authority in terms of ecclesial performances that are faithful to the script, it does not address the need to translate those performances into the cultural categories of the neighborhoods, towns, and cities where churches are located. Every summer in St. Louis, the Shakespeare Festival stages one of the Bard's plays in Forest Park. Young children complain because they cannot understand Elizabethan English. For most of these performances, actors are in period costumes. Their focus is on being true to the script, true to Shakespeare. Year after year as they return, St. Louisans learn the cadence of iambic pentameter that communicates the genius of Shakespeare and his insight into human nature. In autumn, however, the festival stages a different kind of performance.

Throughout most of the year, the playwright-in-residence and her staff research the stories of a particular St. Louis neighborhood, interviewing its citizens. Based on what they learn about life together in that slice of "the

Lou," the playwright interweaves local story lines with a Shakespearean plot to craft a translated, localized script. Not only do neighbors recognize their own voices and experiences in the dialogue, some of them take part in the drama, staged at an iconic, outdoor venue in the neighborhood. They call it "Shakespeare in the Streets."

These performances draw very different responses from kids in the audience than those staged in Forest Park. Having seen their friends, teachers, and a mirror image of themselves onstage they ask, "What is the story behind our story?" They start to realize their local, particular performances express transcultural, transgenerational character traits in Shakespeare's wider canon about what it means to be human.

In like manner, the script of Scripture calls local Christian troupes to stage two types of gospel theater—the more traditional rehearsal of iambic pentameter in the liturgy of the sanctuary, and the more improvisational drama of bearing witness to Christ and his kingdom on the streets. Liturgy is not separate from life, rather it is that part of life that pulls the rest of life into proper orbit.[8] Our calling to be Christlike is our calling to be human, to be image-bearers of the divine.

Gestures of Worship and Witness in the Drama of Discipleship

Worship provides coherence and integrity for our life together in relation to Christ's kingdom and restorative mission. Our gestures in the drama of discipleship have both a worship edge and a witness edge, forging liturgy and life together, reinforcing the bond between God's word and God's world. Each gesture of worship and witness echoes and appropriates an episode of the biblical script. In the course of this study, you and your group will learn six gestures that characterize Christ's body in the world. Each gesture is cultivated, not merely as a practice of individual Christians, but also as a habit of God's people acting together in a local, ensemble performance of the Gospel.

8. See Hauerwas, *Performing the Faith*, 163.

GOSPEL SHOW-AND-TELL

Worship Gesture	Biblical Episode	Witness Gesture
Praise/Thanksgiving	1. Creation	Accepting the Gifts
Confession/Lament	2. Rebellion	Naming the Broken Places
Benediction & Commission	3. Israel	Using Status to Bless
Gospel Proclamation in Word & Sacrament	4. Jesus	Redirecting the Gifts
Offer/Exercise Gifts	5. Church	Working Together
Assurance of Pardon/Testimonies/ Passing the Peace	6. Restoration	Celebrating Little Restorations

G. R. PERRY   C2022

Figure 2—Gestures of Worship and Witness in the Drama of Discipleship

The first gesture of witness in the drama is accepting (not blocking) the gifts that are offered by the people, organizations, and natural resources on our local stages. This gesture respects the image of God in each person and thanks God for all that he has made "very good" (Gen 1:31) in a particular place. In worship, these are gestures of humble praise, counting our blessings with gratitude to God in prayer, in singing and dance. In witness, this gesture can take the form of an asset inventory of the common graces that fill our homes, churches, workplaces, neighborhoods, university campuses, and cities. Moreover, by accepting the gifts, we start our local, ensemble performances at the beginning of God's script—creation. In the beginning, God put man and woman together in a fitting, delightful home "to work and keep it" (Gen 2:15). By cultivating an appreciation for both people and place, we resist the temptation to become problem-focused and become better equipped to identify the resources we will need to sustain the drama of discipleship.

The second gesture of witness in the drama is naming broken places in ourselves, our families and churches, as well as the idols and injustices on our local stages. What isn't the way it's supposed to be?[9] Who is being overlooked, mistreated, or marginalized in our schools, workplaces, and

9. Plantinga's helpful shorthand summary of Augustine's description of sin (as privation of the good) is *Not the Way It's Supposed to Be.*

marketplaces? What natural and cultural resources are being overvalued, wasted, or misappropriated? As you may have guessed, this gesture marks the second major plot point of the ancient script by recognizing the painful consequences of human rebellion against God's good reign. In public worship, this gesture manifests in confessions of sin and prayers of lament that name not only the ways we have sinned, but ways that we and our neighbors have been sinned against. In public witness, this gesture may be expressed in official complaints and public protests on behalf of vulnerable neighbors.

However, knowing our tendency to blame others and complain, our Lord Jesus set a particular order for this gesture: "first take the log out of your own eye, then you will see clearly to take the speck out of your brother's eye" (Matt 7:5). Therefore, in worship we offer our personal confessions in silence before we confess corporately with others. Naming broken places is a needs assessment that hears and records the cries of pain on our local stages, but it is also a call to repentance, a call for change in ourselves, our families, our churches, and neighborhoods.

The third gesture of witness in the drama recognizes different status roles that people play within the institutional structures of our families, churches, schools, businesses, and local governments. Who are the stakeholders? What roles are they playing in our local community? Who leads? How are they using their resources and influence? Who is hosting? Who are our guests? What are the processes for decision-making and communication that affect the quality of life in the places we work, play, worship, learn, and share? This gesture recognizes that we do not act as detached individuals, but as those who live in a variety of relational roles with shifting degrees of status. We are sons and daughters, parents, husbands and wives, employees and employers, hosts and guests, congregants and clergy, students and teachers, citizens of cities—and yet, in all roles, children of God and subjects of Christ's reign.

Using status to bless others on our local stage corresponds to God's election of Abraham's family as a primary agent of blessing for the nations in the biblical drama of redemption. Israel was called to use its status as God's "firstborn son" (Exod 4:22), as a host to "sojourners" (Lev 19:33–34; Deut 10:19), and as a "kingdom of priests" to bless the nations (cf. Gen 12:3; Exod 19:4–6; Deut 4:6–8). After God committed himself to the house and lineage of David (2 Sam 7:4–17), every people group relates rightly to God and his people by relating rightly to their royal representative, David's Son (cf. Ps 2:7–12; 72:8–11, 17–19). Because David's Son "executes justice for the fatherless and the widow, and loves the sojourner," this Lord's people are called to employ their resources and influence for his same purposes.

One of the most formative, character-shaping experiences of the people of God in the biblical script, the exodus, is rooted in the reality that "we, too, were once sojourners in the land of Egypt" (Deut 10:18–19; cf. Lev 19:18, 33–34). At the close of corporate worship, we receive words of benediction to go in peace as instruments of God's peace in his world. Whether in social roles of high or low status, God calls us to "walk humbly" with him and to "act justly with loving mercy" towards our neighbors (Mic 6:8). As Christ's followers, we enter the world "to serve, not to be served" (Mark 10:45). Thus we must consider how we might use our cultural privileges and social capital for God's glory and the common good.

The fourth and climactic gesture of witness in the drama of discipleship is turning to follow the way of life, and redirecting our gifts in accord with the original story line and its aim: "God is reconciling all things to himself through Christ" (cf. 2 Cor 5:19; Col 1:20). In an important sense, this gesture looks both ways along the plotline of Scripture. It is the crucial gesture (cross-and-resurrection shaped) that integrates creation and fall in redemption and anticipates resurrection. In repentance and faith, over- and undervalued resources are redirected towards their intended use. Abused relationships are rectified to display the dignity with which they were created. Human capacities are reenlisted for their original purposes. Though glorious and life-giving, these redirections are painful, partial, and usually slow going.

In Jesus, the story of our life together and of our character as image-bearers makes sense again in the grotesque, yet glorious mystery of the cross. Through gospel proclamations and performances, the Spirit of Christ is "decommissioning the rulers of this age" (cf. 1 Cor 1:26–31; 2:6–13) and liberating humankind from fraudulent, self-serving policies and practices. In the church's worship and witness, Christ is accomplishing his mission by pouring out his Spirit on his people to consecrate and empower us in a continuous drama of redirection (repentance), in which the destructive habits of our old humanity are redressed with good works that produce firstfruits of renewed creation in our churches and neighborhoods.

The fifth gesture of witness in the drama is working together as an ensemble. This gesture is time inefficient, often difficult, sometimes delightful, but absolutely vital to our identity and vocation as God's people. Our fellowship helps us bear life's troubles; our partnership leverages our sanctification and our efforts in mission. In worship, this gesture is expressed as each member of Christ's social body brings "a hymn, a lesson, a revelation, a tongue, or an interpretation" (1 Cor 14:26). Every gift the Spirit gives is important for the church's growth in grace. In witness, we partner with other members of Christ's social body in our network of congregations, across denominational lines, to confront the idols and injustices on our local stage and to promote the flourishing of our cities and towns. As members of a transnational, intercultural household, we also partner with members of God's family in other parts of God's world in ways that either provide immediate relief or in ways that sustain development for a season.

The job of "learning Christ" (Eph 4:20) or "teaching ourselves and others to obey all the things that Christ has commanded" (Matt 28:20) is simply beyond any one of us, any one congregation, denomination, or ecclesial tradition. Just think about how many Spirit-filled and gifted people have mentored you—parents, teachers, scout leaders, coaches, employers, pastors, etc. You heard the old African proverb: "it takes a village to raise a child." Well, it takes not just one, local church, but a network of Spirit-empowered churches to disciple the nations in our neighborhoods. The script of Scripture is written for ensemble, not solo, performances, for a lifetime of learning Christ and imitating him with and before others. Therefore, this discipleship curriculum will put a premium on partnerships that portray Christ's character more fully before the nations, who continue to gather in our global cities.

Sixth and finally, acting in character as the church for the world includes celebrating little restorations. This is the fruit of repentance that demonstrates the release of sins in reallocated resources and restored relationships between women and men, parents and children, wealthy and poor, weak and strong. These are the good cultural works that serve the common good; greater fairness in governmental and economic structures; and the replenishment and sustainable use of natural resources. Like the father who threw a party for his lost-but-found son, the woman who invited her friends to celebrate her recovered coin, and the shepherd who called his friends to rejoice over finding his wayward lamb (Luke 15), we all need the encouragement that comes from celebrating these little restorations of human dignity and meaning! Are habits of addiction being broken and supplanted with life-giving habits of sobriety? Has chronic joblessness ended with a hiring? Has unbelief been shattered with faith and forgiveness, resulting in baptisms? We must "celebrate and be glad, for your brother and sister were dead, but they are alive again, they were lost, but now they have been found!" (Luke 15:32). These little parties pre-enact the eschatological banquet in the new heavens and earth, whether with testimonies and jubilant songs around the Lord's Table in worship or with wine, dinner, and storytelling around your table in witness with neighbors becoming friends.

While key plot points are recorded in God's word and many key lines are rehearsed in our worship, not all of its scenes are scripted. God has made room in your particular neighborhood and its intersection of cultures for your performances together. God has called you out on your local stage. You and I will have to learn our roles in rehearsal and improvise our lines and gestures in cooperation with God's Spirit and mission. But, we do not have to do it alone, indeed we cannot.

The Drama of Discipleship

Many of us have benefited greatly, especially in the early stages of our journey as Jesus followers, when more mature Christians took an interest in our lives. They taught us the disciplines of daily prayer and Bible reading. Some challenged and equipped us to share a summary of the good news with our non-Christian friends or even with strangers. But, we learned most from those who let us in, those who showed us their own need for God's grace in the daily pressures of their work, parenting, and neighboring. These beloved friends showed us that while discipleship is never less than the personal disciplines of prayer, Bible reading, and evangelism, it is much, much more! From Jesus' parabolic teaching about God's reign, we learn that discipleship is the drama of real life that takes place on life's main stages.

Jesus' call isn't merely "learn this set of beliefs and this set of ministry skills," it is "follow me!" (Matt 4:19; 10:38). He was saying to Peter, James, John, and the rest, "If you want to know who I am, what's important to me, and where I'm going," then "go on a walkabout with me." A "walkabout" is an aboriginal rite of passage in which adolescent sons journey with their father through "the bush" for up to six months, living off the land, telling and reliving the stories of their people. Jesus taught his first followers about citizenship in God's kingdom organically and relationally, whilst preparing meals together, sharing a common purse, and by facing the fears and hopes of their neighbors together. The disciples "learned Christ" (Eph 4:20) both by hearing him teach on wealth and poverty, and by seeing him relate to the poor and rich; by hearing the parable of the Good Samaritan, and by following him into Samaria.

From Paul, we see that learning Christ is a life-wide, intercultural process of "taking off [the beliefs, attitudes and practices of] the old humanity" (4:22) and "clothing oneself with the new humanity, who is being created according to the likeness of God in righteousness and true holiness" (4:22). Discipleship is not a spiritual sideshow. Indeed, imitating Christ and discipling all people groups "to obey everything He has commanded" (Matt 28:20) is the church's central, dramatic role! It involves relearning and renewing our role as image-bearers to display God's character in every arena of life, while translating our words and deeds into the cultural vernaculars of the nations that God brings among us or sends us to visit. As Bonhoeffer discerned, "Christ is the man-for-others," so the church acts in character as Christ's social body in a particular place when it acts in the Holy Spirit's power for others.[10]

Every legitimate vocation marks a divine post to display God's image in manufacturing plants, retail outlets, machine shops, government offices, school classrooms, kitchens, households, etc. by treating family members, workers, customers, managers, teachers, students, etc. as fellow image-bearers with dignity and respect, and by making cultural products and delivering services that contribute to human flourishing. Like a son who tarnishes the family's name when he mistreats a client of the family business or a wife who honors her husband and children when she deflects the advances of a co-worker, those who belong to Christ always act and speak as members of him and as members of one another (1 Cor 6:17). Even as I wear my wedding band wherever I go to express my identity as a married man, our baptized bodies bear the name of the Father, the Son, and the Holy Spirit in whatever we do or say.

In other words, every follower of Jesus is engaged in Christian service, and our shared ministry of reconciliation (2 Cor 5:14–21) requires all hands, feet, eyes, and ears (1 Cor 12:12–31) onstage! Our shared mission as church is the trans-generational, intercultural project to "disciple all people groups or cultures" (starting with ourselves) in all the ways of Jesus (Matt 28:18–20), doing all in his name and for his glory (Col 3:17). The aim of this book is to describe the drama of discipleship—both following Jesus and discipling the nations together—as grace with skin on or gospel show-and-tell.

10. Bonhoeffer, *Letters and Papers from Prison*, 501.

Group Activity

Plan and schedule a meal together as a small group. Decide together who will host and who will bring what foods. Share recipes, setup, and cleanup activities. Each group member must bring a portion of the meal and a personal or family story to tell. Intentionally, share foods, stories, or music from your ethnic and family heritages. When you gather, the host should begin the storytelling by recounting an episode of his or her spiritual journey that reveals a unique or important quality about them or their extended family.

Everyone in the group, whether married or not, school-age or retired, introvert or extrovert, will contribute to the storytelling! You may be surprised and delighted by what you learn about each other and how each of you participate in God's grace. Together, you are writing a chapter of your small group's role in the story of God's renovation of the world on your local stage. Select a group archivist and scribe who will collect snapshots or video clips of your group activities to deepen your relationships and awareness of how you are participating in the story of God's mission as it plays out in your community.

Creation

Accepting the Gifts Onstage

HAVE YOU EVER STARTED a movie and have a family member or friend arrive late? The inevitable question is "What did I miss?" It's difficult to explain things in the middle, but that's often what many of us try to do in the drama of discipleship.

Many well-meaning Christians, in their efforts to help others, focus first on the problems that our sins multiply in our attitudes, relationships, and habits. However, this is not the best starting place for someone who hasn't seen the beginning of the "movie." It is hard to know what has really gone wrong with something and how it needs to be mended unless you understand its original design and purpose.

In light of this, we help ourselves and our neighbors when we start at the very beginning, where the script itself starts—with a survey of all that is "very good" about our community. As New Testament scholar Joel Green has observed,

> Beginnings set parameters around the nature of a narrative and its concerns . . . A narrative beginning opens up possibilities, generates probabilities and invites its audience to a full hearing in order to discover its outcome.[1]

The biblical story line is framed at its beginning and end with creation narratives. The covenantal drama between God and the cosmos, mediated

---

1. Green, "Problem of a Beginning," 62.

primarily through human beings, moves from Eden to the new Jerusalem and inextricably ties the heavens to the earth.[2] In other words, the bond the Creator forges with creation is irrevocable (Gen 8:21–22; 9:11–17). Because of the faithfulness and goodness of God, from the moment of creation, the futures of God, humanity, and the earth are bound together.

Most movies start with a wide-angled "establishing shot" to orient viewers to historical, social, and aesthetic contexts, where the main characters live and the action is taking place. Similarly, we will understand our roles and the roles of other actors better when we comprehend the "establishing shot" of Scripture and communicate it to others. In this chapter, we will take a fresh look at the creation narratives in Genesis and what they reveal to us about the first gesture in the drama of discipleship—accepting the gifts on our local stage.

Scripting the Beginning

Origin stories shape a family's, a tribe's, even a nation's understanding of its identity, roles, and place in the world. For many of us, the stories of Genesis are familiar accounts of what happened at the beginning of the human story. While the biblical record does provide a true transcript of God's mediated actions in history, these documents offer more than mere historical testimony.[3] They authorize personal and communal actions, attitudes, and speech that cultivate human flourishing in fellowship with the divine. In other words, God's script provides an improv platform that frames local ensemble performances of Christian living amidst the nations.

But what does this script reveal about God and ask of us? For those who know the biblical narrative well, it is easy to see that this account of humankind's beginning is very different from competing ideas often put forward today. But this was part of its original purpose and dramatic force. Since the creation narrative was conceived as a counter-story, it can help us understand what is unique about Scripture's view of humanity and respond to God's call to live today in light of the orientation provided in the opening words of Genesis.

2. See Richter, *Epic of Eden*, 15–20, 92–136.

3. Building on the work of von Balthasar, both Wells and Vanhoozer explore the metaphor of doing theology as *theodrama* or response to the initiatives of God in history. See Wells, *Improvisation*, 45–57, and Vanhoozer, *Drama of Doctrine*, 35–112.

Moses, traditionally understood as the primary author of Genesis, was a man educated in Pharaoh's court and in all the literature of the ancient Near East (Acts 7:22).[4] He knew well the power of stories to shape one's view of the world and one's place in it. He had heard the stories that the pharaohs told about human origins and saw how they served these leaders' political ambitions and massive public works projects. Ancient Near Eastern cultural orthodoxy was fatalistic and totalitarian, celebrating the power of kings, the only human beings deemed to be "sons of the gods" or "the image of the gods." Their priestly courts organized society in accord with the biorhythms of the gods, planting and harvest seasons. Moses's people, the Hebrews, had been living in Egypt for centuries, and had become schooled or propagandized by Egyptian origin stories and ways of thinking.

The basic plotline of many of the ancient Near Eastern origin stories served the aims of one sovereign, Pharaoh, and his slave economy particularly well. In most of these narratives, junior gods served high gods. Aggravated by their envy of the high gods, the junior gods struggled amongst themselves to improve their servile conditions. The resulting conflict was extremely violent, resulting in the birth of the physical universe from the blood and carcasses of junior gods who had been defeated. The victors created human "savages" to do the hard labor they had once done. In more than a few Egyptian stories and wisdom sayings, a human king is described as a "son" or "image" of a god.[5] With mere humans, especially conquered people groups, under their thumbs to produce enough food and build enough temples for junior and high gods alike, the demigods and their human viceroys enjoyed their leisure. Moses's description of humanity, work, the earth, and God subverted Pharaoh's self-serving stories.[6] The true story of image-bearing that Moses told the escaped refugees, as they fled from Pharaoh across the Sinai Peninsula, answered their longings for dignity and freedom. Remarkably, it did so without demonizing or dehumanizing their Egyptian oppressors.

4. For reasons to discern a primary, prophetic, authorial voice behind the Pentateuch from the era of Moses, see Collins, *Genesis 1–4*, 221–35.

5. I am aware of only one and possibly two wisdom sayings from Egyptian literature that refer to all humans as an image of god(s). But, as Middleton notes, these statements did not find a hospitable atmosphere in royal ideology and were suppressed. See Middleton, *Liberating Image*, 99–104.

6. For a recent discussion of how Genesis 1–11 served as a critique of ancient Near Eastern royal ideologies, see Middleton, *Liberating Image*, 185–231.

Some aspects of the story line in Genesis have clear parallels in ancient Near Eastern literature such as the Enuma Elish, the Epic of Atra-Hasis, and a variety of myths from different regions of Egypt.[7] All of these origin stories feature royal imagery. Creators are sovereigns who build and rule societies through their commands. The Egyptian god Ptah spoke of creatures first in his heart, then created by speaking with his tongue. The Mesopotamian god Marduk created a constellation, then destroyed it by his edict.[8] But the differences between these origin stories and those of the biblical narrative carry great social significance. The creation counter-stories that Moses told were staged on earth, not in heaven. In stark contrast to stories about a violent conflict among junior gods, and the formation of earth from a defeated demigod's dismembered body,[9] Moses described a world with a beautiful array of plants and animals, and a royal garden within it called "Eden," which means "luxuriant" or "place of delight."[10]

In Genesis 1–2, there is only one God who, like any real king, merely speaks and things start to happen: Light shines in the darkness. Dry land appears, setting a boundary of safety against the chaos of the waters. This God forms, then fills, three realms—the heavens, the sea, and dry land—with a teeming variety of birds, fish, animal and plant life, all by royal decree. In marked distinction from a dualistic worldview that sees the material world as evil or a materialistic worldview that sees the universe as autonomous, Genesis 1–2 depicts the Creator present in space and time, working with his own hands in the rich soil of the earth that he made. In a manner of speaking, the God of the Bible isn't afraid to get his hands dirty because the ground God makes is alive and "very good," providing a life-giving, life-sustaining home for his creatures. The royal garden of Eden is especially well-suited for the Creator's representatives, man and woman, who are "co-heirs of the grace of life" (1 Pet 3:7).

Think for a moment about the character of the world, gods, and human beings that these ancient Near Eastern stories imagine. What is the character of these gods? What are their aims? Where does the action of the drama occur? What are the main conflicts? How are human beings and their work described? What kind of home does the earth provide its

7. See Pritchard, ed., *Ancient Near East.*

8. See Middleton, *Liberating Image*, 66.

9. See excerpts of Egyptian, Sumerian, and Akkadian creation myths in Pritchard, ed., *Ancient Near Eastern Texts Relating to the Old Testament*, 3, 37–51, 60–99, 104–5.

10. See Brown, Driver, and Briggs, eds., *Brown-Driver-Briggs Hebrew and English Lexicon*, 726–27.

inhabitants? And, how do human beings relate to these gods? Stories about the beginning of a people, whether on the North American continent or in the ancient Near East, are not merely imaginative tales or projections of the personal qualities of key leaders; they are theo-political stories about core cultural values, values that are inherently religious.[11] These stories imagine a world, who rules it, and how it works.

Rereading the Script

Review Genesis 1–2 and list some of your observations about the *different* kind of God, *different* kind of human beings, and *different* kind of world that Moses described to the company of former slaves who were making their escape from Egypt to the promised land. How was Moses's *different* story "good news" for them?

ANE Origin Stories	Biblical Creation Account
God[s]	
Gods fight amongst themselves.	
Gods secure workers so they can play.	
Human Beings	
Humans are "savages" and "slaves."	
Only kings are image-bearers of gods.	
The World	
The world arises from war or chaos.	
The world is made from a bloody carcass.	

11. Cultural goods, practices, incentives, and sanctions reveal the values of the dominant cultural narrative. As Frame summarizes, "culture is simply the service of God[s] in our lives; it is religion externalized." See Frame, *Doctrine of the Christian Life*, 858.

Covenantal Call and Response

Genesis 1–2 establishes a pattern of covenantal call-and-response that re-sounds in every episode of the biblical drama. Though the word *covenant* does not appear in these chapters, all the elements of a covenant are present. As the senior partner and gracious initiator of the relationship, God provides the stage and resources that his junior partners will need to fulfill their calling and to sustain their mission by multiplying image-bearers to subdue the earth.

The narrative structure of Genesis 1 is highly stylized, like a poem or hymn. Following the framework of a human workweek, the description of each day is presented as a call and response between the Creator and his creation:

> *Call*: And God said, "Let there be . . ."
> *Response*: And it was so.
> *Evaluative Summary*: And God called it . . . and saw that it was good.
>   There was evening and morning of [that] day.

In these opening scenes, the stage is alive and responds to God's call to action. From the lights and fowl that fill the heavens to the swarms of fish in the ocean depths, the organic, living elements of creation not only answer their stage call, they cooperate with their Creator's scripted intent. In counterpoint to the "formless emptiness" of verse 2, God's speech acts form, then fill the earth with an abundant, teeming array of living organisms.

By speaking, God not only creates, he also evaluates the creation as "good." This refrain strikes a tonal note that runs through the opening movement of the score, accompanying God's action. The divine verdict denotes durable craftsmanship and connotes something made lovingly, with life-giving qualities and purpose. There is an aesthetic and moral goodness about creation that articulates God's intention to delight divine and human tastes as well as to give and sustain the lives of His creatures. Life is not merely utilitarian, nor does it just "get by" in luxuriant Eden; it thrives in great varieties and abundance. "Look, I have given you every plant yielding seed that is on the face of the earth, and every tree with seed in its fruit. You shall have them for food" (1:29).

But God has not designed a world where an individual human relates only to God and a beautiful natural setting. Though Adam has "every plant yielding seed" and "fruit-bearing tree," and though God brings him "every living creature to see what he would call them" (2:19), still, he finds "no vital ally who corresponds to him" (2:18).[12] When the refrain of "good" (1:4, 10, 12, 18, 21, 25, 31) is broken, the audience leans in to hear God say, "It is *not good* that the man should be alone" (2:18).

"Not good" must mean "incomplete" in the context of Genesis 2. A vital member of God's living ecosystem is missing, as Adam's exhaustive search demonstrates. The purposeful, life-giving work of humanity's side of this covenant simply cannot be accomplished by one person, one gender, one generation, or even one cultural group. So, God, the great sculptor and animator, completes his work, but chooses a different medium. Instead of the "dust of the ground" (2:7), he chooses Adam's bone and flesh to form Eve. "Bone of my bones and flesh of my flesh" (2:21–23) expresses the inter-gendered, interdependent, covenantal shape of humanity's life and mission as divine image-bearers.

As God made Eve from Adam, for Adam, God made both male and female from his creation, for his creation. Though they are "of the earth," creatures of the sixth day, they are also "like God" in ways unlike earth's other creatures. As we will explore further below, man and woman not only bear God's image, they are God's iconic representatives in the world. The imprint of God's dignity and beauty is on every person, which cements the covenantal and ethical relation between the two great commandments, and Jesus' call to "love your enemies."

"Let Us Make Man in Our Image"

Since Genesis emphasizes that men and women are made in God's image, moreover since accepting the gifts onstage requires that we recognize God's image in others, it is useful to spend some time reflecting further on what the climactic moment of Episode One teaches.

The entirety of 1:26–30 is given to the description of humankind, more space than to any other element of creation. With the repetition of the verb "created" (three times in verse 27) and the noun "image" (three times in verses 26–27), the author uses a change in cadence to signal that readers should linger over God's attention to man and woman.[13] The pattern that audiences have heard echoed to this point is that "God created the great sea

12. Typically translated, "suitable helper" (NIV) or "fit helper" (ESV), *ezer kenegdo*, carries a more robust sense of a "vital ally who is simultaneously alike and opposite" the male. See the excellent discussion by McKinley, "Necessary Allies."

13. See Collins, *Genesis 1–4*, 71–72.

creatures . . . according to their kinds, and every winged bird according to its kind" on the fifth day, then, on the sixth "beasts of the earth according to their kinds, and the livestock according to their kinds, and everything that creeps on the ground according to its kind" (1:21–25). That pattern breaks significantly, however, in verse 26:

> Let us make man in our image and after our likeness. And let them rule over the fish of the sea and over the birds of the heavens and over the livestock and over all the earth and over every creeping thing that creeps upon the earth.

The glory and dignity of man and woman together as God's image-bearers is summarized beautifully by the Apostle Peter, who describes husbands and wives as "co-heirs of the grace of life" (1 Peter 3:7). Shocking ancient sensibilities, Moses's counter-story of creation describes men and women not as "savages" of the gods or "slaves" of Pharaoh, but as God's royal representatives, vice-regents of the greatest king:

> So God created man in his own image, in the image of God he created him; male and female he created them. And God blessed them, and said to them, "Be fruitful and multiply and fill the earth and subdue it. Rule over the fish of the sea and over the birds of the heavens and over every living thing that moves on the earth." (Gen 1:26–28)

Drawing attention to the noble character and calling of every human person, not just pharaohs and other kings, Moses selects the verb "rule over" (1:26, 28) to describe humanity's unique commission from God. Like the other animals (for man is surely a creature of the sixth day), humankind is to "multiply" and "fill" (cf. 1:22, 28). But, distinct from the other animals, man and woman are also "to rule . . . over every living thing" and "to subdue the earth" (1:28). Still, humankind's calling as image-bearers has roots that go deeper than this function. God's call shapes humanity's core identity and structural capacities. We bear God's image because we are God's image.[14]

While some philosophers and theologians have written that to be created in God's image is to be made rational beings, others have identified human creativity and moral capacity. They say language, reason, and spiritual lives of purpose are what separates humans from the rest of the animal kingdom and from lives motivated by mere appetite. But biblical scholar Joel Green discerns that "the quality that distinguishes humanity" is

---

14. See Hoekema, *Created in God's Image*, 68–73.

"not some 'part' of the individual" but "the whole of human existence" in its "relatedness to God."[15] Created in God's own image, human beings are "to exercise dominion . . . in a way that reflects God's own ways of interaction with his creatures."[16] As Bonhoeffer summarizes, humankind's call to "rule over" the earth is a dominion for the earth:

> The soil and the animals, whose Lord I am, are the world in which
> I live, without which I am not. It is my world, my earth over which
> I rule . . . . It bears me, nourishes me, holds me.[17]

To be sure, language and reason are important human capacities, as are creativity and imagination, but they are given within the relational, moral, "intersexual character of personhood" to fulfill the vocational roles of image-bearing.[18] Within the man and woman's covenant with God, each other, and the earth, children are conceived, born, fed, clothed, educated, and discipled in these roles. In the garden of God, parents, children, friends, and neighbors learn and teach how to attend seeds, soils, cycles of planting, and harvest in order "to serve and keep" (2:15) each other, and the earth.

Moreover, by experiencing close communication and generous provision from God, they are taught how to form familial bonds, and wider social relations of neighbor-love that shape practices of friendship, citizenship, and commerce that form and contribute to the common good. Inspired with God's breath, endowed with God's gifts, especially God's Word, human persons and society mediate and embody heavenly wisdom on the earth. God's image is multiplied and the garden is extended through the formation of families and communities, across generations and geography.[19] This is the heartwork and fieldwork of knowing God and being human.

Admittedly in relation to the creation accounts in Genesis, I have elaborated some aspects of image-bearing that are only implied in the text. Indeed, exegetes have long lamented that the terms "image (*selem*)" and "likeness (*demut*)" do not say much about the specific content and meaning

---

15. Green, *Body, Soul, and Human Life*, 63.

16. Green, *Body, Soul, and Human Life*, 63.

17. Bonhoeffer, *Creation and Fall, Temptation*, 42. Moreover, Ellen Davis affirms that "rule" is more like "steward" than "dominate." See Davis, *Scripture, Culture, Agriculture*.

18. Green, *Body, Soul, and Human Life*, 65.

19. Useful summaries of views and the history of interpretation about image-bearing are found in Berkouwer, *Man*, 37–118; Hall, *Imaging God*, 61–112; and Cross, *People of God's Presence*, 66–81.

of the image of God.[20] However, I have followed an exegetical trail marked by Calvin, who wrote, "the image cannot be better known from anything, than from the reparation of [its] corrupted nature," citing Col 3:10 and Eph 4:24.[21] In those texts, the Apostle Paul uses the imagery of disrobing the old, corrupt ways of being human and putting on "the new [or renewed] self," which is "created after the likeness of God in true righteousness and holiness." Indeed, Paul elaborates!

In your role as citizens (see figure 3 below), take off the practice of lying and "speak truth to your neighbor, since we are members of one another" (Eph 4:25). In Christ's kingdom of the renewed covenant, "there is no Greek or Jew . . . barbarian or Scythian" (Col 3:11). Stop stealing from one another, rather, in your role as workers, "labor, doing honest work with [your] own hands, so that [you] may have something to share with anyone who is in need" (Eph 4:28). "Whatever you do, work heartily as for the Lord" (Col 3:23). In your more intimate role as family members, "submit to one another out of reverence for Christ, wives to husbands . . . husbands love your wives . . . children obey your parents" (Eph 5:21–22, 25; 6:1; cf. Col 3:18–20). In your role as gardeners, cultivating natural resources, including your bodies, and "let no one pass judgment on you in questions of food or drink . . . or disqualify you, insisting on asceticism" (Col 2:16, 18).

Moreover, do not practice any form of covetousness, sexual immorality or get drunk with wine (Eph 5:3–5, 18). These practices are idolatrous. Rather, as worshippers of the true and living God, "be filled with the Holy Spirit . . . singing and making melody to the Lord with your whole heart, giving thanks always and for everything to God" (Eph 18–20; cf. Col 3:16). With echoes of Eden playing in his ears, the Apostle Paul redirects image-bearers back to the bonds of covenant with God, each other, and the earth.

---

20. Middleton retraces the history of word studies that examine the linguistic background, semantic ranges, and uses in Scripture of "image" (selem) and "likeness" (demut), then recognizes and explores their immediate syntactical and literary context in Genesis 1:26-28 with the verbs "rule" (rada) and "subdue" (kabas). Read in the symbolic world of ancient Near Eastern royal ideology and as part of the introduction to the book of Genesis, Middleton confirms the established consensus that the image of God in humans refers to the delegated or representative rule we are called to have in the world on God's behalf. See, Middleton, *Liberating Image*, 43–90, and Hart, "Genesis 1:1–2:3 as a Prologue to the Book of Genesis."

21. Calvin, *Institutes*, I.15.4.

Five Roles of Image-Bearing

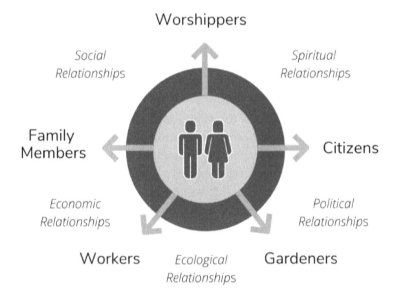

Worshippers

Social Relationships

Spiritual Relationships

Family Members

Citizens

Economic Relationships

Political Relationships

Workers

Ecological Relationships

Gardeners

Figure 3—Five Roles of Image-Bearing

The garden is not only a royal habitation (for only kings had such gardens in the ancient Near East), it is also a sacred space, a temple for God and his priests, who "serve" and "keep" it. These five dimensions of image-bearing—worshipper, worker, gardener, family member, and citizen—can be distinguished, but they cannot be separated as they weave together the fabric of human life, given by God and sustained in God's own life.[22] This account of beginnings has remarkable explanatory power for the sense of dignity and moral obligation in human beings over against any anthropology rooted in evolutionary naturalism or resulting from violent conflicts between primordial gods. Most remarkable to the ears of the Hebrew refugees escaping Egypt, Genesis told them that they, too, were sons and

22. See the discussion of the "complementation" of the "creation ordinances" which "interpenetrate each other" in Murray, *Principles of Conduct*, 27–44. Bonhoeffer identifies "four mandates: labor, marriage, government and the Church" (see Bonhoeffer, *Ethics*, 207–13). As I noted above, he also underscores humanity's care for the earth, a characteristic of image-bearing explored more fully by Wright, *Mission of God's People*, 48–62.

daughters of God, the High King of heaven, and that Pharaoh's claims and commands were not in keeping with their character at the beginning.[23]

The first covenant of life, freely offered by God and embraced with integrity and innocence by humankind, sets the trajectory for future covenants. As we will see throughout our rereading of the script, image-bearing is at the heart of humanity's side of covenant-keeping. When we, humans, go rogue by seeking to determine "good" for ourselves, we deny and deform our covenantal relatedness to God, each other, and the rest of creation. We act inhumanely and, thus, ungodly. We deface God's image and bear false witness about God's reign over the world and creatures he made. When God reestablishes his purposes with creation through Noah and his offspring after the flood, he repeats humanity's commission of image-bearing and, this time, Moses describes it repeatedly as a "covenant" (*bryt*; Gen 9:1–17, especially verses 9, 11–13, 15–17). According to the book of beginnings, the very shape of reality is covenantal.[24] Both offspring and land, people and place are gifts of the covenant.

Beginnings set trajectories. In Genesis 1–2, Adam and Eve are real partners with God and each other. While they are not equal partners with God, neither are they God's puppets or slaves. Their interdependent work is meaningful and material. What man and woman do or fail to do together really matters. Their words and deeds leave marks on God, each other, and the world. Though their story forms the climax of the creation account, Adam and Eve are not its goal. They share a mission—the heartwork and fieldwork of extending the borders of Eden by multiplying God's image and cultivating the earth in accord with heavenly wisdom. We share their heartwork and fieldwork in the ongoing drama of discipleship.

Covenantal Dynamics on Every Page and in Every Scene

Genesis 1–2 is quite clear that human beings are not gods, but dependent on God and interdependent with each other and the earth. Indeed, along with all their positive responsibilities and abundant resources, Adam and Eve are given one negative stipulation that carries a devastating sanction: "You shall not eat of the tree of the knowledge of good and evil, for in the day that you eat of it you will surely die" (Gen 2:17). As Old Testament

23. The point holds whether you date Genesis with evangelical scholars to the time of the exodus or with critical scholars to the time of Israel's return from exile.

24. Brueggemann, *Genesis*, 17.

scholar Sandra Richter summarizes, Adam and Eve are free to do anything but decide for themselves what is good and what is evil. Yahweh reserves the right (and the responsibility) to name those truths.[25]

With these abundant provisions and this stipulation—represented by the two trees, the tree of life and the tree of the knowledge of good and evil (2:9)—humankind's first parents are reminded that God's words form the script of life.[26] To defect from the script is deforming and, ultimately, deadly. The covenant's provisions and sanctions have been listed, its related parties named, and its purpose emphasized in their responsibilities. Finally, God pronounces all he has made "very good" and establishes a weekly covenant renewal event—the Sabbath.

Genesis 2 combines "the Lord" (*yhwh*), the covenant name of Israel's God, with "God" (*ʾel*), a common Semitic designation for the Canaanite high god. So, the Lord is not limited to geographic borders like other tribal deities. Israel's God is also the maker of heaven and earth, "the Lord God" of all humankind. The seventh day, the Sabbath, poignantly reminds Moses's first readers they are no longer work units in Pharaoh's false narrative, but image-bearers of the living God with whom they share life, work, and rest.

This covenantal dynamic appears throughout the Bible as both God's initiatives and humanity's responses shape events on the world stage.[27] In other words, according to Scripture, the work of being human occurs simultaneously in relation to God, oneself, other humans, and to the rest of the created order. Some theologians describe this covenantal dynamic as concurrence or compatibilism, referring to the cooperation between God and humankind.[28] To be sure, divine and human wills are not of equal capacity or consequence. Nevertheless, each partner's choices affect the other,

---

25. Richter, *Epic of Eden*, 104.

26. As Blocher notes, "two trees in the garden correspond to the two clauses in the contract." Indeed, it is "strange that some commentators assert that [Adam] had not eaten of [the tree of life]" before he sinned with Eve by partaking of the forbidden tree. The tree of life represents the central gift of the covenant, sustained by the tree and by all other covenantal provisions. Surely, it was a primary resource for the couple until God's censure in 3:22, which symbolizes the sentence of death, and does not imply that the couple had never eaten from it. See Blocher, *In the Beginning*, 122–23.

27. Brueggemann, *Genesis*, 17.

28. For an accessible discussion of God's sovereignty and human responsibility in *compatibilism*, see Carson, *How Long, O Lord?*, 199–228. It is important to note with Berkouwer and others that a robust understanding of God's providence must not be limited to his role as Creator, but finds fuller expression in his redeeming work as the Savior of the world. On concurrence, see Berkouwer, *Providence of God*.

as well as the resources onstage. Indeed, divine and human agencies affect the living stage itself. The world which was cursed because of man and woman, also will be liberated and restored because of man and woman (cf. Gen 3:17; Rom 8:19–21).

Most decisively, the Last Adam or Definitive Human Being (cf. John 1:14; Gal 4:4) entered the stage to secure the goal of history—the first Adam's original mission—to cultivate the whole earth under "the reign of God" (cf. Gen 1:26–28 à Rev 11:15). God's work with and through us is both heartwork and fieldwork. Human beings are designed for covenant relationship with God, each other, and the created order. According to Genesis, we were and remain bound together in the covenant of life. Our knowledge and experience of God is not, nor can it be, gained independently, merely for ourselves. It is gained in the field, in interdependent, interactive practices of image-bearing.[29] Therefore, in each episode of the drama of discipleship, we will seek knowledge and experience of God in the interactions between the Spirit, who is speaking through the script, and the Spirit, who is working through image-bearers on our local stage.

As Calvin began in his *Institutes*, "Our wisdom, in so far as it ought to be deemed true and solid wisdom, consists almost entirely of two parts: the knowledge of God and of ourselves."[30] This agrees with the Lord Jesus' assertion that our love for God and our love for neighbor are intertwined. One cannot grow richer or truer without the other. The drama of discipleship is not merely interior, it is also exterior. It is not only heartwork, it is also fieldwork. So, in each episode of our journey together, we will exegete both the script of God's word and the stage of God's world. Moreover, we will develop our observation and interpretive skills for understanding their interaction. Each episode not only invites a "table reading" of the script together, it also offers group activities for a "walk through" of each episode on the local stage.

First Gesture: Accepting the Gifts Onstage

Like creation itself in Genesis 1–2, the church is constantly responding to God's call—God's prior, gracious initiatives of creation and redemption. Our group performances, both public and private, not only attest to God's faithful actions in the past, they also extend our covenantal future. Admittedly, the church's improvisational interpretations of the script are

29. See Scharen, *Fieldwork in Theology*, 65–90.

30. Calvin, *Institutes*, I.1:1–3.

partial, impoverished, and deeply compromised by its own sins. Inasmuch, however, as its performances are resourced by the Holy Spirit's gifts, and offered in humility and love to God and neighbor, they remind the world of humanity's true origin and offer foretastes of its new creation.

The first gesture of gospel show-and-tell is accepting the gifts offered by the people, organizations, and natural resources of our local campuses, workplaces, and neighborhoods. This gesture respects the image of God in every family member, co-worker, neighbor, or stranger, and recognizes aspects of God's good design in the particularities of each place. By cultivating appreciation first, we resist our tendency to start with what's wrong and begin, instead, where God's Script begins—with what's good and right about this place and its people.

Accepting the gifts on our local stage involves more than just passive acknowledgement that creation is beautiful or that every person is worthwhile. It is a habit that we learn and cultivate with practice, just as actors develop behavioral habits that make them successful onstage. For instance, an ensemble of actors often warms up with a series of improv games that strengthen their connection. The first rule is "no blocking." "No blocking" means that no one is allowed to reject someone else's contribution to the emerging scenario. If your partner says, "Look at this beautiful apple that I picked up at the corner market!" while gesturing as if pulling the fruit out of a shopping bag, you do not serve her well by responding, "No, actually, it's a truck." "No, actually" breaks the connection between actors, making it difficult, if not impossible, to move forward in the scene.

However, "Yes, and . . ." expresses solidarity and adds something valuable to what your fellow actor has brought to the action. For example, a response like—"That looks delicious! Let's cut it up and dip the wedges in a jar of peanut butter!"—accepts the gift, then reoffers it with collaborative opportunities.

But wait, you are probably thinking, what if this apple is in a scene with Adam, and Eve is making the offer? Aren't there some situations when it is fitting and best to reject what others are offering? Aside from the fact that Genesis does not tell us what kind of fruit the forbidden tree produced, it is true that the significance of our actions relate to a wider story that defines what it means to "act in character." To accept the gifts does not mean simply to affirm everything without discretion, but rather to find what is good in a situation and build on it, recognizing aspects of God's creative intent for that person, community, or setting.

I offer an example in the following dialogue I once had with a student during a class discussion on accepting the gifts:

> *Student:* "What if a colleague asks me to go to a strip club with him after work? Shouldn't I block that offer?"
>
> *Me:* "Bryan, why do you think your colleague asked you, when he could easily go to the club by himself?"
>
> *Student:* "I guess he wanted some company."
>
> *Me:* "Good. So, how might you look past the words on the surface to find something in his request to affirm?"
>
> *Student:* "I could say, 'I'd love to hang out sometime. Would you like to grab dinner after work next Tuesday at that new taco place in the Loop?'"

Notice how different this response is from one where the student simply says, "No, I would never go to a strip club" or even more strongly, "Why would you ask me to do that?" Accepting the gifts means looking for what is good in this situation and cooperating with God's creative intent.

My dialogue with Bryan is an example of what some improv actors describe as "walking backwards onstage."[31] This involves taking a step back to gain new perspective on whatever is happening in front of us. As an actor gains a wider perspective onstage, [s]he perceives viable alternatives to redirect or delay the action in a way that maintains connection with the ensemble, but also remains true to the character. For instance, if it has already been established that one character has no money, but another character approaches her to try to sell her some Girl Scout Cookies, the first actor doesn't just say "No, thank you," effectively stopping the action. Instead, she "walks backward onstage," imagining ways that she can still interact with her fellow actors.

She might say, "Oh, I love those coconut covered cookies. I buy them from my niece's scout troop every year. What are they called again?" Or maybe she says, "I've cut sugar out of my diet, but do you see that house over there on the corner? The man who lives there has a sweet tooth. I'm pretty sure he will order a box or two." By viewing the situation from a wider perspective, the actress enables both herself and her fellow actors to move the drama forward while acting in character.

The same opportunity presents itself when we as church members relate constructively towards our neighbors or we as congregations engage

31. Jones, *Off/Camera Show.*

other groups or institutions in our neighborhoods for the common good. Whether interpersonally with fellow citizens, who share workplaces, schools, or playgrounds, or by inventorying the many assets on the local stage itself, accepting the gifts is a vital gesture that reveals the character of divine image-bearers and the opening chapter of the story the local church is called to embody.

With the press of human need every day, it is easy to fall into a reactive pattern of ministry that starts with the problems caused by human sin. But the first word about human beings in the script is not *sinner*, it is *image-bearer*. Indeed, "God saw everything that he had made, and behold, it was very good" (Gen 1:31). Sometimes pastors and other lay leaders who deal with needs daily, up close and personal, are the ones who most need to "walk backwards on the stage" in order to gain a wider perspective, rooted in how the human story begins.

At a church-wide meal following his Pentecost Sunday sermon, Pastor Michael Mather was drawn into a conversation with a long-time parishioner who worked in the church's food pantry. "If God's Spirit fell on the church at Pentecost, shouldn't everyone have something to give?" she asked as she pushed a piece of paper across the table around their overflowing plates. Looking down, Pastor Mather saw the needs assessment their church used to determine eligibility to access the pantry. Puzzled, he said, "Yes, but help me understand how these things go together?" "With every line on this piece of paper," she exclaimed, "we are asking our neighbors to prove what they don't have—a job, money, family support. We assess needs, but not the gifts they have to offer their neighbors, and our church community." Surprised by such an immediate application of his sermon, Pastor Mather put the paper in his pocket and arranged a follow-up conversation with his thoughtful parishioner later that week.

Taking his sister's application of his sermon to heart, Pastor Mather offered a new survey that includes this question: "What three things do you do well enough that you could teach others?" One of the early applicants for the food pantry to use the new form, Adele, wrote down, "I could teach someone how to bake cookies!" After her cookies found their way to Pastor Mather's office, the church hired Adele to cook in their kitchen for church-wide events. Her reputation grew so much that she started a catering business, and today Adele owns her own restaurant in Indianapolis.[32] Without ignoring our needs and those of our neighbors, we engage the

---

32. This story is told by Ziegenhals, "Living Out of Abundance."

more complex, bigger, truer story of being human when first we learn to recognize and accept the gifts God gave at the beginning.

Group Activity: Take an Asset Inventory

The purpose of this study is to find our place as God's continuing covenant community in this script about divine image-bearing on this stage, the place where God has brought you and your neighbors as worshippers, workers, family members, citizens, and gardeners. In every generation throughout his world, God calls, directs, and equips his people by his Spirit to develop their own gospel show-and-tell, their own mission improvs. Together, we will learn and practice six characteristic gestures of image-bearing, that is, acting in character as God's people. First, as those who have arrived on the stage only recently, we must identify and accept the gifts that we have inherited. To respond to and riff on that which is being handed on, we will first need to observe, to listen, to respect the resources and people with whom we share our local stage.

An exercise that actors use to warm up is space walking. To develop their awareness of the stage, its dimensions, scenery, and props, as well as the presence of their fellow actors, an ensemble starts by exploring the stage. What are the props, tools, and other "very good" resources that already have a place on your local stage? What's "very good" about your city, neighborhood, workplace, school campus, home, or church? What do you love about being there? Start making a list or drawing a map. As the old hymn says, "count your blessings; name them one by one." Or, as asset-based community developers describe it, "take an asset inventory." While it will be important later to ask, "What's wrong?" we must first ask, "What's right?"

In consultation with your leaders, delineate the boundaries of your local stage. Will you focus on your neighborhood, your campus, or a part of your city that your leaders have identified for partnerships in your ministry? Once you have identified the boundaries of your place of service, develop an asset map of your local stage. Schedule a Saturday or other agreeable time in the near future when your group can walk through the space during daylight hours, when your fellow citizens are out and about. As the asset map in the figure below shows, you will document three types of assets: individual gifts, voluntary associations, and local institutions.

Community Assets Map

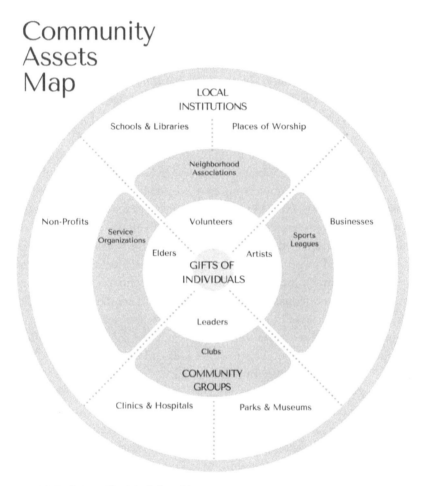

FIGURE 4 - The Drama of Discipleship, Dr. Gregory R. Perry
Based on the assets map by John Kretzmann and John McKnight,
Building Communities from the Inside Out (1993).

Figure 4—Community Assets Map

How is God already present and at work? How can your group find out how to cooperate with the flow of the Spirit in and through your local space and its citizens, your fellow image-bearers? Like improv actors, you will need to develop your awareness with careful observation and listening skills. Ask your neighbors, "What do you love about living here? What are some of your favorite places and community events?" This is the first phase of discerning how the story of redemption is playing out on your local stage (see the final chapter, "Closing Notes and Additional Tools for State Directors in the Drama," to learn how to conduct a neighborhood survey).

You may decide to divide your group into subgroups of twos or threes to space walk different areas of your local stage. Each group member should have an asset map to fill in. Institutions like schools and businesses are easiest to spot first and document fairly quickly. But, take a few moments to give thanks as you are writing down the names of local parks, clinics, grocery stores, etc. Praise God for the image-bearers who work there and for the good they identify and bring to your area. Voluntary associations are a little harder to list. Some of the easiest to identify are places of worship. Some members of your group may be members of neighborhood or business associations, sororities or fraternities, clubs, sports leagues, scouts, or a community garden. You will learn more if you do a little online research before or after your space walk. Again, give thanks for the value these groups add to your campus or neighborhood. Finally, while you are space walking in the local park, family-owned restaurant, or coffee shop, you will notice individuals who are making a contribution—the lady who leads an exercise class in the park or the coach who is leading practice on the ballfield; business owners who have a sign in the window offering jobs; or a tutor sitting in the local library with kids and their books after school hours. Note and give thanks for them as well.

After your space walk, your group may decide to divide the list and do a little more online research to fill out your asset inventory and praise list. Choose a group scribe or rotate that responsibility so you can archive and update your asset inventory, keep and add photos, keep a calendar of community events, and keep a praise list to include in your prayers. Once you find out what good things are happening on your local stage, you may decide to support one or two of them in ways that fit your group's gifts and/or growth areas. For example, you might adopt a school or other nonprofit in your neighborhood by supporting their volunteer programs. Or, you may decide to build a relationship with a particular group or club on campus. Above all, thank God for these community assets and ask how you can join what his Spirit is already energizing.

Rebellion

Naming the Broken Places with Tears

THE STAR WARS SAGA depicts good and evil as two opposing forces locked in an endless tug-of-war. From time to time, the balance shifts toward the "dark side," and heroes and heroines rise up to resist. But their brave actions, at best, only restore balance in "the Force." They never vanquish evil.[1]

Many people, and even many Christians, have bought into the idea that the conflict between good and evil is a fundamental feature of our stage. But, according to the biblical script, this is not the true story. As we saw in Episode One, the script begins with creation. God surveys all that he has made and pronounces it "very good." Remarkably, evil is not part of these opening scenes. It is not a given in the biblical story line. Rather, evil is a distortion of God's original design.

As North African preacher and theologian Augustine (354–430) explains, sin and evil are parasitic and perverse, a misdirection and misuse of all that God accomplished in creation. With no independent, self-sustaining power, sin and evil spread only as God's creatures, both angelic and human, bend the good creation away from its original design and purposes.[2] This terribly sad second episode of the script describes the rebellion of humanity against the Creator and the consequent advent of devastation and death. Every pool of life is polluted. Every relationship spoiled. Despite humanity's

---

1. Lucas, dir., *Star Wars: Episode IV—A New Hope.*

2. Augustine, *Confessions*, 3.7.12 as cited in Plantinga, *Not the Way It's Supposed to Be*, 89. Evil has no independent existence "except as a privation of good."

best efforts to appreciate and accept the good, the effects of sin often dominate our stage and our news cycles.

In this episode, we will consider what our script tells us about the nature of evil and our appropriate response to it. The script doesn't call for us to be heroes and heroines who overcome evil, for, as humans, we do not have the strength or the status to win that war. But neither does it call for us to ignore evil and insulate ourselves in a corner of the stage where things seem good and right. The word of God calls us to imitate Jesus' actions by identifying with sinners and those who are sinned against, by naming the broken places in our world with tears. Ironically, not by trumpeting our goodness, but in confessing our sins, in lamenting its devastating effects, and in ongoing repentance, the church is most like the one who became sin for us.[3]

The Shalom of God

Genesis 1–2 gives us a glimpse of a world unaffected by evil. Eden, "the LORD God's" masterpiece, was "very good" but incomplete, making room for the culture-making practices of his image-bearers and covenant mediators. Adam and Eve learned wisdom as they plowed, planted, parented, negotiated, governed, irrigated, prayed, harvested, celebrated, redirected wildlife, and replanted seed. By recognizing and cooperating with the patterns of God's creative design, they experienced its purpose—overflowing life, wholeness, peace. "*Shalom*," the Hebrew word often translated as "peace," is better understood as "well-being" or "flourishing." Cornelius Plantinga provides this robust definition:

> The webbing together of God, humans, and all creation in justice, fulfillment, and delight is what the Hebrew prophets call *shalom* . . . In the Bible, *shalom* means universal flourishing, wholeness, and delight—a rich state of affairs in which the natural needs are satisfied and natural gifts fully employed, a state of affairs that inspires joyful wonder (or worship) . . . . In other words, *shalom* is the way things ought to be.[4]

Adam and Eve were "fearfully and wonderfully made" (Ps 139:14) and abundantly resourced to delight in God, one another, their children, neighbors, garden, home, and work. According to God's original design, the loves and tastes of the first humans were calibrated to cultivate life,

3. See the powerful argument and witness of McBride, *Church for the World.*

4. Plantinga, *Not the Way It's Supposed to Be*, 10.

create equitable practices of exchange, love that which is lovely, and delight in the goodness of God. To do these things together, in covenantal interdependency, is to experience *shalom*.

To this day, "*shalom!*" is a greeting used in the Jewish community to communicate good wishes that a family member or neighbor is enjoying good health, or that all is going well. This use is reflected in Scripture, for example, when Joseph asks his brothers (who had not yet recognized him), "Is your father doing well?" "Yes," they assure him, "our father, your servant, is alive and well" (Gen 43:27–28).

Beyond mere well-wishing, however, *shalom* may signify harmonious relations, as in the interaction between Joseph's grandfather, Isaac, and the Philistine king, Abimelech, recorded in Genesis 26. Having been sent away from Gerar by Abimelech, Isaac encamped at Beersheba, where the LORD appeared to him and reaffirmed the covenant that he had made with Abraham (Gen 26:23–25). After a period of conflict, Abimelech approached him there to reestablish mutually beneficial relations, saying,

> We see plainly that the LORD has been with you. So, we said, . . .
> let us make a covenant with you, that you will do us no harm, just
> as we have not touched you and have done only good to you, and
> have sent you away in peace. (Gen 26:28–29)

After sharing "a feast" and exchanging their oaths, they parted ways "in peace" (Gen 26:31). Because of the LORD's blessings, as well as their own promise-making and promise-keeping, Isaac and Abimelech shared the things that make for peace, as Romans 14:19 encourages us to do. *Shalom* is the fruit of covenant faithfulness and its life-sustaining aim.

One additional example from the script demonstrates that, among the people of Israel, *shalom* was preserved not only when interpersonal covenants were made and kept, but also when the community elders settled disputes justly in relation to God's law. Jethro, Moses's father-in-law, established a judicial system when he advised Moses to select "chiefs of thousands, hundreds, fifties, and tens" who "fear God, are trustworthy, and hate a bribe" to decide most matters and to limit his own involvement to "great matters" (Exod 18:21–22). This representative system was closer to events happening on the ground, resolved matters more quickly, and eased the weight of responsibility on Moses.[5] As Jethro summarized it, "If

---

5. Catholic social teaching articulates something like this as the principle of *subsidiarity*. See Pope Pius XI's encyclical, *Quadragesimo anno*, and the National Conference of Catholic Bishops, *Economic Justice for All*.

you do this, God will direct you, you will be able to endure it, and all this people will go to their place in peace" (Exod 18:23). When used in this sense, *shalom* entails equitable sharing of image-bearing responsibilities and God's life-sustaining goods throughout the community. *Shalom* aims at well-being, establishes mutually beneficial relations, then adjudicates the material and relationships that sustain communal life equitably. *Shalom* resonates with God's original design.

Sin Wrecks Shalom

A quick glance at the front page of a newspaper or the latest update on our Twitter feed makes it clear that, in the world at large, *shalom* is in short supply. The scarcity of *shalom* affects us on a personal level when we hear the pain-filled cries of our neighbors and experience our own struggles with sorrow, conflict, and injustice. The script reminds us that all of these are the effects of sin.

From the first moment of Adam and Eve's rebellion in Genesis 3, the fall away from *shalom* towards death is rapid and steep. Cain, their first-born, murders his own brother, Abel. Lamech boasts to his wives of the revenge he has taken through multiple murders. By the end of Genesis 4, the inexplicable, irrational absurdity of sin is in full bloom. Genesis 6:5 provides the narrator's devastating evaluation, "The LORD saw that the wickedness of man was great in the earth, and that every intention of the thoughts of his heart was only evil continually." In relation to the five roles of image-bearing, outlined in the first episode of creation, sin alienates every relationship and corrupts every role.

Five Image-Bearing Roles Affected by Sin

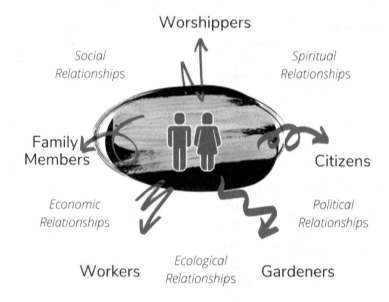

Figure 5—Five Image-Bearing Roles Affected by Sin

Genesis 3–11 offers a robust narrative of the total depravity of human-kind. Total depravity does not mean every human action is evil, but it means every human endeavor in every arena of life is stained with our sins. Mixed motives hide behind seemingly good deeds. As Chris Wright summarizes,

> Women enjoy the gift of childbirth along with suffering and pain. Men find fulfillment in subduing the earth, but with sweat and frustration. Both enjoy sexual complementarity and intimacy, but along with lust and domination . . . Technology and culture are advancing, but the skill that can craft instruments for music and agriculture can also forge weapons of violent death.[6]

The violence and destruction of sin not only affects us, our families, work-places, and governments, it affects the ground we are called to cultivate.

The commands—"Be fruitful, multiply, and subdue the earth"—that were intended to bring delight and glory to human beings as God's

---

6. Wright, *Mission of God's People*, 65.

image-bearers now carry painful reminders of covenant-breaking. Through the pain of childbirth, Eve is "the mother of all who live" (Gen 3:16, 20). In resistant soil, through frustrating toil, Adam plants, cultivates, and harvests a livelihood (Gen 3:17–29). When Cain murders his own brother, Abel, the ground no longer produces fruit from his labor. Instead of a home in a garden, Cain wanders the earth as a fugitive, driven from God and, like his parents, alienated from the ground (Gen 4:11–16). Instead of *shalom*, humankind experiences estrangement and pain; instead of peace, human beings perpetrate conflicts with God, with each other, with the earth, even against themselves. "Sin wrecks *shalom*."[7]

What does sin look like in practice? In *Creation and Fall*, Dietrich Bonhoeffer suggests that sin is a human being's attempt to reach behind God's word to snatch life for his or her self on their own terms. There is a false possibility contained within the serpent's question, "Did God say?" (Gen 3:2). Within it, a human being's basic posture as a creature in relation to the Creator is under attack. "Man is expected to judge God's Word instead of simply hearing and doing it."[8]

As we learned in Episode One, divine call and human response characterize the covenantal shape of reality. God's word is primary, shaping the setting and its characters, and giving them life and boundaries to cultivate it. At its root, then, sin is faithlessness, a personal affront against God and a misuse of the goods of creation as God intended. Powerful human capacities of creativity, reasoning, sexuality, and more are directed away from God's mission towards one's own ends. Instead of fulfilling our vocation as representatives of God's kingdom and mediators of heavenly wisdom, we craft our own messaging, build our own brands, platforms, and kingdoms. As Plantinga explains,

> Sin is a culpable and personal affront to a personal God. . . . God is not, after all, arbitrarily offended. God hates sin not just because it violates his law, but, more substantively, because it violates *shalom*, because it breaks the peace.[9]

The term *sin* is one we often hear in church, but not on the streets or in the marketplace. In *The Road to Character*, David Brooks laments that "the word 'SIN' has lost its power and awesome intensity" in late modern

---

7. Plantinga, *Not the Way It's Supposed to Be*, 14.

8. Bonhoeffer, *Creation and Fall*, 74.

9. Plantinga, *Not the Way It's Supposed to Be*, 13–16.

culture.[10] In advertisements and on menus, decadent desserts are "deliciously sinful," and "it's a sin" if you don't take advantage of this "once-in-a-lifetime offer." Though it has been ruined by many misuses, Brooks argues for putting the word *sin* back in circulation, because

> We really do have dappled souls. The same ambition that drives us to build a new company also drives us to be materialistic and to exploit. The same lust that leads to children leads to adultery. The same confidence that can lead to daring and creativity can lead to self-worship and arrogance.[11]

When we sin, we attempt to define our own lives, apart from God's word. But, to do so, we must borrow capital from God's good creation. The worldview of this episode is less like the latest release in the Star Wars series, and more like *The Matrix*, where a false world created to exert control over its inhabitants, but dependent on a larger, more real world.[12] When we sin, we create our own virtual worlds. Instead of putting on Christ and his armor, we choose an alternate wardrobe and, with it, an alternate reality. Donning helmet, visor, bodysuit, and gloves, we enter the matrix, a virtual reality game that seems real enough, but that blocks our view of the real world. We assume the role of Creator to design game scenarios for ourselves that meet our own definitions and standards of what is "good" and what is "evil."

Rereading the Script

Within our virtual worlds, the game of life seems to work on our terms. Inevitably, however, these scenarios must end. We must remove our virtual suits; pay the webmaster for the use of his electricity, software, and time; and reawaken to the real world (which we never left), where boundaries are firmer than we had thought. When we try to alter the terms of God's covenant with creation, we deny our creatureliness, tamper with the hardwiring of our humanity, and short-circuit our design as divine image-bearers to cultivate *shalom*. In short, we deceive ourselves. True freedom belongs only to God, the one whose Word bounds and shapes all

---

10. Brooks, *Road to Character*, 53.
11. Brooks, *Road to Character*, 55.
12. Wachowskis, dirs., *Matrix*.

that's real. God's life is the only source of lasting *shalom*. Take time to reread Genesis 3:1–24 slowly. Consider what this chapter teaches us about the nature and effects of sin. In verses 1–7, how are the serpent, Adam, and Eve creating a virtual world that does not align with the structure of reality set forth in Genesis 1–2? In verses 8–24, what are some of the signs that *shalom* in the real world is being wrecked? _____

_____

_____

_____

Second Gesture: Naming the Broken Places with Tears

What is a human response to destruction and death, to violent attacks against Muslims at prayer in the mosques of Christchurch, New Zealand, to the burning of Black churches in Louisiana, to the bombing of worshippers in Sri Lanka? Anger and tears. The gospel frames our cries of pain and our complaints about the devastating effects of our sin and the ways our neighbors are sinned against in confession and lament. These constructive channels for venting the pressure of our grief and anger are necessary for our mental, spiritual, and physical health, because they express the pain that results from the rupture of the covenantal shape of reality. We act in character as the body of Christ when we name the broken places and "weep with those who weep" (Rom 12:15).

We are tempted, however, to complain only about the ways we are sinned against, or how we think others have sinned. Yet "no one is righteous, no not one" (see Ps 14:3; Rom 3:10). Perhaps our greatest temptation is to cast ourselves as the heroes of the story. But, as David Brooks has reminded us, "We are all sinners together."[13] Any pretense that we, the church, are the answer and not part of the problem is a denial of the gospel. As we name the broken places in our neighborhoods, workplaces, city councils, and courts, we must remember the sequence Jesus taught his followers: "First, cast the

---

13. Brooks, *Road to Character*, 54.

plank out of your own eye, then you can see clearly to remove the speck out of your brother's eye" (Matt 7:5).

In confession, we enter the grief of loss caused by our own sins. But, before any assurance of pardon or acts of restitution, we must sit in the grief with God and with those we have wronged. Confession cuts one of sin's greatest supply lines—silence. By naming the broken places in ourselves and in our neighborhoods, we begin to understand a few things about how they came to be broken in the first place.

The habit of confession in the church is often approached as a personal, private, and sometimes silent practice—something that happens between the individual and God, or between the individual and one or two leaders in the church. But confession should also be approached corporately, publicly, and vocally. One way we see this is in scripted prayers that a congregation reads aloud during a worship service. We are called to confess and lament in the streets beyond our sanctuaries as well. Too often, we equate ministry and witness with "fixing it." But confession and repentance are integral and ongoing practices for mending our covenant with God and the world.

Cracks and Confessions in the Streets of St. Louis

I experienced this on the streets of St. Louis in the spring of 2015. By late March, the rate of deaths due to gun violence was already outpacing motor vehicle accidents and the record-setting murder rate from the prior year. On their weekly phone calls, Nikki Shockley was telling her son, Brandon Ellington, about the constant news stories and regular sounds of gunshots in his old neighborhood. She asked him to stay in South Bend, Indiana, with the network of friends and co-workers he had built there. But the father of six wanted to live closer to his oldest children, as well as his aging parents, so he packed his belongings and moved back to St. Louis. Brandon provided a stable, guiding presence not only for his children, but also for kids in the neighborhood around his mother's house. Tragically, on March 22, 2015, one of those kids would steal his life and his tax refund money at gunpoint.[14]

Nikki Shockley's tears for her son, Brandon, streamed with those of 188 other mothers whose children had died due to gun violence in St. Louis in 2015, a rate per capita higher than any other city in America. After

14. Lartney, Diehm, and Aufrichtig, "Grasping for Change on America's Most Violent Streets."

the news of Brandon's death, my phone rang. A former student, Michelle Higgins, now ministering as a pastor and community activist in St. Louis, called to ask if I would participate in a march planned for April 4. It was Easter weekend, Holy Saturday, a day of confession, lament, and reflection for Christians about the devastating effects of sin in ourselves, our families, and neighborhoods. It was also the forty-eighth anniversary of Dr. Martin Luther King Jr.'s assassination, who wrote, "He who accepts evil without protesting it is really cooperating with it."[15]

Michelle described the planned action as a mourning march of lament. She explained that members of several city congregations would gather at a local church on Delmar Boulevard with family members whose loved ones had been shot to grieve the loss of human life. The lines of our liturgy would stretch into the streets. We would pray with our lips, our tears, and our feet. When the bright, cold morning came, we marched down the Delmar Divide toward the Central West End, stopping twice along the way to amplify the witness of our neighbors' grief. In a rhythm of complaint, confession, and petition, again and again, we cried out, "Why?" and "How long, O Lord?" These are the insistent questions of psalms of lament (cf. Pss 10, 13, 22). By intentionally disrupting business as usual, we called our neighbors to pay attention to the pain, to stand and pray against the violence, and to love all the streets of St. Louis, not just those of their own neighborhood.

Michelle's request resonated with me as part of a much bigger story than the narrative of our teacher-student relationship during her years at the seminary on the western rim of our city. The lines of racial and socio-economic division that run through the history of my branch of the Presbyterian church and our city were colliding in me with the larger arch of the gospel of Christ's kingdom. My role as a minister and seminary professor was being called out from behind pulpits and lecterns into the streets to confess and bear witness to Christ's royal claim on me and my neighbors there. In my mind's eye, I could picture an on-location Bible study where Jesus and his disciples sat at the city gate watching their neighbors approach the city elders and judges, petitioning for justice. The same woman came day after day with the same request. Though the judge did not fear God, nor care about the interests of his neighbors, he gave in, worn down by the persistence of this widow pleading for justice (Luke 18:1–8). When Jesus told his disciples to pray like this, he was not merely saying "persevere in prayer," he was also commenting on how to persevere: seek justice like this widow by

15. King, *Stride Toward Freedom*.

praying with your feet. These claims on my identity—my role as Michelle's brother in Christ, my roles as teacher of the Script, minister, neighbor, and image-bearer—shaped the prayers of my mouth, heart, and feet.

Brittany, one of the young women marching with us that morning, lifted the bullhorn to ask the central question of lament before the Great Judge, "Why? Why have we lost so many of our young Black men? Trayvon Martin, Dontre Hamilton, Eric Garner, John Crawford, Michael Brown, Ezell Ford, Dante Parker, Akai Gurley, and Tamir Rice were unarmed. Why are they dead? Do you see our tears? Do you hear our cries? Why are our neighbors silent? Why is the church silent?" Later that very day, we heard news of yet another shooting of an unarmed Black man, Walter Scott, in North Charleston, South Carolina.

The police began calling for us to move out of the intersection, where we had arranged with them ahead of time to circle. We stood our ground, disrupting business as usual, and I lifted the bullhorn with a prayer of confession.

> Hear our confession, Lord, and show us your mercy. Forgive us for neglecting the pain of our neighbors. For treating you as our own personal Savior, but not as the Lord of our city. Enable us with your forgiveness and the gifts of your Spirit to bear the fruit of repentance, that we might love our neighbors not in word only, but by working for justice in our courts, in our grand juries, in our policing practices, and in the opportunities of our schools and marketplaces. For you've told us clearly through your prophets, Lord, that the kind of worship you receive is "to break the bonds of oppression, to pay fair wages, to declare to everyone the year of the Lord's favor" (Isa 58:3, 6; 61:2).

Our mourning march of confession and lament, like the persistent widow's cry and all cries for justice seek at least two things: 1) a specific acknowledgement of wrongdoing and 2) a process wherein some form of restitution in whole or in substantial part is granted to the wronged party by those who are responsible for causing the injury or loss. This understanding of restorative justice, not mere retributive justice, is rooted in the biblical script, where the judgment and grace of God consistently confronts the destructive, death-dealing power of evil in us, in our neighbors, and in our social systems.

Restorative Justice

The injustices of one or more human beings against others does violence to the dignity of all, dislocates the life-giving purposes of creation, and breaks the heart of God. As Calvin commented, "No one can be injurious to his brother without wounding God himself."[16] The righteousness of God, that is to say his good character and rightful authority, demands a confrontation with sin and evil in the world he made. On the one hand, God's judgment is punitive, deconstructing deformed misuses of creation. On the other hand, God's judgment is gracious, renewing and redirecting creation back to its original story line. God's judgment seeks both justice and redemption.

Nothing escapes God's penetrating gaze and providential care. Genesis 6 underscores this truth repeatedly: "the earth was corrupt in God's sight, and filled with violence. And God saw the earth, and behold it was corrupt, for all flesh had corrupted their way on the earth" (Gen 6:11–12). The covenantal nature of this truth is revealed by God's evaluation of both the earth and His covenant representative or mediator, humankind: "The earth is filled with violence through them. Behold, I will destroy them with the earth" (Gen 6:13). Readers are relieved to hear a note of hope resound through the name "Noah, who found favor in the eyes of the LORD" (Gen 6:8).

In Episode One, we noted the significance that Hebrew names often carry in our study of "the LORD God" in Genesis 2:4. Introducing Noah in a genealogy, Moses explains that his name sounds like the Hebrew word for "rest" or "relief." Lamech called his son Noah, saying, "Out of the ground that the LORD has cursed this one shall bring us relief from our work, from the painful toil of our hands" (Genesis 5:28–29). By sandwiching Noah's name between the curses of chapter three and the renewal of the covenant in chapter nine, Moses makes a vital theological point: covenant-making in Scripture is about restored image-bearing. God's covenant with Noah provides relief not only in the form of deliverance for his family, but also for the renewal of creation! Though spoiled, the original covenant relationship is not utterly destroyed. Adam and Eve are evicted from the garden. Nevertheless, in mercy, God provides animal skins (cf. Gen 22:13) to cover the shame of man and woman (Gen 3:21). Graciously, God gives our first parents a child in fulfillment of their original commission to "be fruitful and multiply!" (Gen 3:20, 4:1). Because of humanity's rebellion, a new, second act of covenant-making is necessary with Noah, his offspring, and the earth.

---

16. Calvin's *Commentary on Genesis* as quoted by Wolterstorff, *Hearing the Call*, 118.

The flood is an act of cleansing judgment that addresses both human-ity's sin and original commission as image-bearers. Nevertheless, this new act of covenant-making is not unlike the original covenant. Like Adam's family, Noah's family is to "be fruitful and multiply and fill the earth" (Gen 9:1). They are to care for and to cultivate the earth and its wildlife. Covenants are peace treaties, oaths which require the cost of peace to be dramatized at their formation, and which threaten pain of death should they be vio-lated. From this point forward in the biblical story line, after humankind's rebellion, the LORD initiates costly covenants to restore human beings to their image-bearing vocations, and to renew the original bond of intimacy with himself. This rebirth begins with confession and laments that "all flesh [have] corrupted their way on the earth" (cf. Gen 6:12; Rom 3:9–18).

Confession Is the Door for Restoring Community

In his devotional classic, *Life Together*, Dietrich Bonhoeffer marks public confession as the door through which we must pass if we are to experience genuine community, access the cross of Christ, receive true forgiveness, and participate in a new, resurrected life. He writes,

> Those who remain alone with their evil are left utterly alone . . . . Sin demands to have a man by himself. It withdraws him from the community. The more isolated a person is, the more destructive will the power of sin be over him. . . . In confession, the breakthrough to community takes place. Since the confession is made in the pres-ence of a Christian brother, the last stronghold of self-justification is abandoned. The sinner surrenders; he gives up all his evil.[17]

Public confession is not merely an act of interpersonal communica-tion for Bonhoeffer, but also a corporate gesture.[18] Again, the church's wor-ship and witness are interdependent, mutually informing. Our prayers of confession, whether personal or corporate, must not stay cloistered behind church walls; they must proceed to Golgotha, a place of public shame. As Bonhoeffer put it, "We cannot find the cross of Christ, if we are afraid of going to the place where Jesus can be found, to the public death of the sinner."[19] Remarkably, Christ was willing to take on the responsibility for

17. Bonhoeffer, *Life Together*, 100, 102
18. McBride, *Church for the World*, 131.
19. Bonhoeffer, *Life Together*, 104.

our sins, to stand in our place. Still, he is willing to identify publicly with a sinful society, the church. But, if we are to be his true witnesses and instruments of his transformative power in the world, we must "reciprocally take Christ's form, the form of the penitent in fallen flesh, who accepts responsibility for sin."[20]

In confession, we enter the grief caused by our sins. If we confess our sins specifically, concretely, and publicly, we put to death our personal and corporate attempts at being human apart from covenant relation to God and neighbor. Like my prayer on Holy Saturday in our mourning march, our prayers of confession articulate sins of shared responsibility in economic, judicial, and educational systems, where we either act or avoid acting together. With Bonhoeffer, we confess,

> The church was mute when it should have cried out. . . . The church has withheld the compassion it owes to the despised and rejected; the church has not resisted strongly enough the misuse of the name of Christ for political ends; the church has coveted security, tranquility, prosperity, to which it has no claim.[21]

Like the Psalms, our prayer journals, hymnals, newspapers, and books must record both personal and corporate prayers of confession, corporate and personal laments. In lament, we join the painful cries of those who are being sinned against, giving voice to our shared longings for a resurrected way of practicing human community.

Group Activities: Conducting a Needs Assessment and Practicing Lament

In light of our study of the terribly sad, second episode of the biblical script, your group is equipped to take a needs assessment of the stage where God has placed you (i.e., your campus, neighborhood, city). However, before you walk or drive through your neighborhood identifying the broken places, begin with personal and corporate confession. Write a prayer of confession in your journal describing the ways you have entered your own virtual reality, depicted yourself as the hero, and/or built your own platforms, instead of following the divine script. Though it's still early in your relationships with group members, carefully consider with whom you might share at

20. McBride, *Church for the World*, 119.
21. Bonhoeffer, "Report on the Mass Deportation of Jewish Citizens."

least a portion of your journal entry. The wise letter from the Apostle James counsels Christians to "confess your faults to one another, that you might be healed" (Jas 5:16). Remember, the drama of discipleship is not a solo performance, nor can we hide in the shadows. Gospel show-and-tell calls us out onstage with the ensemble of the church.

FIGURE 6 - The Drama of Discipleship, Dr. Gregory R. Perry
Based on the assets map by John Kretzmann and John McKnight,
Building Communities from the Inside Out (1993).

Figure 6—Community Needs Map

Last week as you drove and walked through your communities, you listed its assets and counted your blessings on three levels, that of individuals, groups or associations, and institutions. Retrace your steps, using your Community Needs Map to begin naming broken places on your stage. When you see the same neighbors you ran into last week (remember the yoga instructor or coach in the park, or community gardener from Episode One?) or when you meet new neighbors, ask them to identify two or three key issues that "aren't the way they are supposed to be." Which groups are being overlooked? Which neighbors are most vulnerable when trouble comes? What are the biggest needs in our community?

As you journey on this week's prayer walk, add confession and lament to last week's praises. Identify and confess ways in which historic lines of division in our society collide with the reconciling arch of the gospel in you. Notice the empty storefronts, the trash-filled lots, the broken playground equipment. Think about how these abandoned spaces represent empty, idle time for adults and kids who have no place to work or play. As you are completing this activity, resist the urge to start problem-solving and planning. Instead, simply feel the grief and express your pain together to God.

Lament not only names the broken places; it brokers relations with the One who can heal. Lament connects the painful reality of the world to the broken yet able heart of God. The literary form of lament is gospel-shaped—in our need, even complicity, in a disordered world, we must call and rely on the power and provision of God, our Savior. The biblical formula for lament includes five common elements: addressing God, articulating questions and complaints, confessing, expressing our petitions, and making a vow of praise.

Address: Lament begins by addressing the disorder in human hearts and communities to the one, true God. The psalmist often chooses metaphors that highlight the very aspects of God's character he needs! In need of guidance, the worshipper calls upon God as the light. In need of protection, the petitioner identifies God as a fortress or the Lord of the armies.

Questions & Complaints: In this portion of lament, the worshipper describes terrible realities in the world, the ways they affect people and places s/he cares about, as well as the feelings it provokes in him or her. Because of the great gap between God's character and these realities, the worshipper asks God repeatedly, "Why?" and "How long?" This is the absurdity of sin—things are "not the way they are supposed to be."

A Confession of Faith: These questions lead to a confession of faith, the worshiper's finds motivation for his or her petitions in God's past actions and the testimony of others about God's faithfulness. Documented both in

Scripture and in the memories of those gathered for prayer, God has acted with rescuing power, provision, goodness, and mercy towards his people. By remembering, we are not merely recalling, we are facing the present difficulty or threat on the basis of God's character. We are placing ourselves in God's hands.

Petition: No mere request for God's attention and action, petitions are also confessions of helplessness and/or failure. In other words, petitioning God to "save," "deliver," "forgive," "guide," "restore," etc. is another form of confessing faith.

A Vow of Praise: With rare exception (see Ps 88), psalms of lament end with promises to tell everyone when God answers our cries. Again, this affirms the covenant bond between God and the world as well as the worshipping community's role as God's covenant representatives to bear witness to the nations.

Prayers of lament are not to be relegated to some private sphere. They are living parables of the gospel. In prayer—especially when we pray with our mouths and our feet like the persistent widow—the church identifies with the pain of the world, the sin that caused it, and the only One who can do and has done anything about it.

With the Holy Spirit bearing witness in and between each member of your group, chances are this needs assessment will reveal particular broken places in your community or on your campus that burden two or more of you. A template is provided below to facilitate your prayers of lament.[22]

---

22. Taken from Pratt, *Pray with Your Eyes Open*, 79–90, esp. 90.

A FORMAT FOR WRITING PRAYERS OF LAMENT

1. Address: "Holy LORD, you are _____

_____

_____.

2. Questions & Complaints: Yet, when we see (hear, think about)

_____

_____,

our hearts are _____

and we feel _____.

Why, O LORD _____?

How long, O LORD _____?

3. Confessing Faith: But, because of your _____

and, _____

_____.

4. Petition: In our helplessness, we turn to you for _____

_____.

Hear our cries, and save/guide/help/provide us _____

_____.

5. Vow of Praise: When you respond, we will tell of your _____

_____

_____. Amen."

Figure 7—A Format for Writing Prayers of Lament

Israel

Using Status to Bless Others

NELSON MANDELA IS A "great name," not only because it is known through-out the world, but because of the respect the first Black president of South Africa gained for leading the work of national reconciliation and disman-tling of apartheid. But "Nelson" was the name assigned to Mandela in a British school by his first teacher. "Rolihlahla" was the name his father gave him, a Xhosa tribal word that means "troublemaker."[1] He was a *royal* troublemaker. Mandela's great-grandfather was king of the Thembu people. After his father died of lung disease when Mandela was only nine years old, his mother took him back to the royal house, where he was adopted by Chief Jongintaba and his wife, Noengland. Mandela's biological mother, Noeskeni Fanny, was a devout Christian, who had Rolihlahla baptized in the Methodist church as an infant and taught in Methodist schools as a child. Even after his return to the royal house, Mandela continued to attend church services and never renounced his Christian faith.[2]

Critics of Mandela highlight his three marriages, reported affairs, and his part in Umkhonto we Sizwe (MK), an armed wing of the African Na-tional Congress, which he formed in the wake of the Sharpeville Massacre. The MK sabotaged government property and communications, actions that led to Mandela's arrest and long imprisonment.[3] But the script of Scripture

1. Mandela, *Long Walk to Freedom*, 3.
2. Mandela, *Long Walk to Freedom*, 13.
3. Mandela, *Long Walk to Freedom*, 356.

profiles others who had multiple wives and destroyed property to confront oppression. As we saw in Episode Two, sin has infected every part of us, every human relationship and institution. Still, human beings are God's chosen agents to reclaim the world. What is the longer arc of our lives? How do we deal with our sins and the ways we are sinned against? How do we steward our suffering and our power to leave marks on the world?

When Mandela was elected to the presidency, he used his power to assist the formation of the Truth and Reconciliation Commission (TRC). The TRC established a process designed to investigate human rights abuses, receive confessions of gross injustices, and create a forum in which to seek forgiveness and offer reparations. This courtlike process required the participation of all parties in the conflict over apartheid with the aims of restorative justice and national reconciliation.[4] Shortly after his election, Mandela presented the Rugby World Cup trophy to the white Afrikaner captain of the South African team, Francois Pienaar. Though there were many old South African flags blowing in the wind that day, Mandela donned the hat and jersey of the team to make the presentation. South Africa had beaten the All-Blacks of New Zealand. Receiving the trophy from his president, Pienaar said, "Thank you, Madiba for all you are doing for our country." "Madiba" is a clan name from Mandela's Xhosa tribe. Deeper than a surname, its use is the customary way to show the highest respect. It means "father."[5]

In Genesis 12 and following, God makes extravagant promises to Abraham and Sarah. One of the promises he makes is, "I will make of you a great nation, and I will bless you and make your name great" (v. 2). Why does God promise such things to Abraham? The answer is revealed when we read the rest of Genesis 12:2–3: "I will bless you and make your name great, so that you will be a blessing . . . In you all the families of the earth shall be blessed." God's purpose in blessing Abraham is to extend that blessing beyond Abraham's house to "all the families of the earth." God's promises to Abraham, Sarah, and their children mark a new beginning for humankind. Abraham's importance is recognized in each of the so-called "Abrahamic" religions—Judaism, Christianity, and Islam—where he, much more famously than Madiba, is known as "father."

In Genesis, we see that God calls Abraham and gives him a special status in relation to other people. He is chosen, set apart. These narratives about Abraham are more than mere records of a past epoch. They

4. Allen, *Rabble-Rouser for Peace*, 343–45.
5. See Eastwood, dir., *Invictus*.

also provide stage directions for how we should act in the present, because they are intended to shape the character of God's people. In particular, they script the third gesture we will consider together: using our privileges, status, even our sufferings to bear witness to Christ and bless our neighbors.

We also learn about the purposes of God's blessings upon his people from Paul, who retells Abraham's story in new contexts to highlight how God's particular promise to Abraham's family reaches its intended goal of universal blessing to the nations. In doing so, Paul not only helps write a new chapter in the script, he teaches us that the doctrines of election, justification, and adoption are more than mere descriptions of our identity, they also carry with them instructions for their proper use. As we will see, the benefits of God's covenant are not for mere consumption—they are intended for extending the borders of God's kingdom.

The God of Glory Calls Abram in Mesopotamia

In Episode Two, we followed Moses's story of "total depravity," and the progressive and pervasive effects of sin, in Genesis 3—11. Against this bleak backdrop of blame-shifting, fratricide, abduction, rape, and the pursuit of human autonomy at Babel, Genesis 12 opens with surprising words of hope, an echo of Eden. In sharp contrast to the arrogant assertions of human capability at Babel—"let us make a name for ourselves"—the creative, life-giving God speaks a word of promise into the grief of one family's barrenness—"I will make your name great!" It's such good news that Paul describes it as "the gospel in advance to Abraham" (Gal 3:8).

This crucial moment in the script's plot begins with a call for Abraham to follow God's lead:

> Now, the LORD said to Abram, "Go from your country and your kindred and your father's house to the land that I will show you. And I will make of you a great nation, and I will bless you and make your name great, so that you will be a blessing. I will bless those who bless you, and him who dishonors you I will curse, and in you all the families of the earth shall be blessed." (Gen 12:1–3)

As we will elaborate below, it is a call back to the place and original purposes of Eden. In *The Mission of God*, Chris Wright points out that this covenantal moment is so pivotal for the book of Genesis that it is referenced "five times altogether, with minor variations of phraseology (cf.12:3; 18:18;

22:18; 28:15)."[6] Moreover, God's promise to Abraham's family resounds throughout the script in later covenant events, like that with David's house (cf. 2 Sam 7:8–17; Luke 1:31–33, 54–55, 68–79; 2:29–32). It vibrates through temple worship as a call to worship for all nations (e.g., Ps 22:27–28; 47:9; 67; 72:17; 86:8–11; 105:5–11; 117). And it forges the hope of a besieged, then exiled people in their Lord and Savior, who will one day establish his reign over all the nations (e.g., Isa 19:19–25; 45:22–23; 49:1–6; 56:3–8; 60; Jer 4:1–2; Zech 2:10–11).[7]

As we follow the script into Episode Three, novelist Dorothy Sayers reminds us that the narrator is doing more than recounting events, he is recounting these events in this way in order to shape the imaginations and choices of his audience: "The Christian faith is the most exciting drama that ever staggered the imagination of man—and the dogma is the drama."[8] By retelling the story of God's painful yet productive relationship with Abraham's family, Moses and his apostolic readers dramatize the doctrines of election, justification, and adoption. They do not use Abraham's story merely to illustrate doctrinal points. Rather, Abraham and Sarah's covenantal drama with the Lord is the point—the good news that is still spreading across generations and geography for the sake of all the families of the earth. As distinguished Ghanaian theologian Kwame Bediako wrote, "Scripture is the living testimony to what God has done and continues to do . . . . [It] is not only something we believe in, it is something we share in."[9] Biblical authors and Christian readers proclaim, practice, and improvise the story they are living in covenant with the Creator and Redeemer of life.

As we will see, God's particular covenant with Abraham's family binds its salvific benefits with its commission to bless all nations. That is not to say that God's people must bless others in order to merit the benefits of salvation; rather, it is to say that God's grace is given to them to restore their original, human role as divine image-bearers, whose practices of culture-making bless their families and their neighbors (cf. Exod 19:4–6; 1 Pet 2:9–10). For Abraham's family, later constituted as the exodus community, salvation is not merely a covenantal and redemptive event, a deliverance from the idols and injustices of Egypt; it is also a redemptive process of deliverance for restoring human vocation in the land, a land cultivated as

---

6. Wright, *Mission of God*, 194.

7. Wright, *Mission of God's People*, 74–75.

8. Sayers, *Creed or Chaos?*, 3.

9. Bediako, "Scripture as the Hermeneutic of Culture and Tradition," 3–4.

sacred space in God's presence. Indeed, redemption is a process of rein-corporating all cultural expressions of human life into a restored covenant relationship with Abraham's God and renewed social relations with God's people. By attending to the story of God's covenant with Abraham's family, we find ourselves implicated in its call to employ our endowments, our status roles, our privileges and resources, and indeed, all the benefits of our salvation for their scripted purpose—blessing and discipling all nations.

The Importance of Rereading the Script with Others

Every Bible study is an "on-location" Bible study. Because we read Scripture through the lenses of a particular language and culture, we must sometimes read with Christians who wear other lenses, if we are to see more of what is in the text and more of our cultures under the light of the text. Kwame Bediako writes, "When our cultures pass through the prism of Scripture, we see them in a new way. We are no longer defined merely by our traditions, but are allowing Scripture to interpret those traditions." Bediako understood that this illumina-tion and discipleship of cultures is taking place because "the people in the Bible will not be made perfect without us (Heb 11:40) nor we without them."[10] How do those from different cultures read God's call for Abram and Sarai to leave country and kinsman?

As we read the history of our forefathers and foremothers, we will be helped if we sit near our brothers and sisters who have made similar journeys as refugees and immigrants. Zam Khat Kham and Daniel Murphree, co-pastors of a Burmese refugee congregation within New City Fellowship of St. Louis, ask, "Do you know what it feels like to be uprooted from your native soil and family connec-tions like Abraham? To fear for your wife's safety or even for your own life like Abraham and Sarah, when they 'sojourned in Egypt' (Gen 12:10–20)?"

Many brothers and sisters, offspring of Abraham's family, in the congregation of New City have followed a similar call into refugee camps and again to new lands with strange languages. Their desire to teach their children the story of Abraham and Sarah in their na-tive tongue and their willingness to sing praises to Abraham's God

---

10. Bediako, "Scripture as the Hermeneutic of Culture and Tradition," 3–4.

in many languages marks their courageous struggle to identify first and foremost as disciples of Jesus, the Lord of all peoples and places.

Perhaps you have worked with refugees in the past or have even yourself faced displacement or significant personal transition. What have your own experiences taught you about Abraham's situation and choices in the Genesis account? I encourage you to go deeper into these questions by talking with someone who has a different perspective than you do on adapting to a new culture. Do you know international students on your campus or immigrant families in your community? Are you regularly in contact with cross-cultural missionaries? Whether over coffee locally or via email or a video-conferencing app globally, set up a series of two or three meetings to discuss Abram's call and journeys (Gen 12–15) as well as the beliefs, attitudes, and actions that are necessary for leaving and for pressing forward on the basis of hope. How do you read similarly and yet differently? _____

_____

_____

_____

_____

The Drama and Purpose of Election

In the Christian theological tradition, the term *election* refers to God's choosing or selection of those who are members of Christ's body, the church. The doctrine was first articulated by Augustine in his writings against the teachings of Pelagius to highlight God's bestowal of grace on sinners as the necessary cause of their salvation. In the Reformed, Calvinist branch of the church, this election is described as "unconditional" to emphasize that God does not choose his people based on anything good or potential good in them. Rather, God chooses his people freely in accord with his plan. Adults and children who are unsure about their standing before God may look at the doctrine of election as a comfort or struggle over its implications for themselves and their loved ones.

Using Status in the Lord's Economy

We get a glimpse at the function of status in God's covenant with Abraham's family in an upside-down bargaining encounter between them and the Lord. The scene opens with the narrator's description, "the LORD appeared to [Abraham] by the oaks of Mamre," but then describes "three men [who] were standing in front of him" (Gen 18:1–2). Do all three men together represent the Lord, or is the Lord only one of the three, who has come to Abraham in human form? Careful readers are left in suspense as Sarah and Abraham prepare a meal for the men, until two of the three "turned from there and went toward Sodom" (18:22). What happens next provides a stunning incarnation of choosing status roles in relation to others that are consistent with Abraham's new identity and vocation as one through whom God will bless all nations.

In Hebrew, the second half of verse 22 reads, "The LORD remained standing before Abraham." Sensing impropriety in this role reversal, ancient scribes switched the subject and object in the sentence to provide what our English translations read today, "but Abraham remained standing before the LORD" (see NIV, ESV, et al.).[15] Contextually, however, the Lord's choice to lower his status "before Abraham" sets up their reverse bargaining dialogue perfectly, and exemplifies an important character trait for God's people—the use of status, power, and authority for the benefit of others. The perceived difference between the Lord's true status and that which he chose to play with Abraham not only heightens the gap between the Lord's mercy and the "very grave" sins of Sodom and Gomorrah, it also dramatizes Abraham's role as intercessor.

Acknowledging the requirement of righteousness, Abraham starts by asking the Lord, "Will you sweep away the place and not spare it for the fifty righteous who are in it?" (Gen 18:24). A typical bargaining partner would respond by increasing the number to allow room for negotiation, but the Lord surprises Abraham, readily agreeing to his terms. Abraham underestimated God's justice and mercy so badly that he must lower his status with great deference to his partner if the number is to go any lower. The extent to which Abraham discounted God's mercy becomes apparent

---

15. The Hebrew of Genesis 18:22 is ambiguous. Bill Arnold points out that it is "one of the rare occasions when the earliest Jewish scribes altered the text. . . . They presumably thought it inappropriate for YHWH to stand before Abraham, so they reversed the order, leaving Abraham to stand before the YHWH." See Arnold, *Genesis*, 181.

with each round, until the number of the righteous men required by God to avoid citywide punishment is reduced from fifty to ten.

Remarkably, the Lord and Abraham "stood before" one another in a mediation of mercy, but alas, the wickedness of Sodom and Gomorrah was equal to "the outcry" against them. "The outcry" reverberates across the generations in the book of Genesis to the blood of Abel "crying out from the ground" (cf. Gen 4:10; 18:20–21), signifying the interdependence of humankind and the earth. Though the cities of Sodom and Gomorrah have "filled up their sins," God's and Abraham's mediation deliver a future for Lot's family and the nations who would flow from them. God called Abram out of Mesopotamia and mercifully chose to bless him, Sarai, and their family in order that they might use their status to bless Mesopotamia and all the families of the earth.

Third Gesture: Using Status to Bless Others

All human relationships are characterized by status. Identity, both personal and communal, is complex. Many status relationships are often in play at once. Every day, we take on many roles in relation to others: professor, student, parent, child, spouse, boss, employee, customer, neighbor, colleague, counselor, and friend. For example, my friend and former colleague Mike Higgins is a husband and father, an ordained pastor, seminary chaplain, and an honorably retired colonel in the US Army. Needless to say, he wears many hats. He plays many roles.

Due to his status as a Black male, he was stopped regularly by St. Louis-area police until he decided to advertise his status as an Army colonel and Purple Heart recipient on his license plates. By choosing to lift his status, he saved himself a great deal of hassle and restored a sense of proper respect in the way local police related to him. During the Ferguson protests, Mike crossed a yellow police tape to enter a government building, which he had a right as a citizen to enter during posted business hours. Along with other peaceful protesters, he was arrested, booked, and jailed for twenty-four hours. By lowering his status to become a prisoner, Mike underscored the injustices of a system that did not want to recognize its accountability to its citizens.

As Sam Wells states, "'High' and 'low' status are not moral designations."[16] They are an ordinary aspect of every human interaction. The crucial question is "For what purpose do you choose a higher or lower

16. Wells, *Improvisation*, 94.

status?" Does it align with the purpose of status in God's covenantal story to form a people who will "bless all the families of the earth"? Jesus used his choices of "higher" and "lower" status to move relationships toward the plotline of redemption and the values of God's kingdom. When confronting powerful demons or proud leaders, Jesus asserted his power and status. When those on the margins needed someone to search for them or when those who followed him needed an example, he shared his power and chose "low" status as a servant. What status roles, what use of power and position is needed in this moment to signify the character and kingdom of God?

Having discerned God's wider, redemptive purpose for the nations in the gifts of Abraham's elective casting call, the script leads us to consider the character of Abraham's justification. Paul not only retold Abraham's story to shape the attitudes, beliefs, and practices of intercultural, interclass, urban Messianic congregations; he embodied that story himself.

Paul's Retelling of Abraham's Justification

Having once interpreted his Jewish cultural privileges as expressions of his righteousness, Paul came to see that continuing to interpret them as such made them obstacles to the righteousness that comes as a gift through the faithfulness of Christ (see Phil 3:1–11). As a bearer of Abraham's promise, however, he did not discard his status and cultural privileges entirely, but redirected their use to advocate for the acceptance of Gentile Christians as Gentiles into the covenant community on the same basis as Abraham—faith.

Notably, Moses's account of Abraham's justification does not focus on his need for forgiveness or acquittal before a divine judge. Instead, it contrasts Abraham's impotence and nomadic exposure with God's power to create the stars and dramatic royal assurances to provide Abraham with offspring and land—the resources he and his family needed as covenant partners in God's mission to renew the earth. Many, many years had carried the couple well past their childbearing capacities. Abraham described his situation to the Lord as a matter of biological and legal facts: "You have given me no offspring, and a member of my household will be my heir" (Gen 15:3). Not unlike the lesson for Job in God's power, wisdom, and righteousness (Job 38:7, 18–20, 24, 31–33 à 40:8–14; 41:11), the Lord shows Abraham the heavens and asks if he can count the stars (Gen 15:5). Like Job, Abraham goes quiet, seemingly covering his mouth. However, the narrator speaks on his behalf, describing the significance of his silence: "Abraham believed God and it was credited to him as righteousness" (15:6).

The narrator's assessment of Abraham's faith is not lost on Paul. Yet, as commentators have focused on Paul's repeated reference to Genesis 15:6 (Rom 4:3, 9, 23), they have sometimes missed the harmonic overtones of his three-note chord from Abraham's story (Gen 15:6 [Rom 4:3, 9, 23]; Gen 15:5 [Rom 4:18] and 17:5 [Rom 4:17, 18]), and his central characterization of Abraham as "father" (4:1, 11, 12 [2x], 16, 17 [2x], 18). Paul not only elaborates on Moses's connection between justification and the promise of offspring; he also extends that connection to the land grant treaty. Abraham's justification is not about him in isolation. He is not justified in a corner or facing charges alone before a judge in a courtroom. Rather, like his election, Abraham's justification is about his covenantal relationships with God, Sarah, their miraculous offspring, and the land of promise.

With Moses, Paul's redemptive vision is bifocal. He describes God's grace to the person Abraham, but always in relation to the wider, public purpose of his covenantal participation. In other words, Paul's renarration of justification is about life out of death (4:19), birth out of barrenness, a land inheritance out of wilderness wandering—not merely for Abraham's family, but for all the families of the earth (4:13).

Why, then, is forgiveness of sin a focal point in Paul's renarration of justification? Having reviewed the way Paul rereads Moses's description of Abraham's justification in relation to God's promise from a perspective before the Law was given, we are now in a better position to understand Paul's rereading of Abraham's justification from a perspective after the Law was given and broken. Sadly, the Law's sanctions anticipated Israel's return to Ur (i.e., Mesopotamia) and Egypt in exile (Deut 28:15–68). The exodus was reversed because the people of the covenant did not keep faith with the Lord alone as their God and display his righteousness to each other and to the nations. Indeed, they became indistinguishable from their pagan neighbors (Ezek 5:5–7). God's plan with Abraham's family for the sake of the world was threated again by the death-dealing sins of idolatry and injustice. The Law had a sentence for punishment, but no solution for starting again.

Paul's renarration of God's promise to Abraham in Romans 4 and Galatians 3 exposed Israel's need for forgiveness as equal to that of the nations, answering a human need for new life through the life, death, and resurrection of Jesus the Messiah.

What, then, was the purpose of the law? It was added because of transgressions until the Seed to whom the promise referred had come . . . Is the law, therefore, opposed to the promises of God? Absolutely not! For if a law had been given that could impart life, then righteousness would certainly have come by the law. But, the Scripture declares that the whole world is a prisoner of sin, so that what was promised, being given through the faithfulness of Jesus Christ, might be given to those who believe. (Gal 3:19, 21–22)

Slavery to sin is a metaphor with which Paul describes the living death of all humans, Jew or Gentile, who are imprisoned in "the present evil age" (Gal 1:3). Like the exodus community, Paul's audience had been liberated from "the elements of the universe" that shaped their circumstances (*stoicheīa*; Gal 4:3, 9).[17] The plagues, culminating in the death of the firstborn, were the Lord's instruments of war on the gods of Egypt as he redeemed his covenant people. Just as the blood of the Passover lamb had liberated the firstborn of Israel, "Christ our Passover" (1 Cor 5:7) delivered Paul's readers into "a new creation" (Gal 6:15; cf. 2 Cor 5:17) from slavery to "the elements of the universe" that ruled the Roman world.

With the arrival, death, resurrection, and enthronement of the Messiah of Israel, a new cosmic order dawned over Jews, who had been under "the Law's curse" (Gal 3:13), and Gentiles, who were enslaved to "the elements of the universe." "For freedom, Christ has set us free!" (Gal 5:1). But how? To explain the liberation of Jews and Gentiles from sin, and their mutual incorporation into God's family and mission, Paul chooses a practice in status-conscious Roman society that effected a radical change in status, but not for the reasons that readers in the late modern West might expect.

Adoption Effects a Radical Change of Status

On Paul's Greco-Roman cultural stage, someone without an heir would often adopt an adolescent male as his son, one who would care for him in his old age and continue his business interests, political relations, and religious obligations after his death. The well-being of the paterfamilias and

---

17. John M. G. Barclay writes, "recent research has confirmed that *ta stoichea tou kosmou* most likely refers to the physical elements of the world \ . . . . Paul represents both Torah-observance and pagan religious practice . . . as beholden to the natural order of the cosmos through alignment to its elemental, physical components." See *Paul and the Gift*, 409.

continuation of his interests, not those of the child, was the focus of concern.[18] An important exception to this motivation was found in heavily indebted families. Nevertheless, to avoid passing on their debts and subjecting their children to a life of slavery, parents would sometimes commend them for adoption within their network of extended family members or patrons, because, legally, debts could not follow them into their adopted family.

Modeling a pattern of interpretive improvisation, Paul articulated connections between God's scripted promises and his missional stage. Though unknown in ancient Jewish jurisprudence and social convention, adoption was tied to inheritance law in the Roman world. Paul picked up on the reversal of status in Roman adoption law, from slavery to freedom, from poverty to inheritance, to summarize the drama of the gospel:

> When the fullness of time had come, God sent forth his Son, born of a woman, born under the Law, to redeem those who were under the law, so that we might receive adoption as sons. And, because you are sons,God has sent the Spirit of his son into our hearts, crying, "Abba! Father!" So, you are no longer a slave, but a son, and if a son, then an heir through God. (Gal 4:4–7)

The sanctions of the Law condemned Israel to barrenness and dispossession, a return to Abraham's and Sarah's condition at the time of their calling and election. Like their forebearers, condemned Israel was incapable of a do-it-yourself reboot.

Picking up on the word *heir* in Genesis 15:3, Paul saw that God's choice of Abram's family out of paganism was similar to the adoption provision in Roman inheritance law. As Robert Brian Lewis has shown, Roman adoption law not only brought about a change of status, but a change of family divinities. Adoption was not only legal, economic, and familial; it was also religious. As Lewis put it,

> When someone was adopted, not only did family relationships change, worship changed also. The adoptive family spirits became the spirits of the adoptee. The adoptee was expected to preserve the family cult and celebrate the genius of his new family.[19]

Connecting God's past promises in the text to God's presence and mission in his social context, Paul also built his exegesis on the Galatian

18. See the summary discussion on Roman adoption law in Heim, *Adoption in Galatians and Romans*, 1–23.

19. Lewis, Paul's *"Spirit of Adoption" in its Roman Imperial Context*, 56.

Christians' experience of the Holy Spirit, who cried out, "Abba, Father!" among them (Gal 4:6). He asked them:

> Does he who supplies the Spirit to you and works miracles among you do so by the works of the Law or by hearing with faith—just as "Abraham believed God and it was credited to him as righteousness"? (Gal 3:5–6)

To the Galatian Christians, who were being told they must observe the practices of Torah to be counted among Abraham's sons, Paul pointed to the Messiah and his gifts of the Spirit and wonder-working power to say, "If you have God's Spirit, you are already sons and, thus, heirs according to the promise" (cf. Gal 3:26—4:7; Rom 8:15–17). For Paul, the presence and practices of life in God's Spirit are the proper peak of Abraham's story in new exodus and new covenant, because no law can impart life (cf. Acts 13:36–39; Gal 3:21; Rom 4:16–22). Only the Resurrected One, who pours out the life-giving Spirit, has power over barrenness and death to make things new.

Even as her election in Abraham was missional, so Israel's redemption in Abraham's seed, Christ, was not merely for her own sake but "that the blessing given to Abraham might come to the Gentiles" (Gal 3:14). So Paul emphasized Abraham's role as "the father of many nations" (cf. Gen 17:5; Rom 4:16, 18). Remarkably, those of us who believe among the nations are also Abraham's offspring, sharing in Israel's adoption, redemption, and mission as children of Israel's God through Christ (cf. Exod 4:22–23; Hos 11:1; Rom 8:15–17, 23; 9:4; Gal 4:5).

As we have learned, adoption was not part of Jewish jurisprudence. Paul's improvisation in Romans 9:4 incorporates the redemptive dimension of adoption in Roman law. Occasionally, adoption and redemption (that is, manumission) intersected in court when a master would extend his name and serve his interests by adopting the son of a trusted slave. Not only did this liberate "his son," granting him new rights of citizenship and inheritance; it also ensured great loyalty to the former master's household.[20] Paul integrated elements from Israel's script and the Roman stage, because the Word of God not only called creation into existence, it also liberates both Jew and Gentile

---

20. While manumission or redemption, in the case of sacral manumission, did not necessarily secure citizenship or inheritance rights, the strict terms of adoption did. See the brief discussion of slavery and manumission in Gorman, *Apostle of the Crucified Lord*, 15–16. For more detailed discussions of Galatians 3–4 in relation to slavery and adoption, see Glancy, *Slavery in Early Christianity*, 34–38, and Heim, *Adoption in Galatians and Romans*, 148–99.

as God's adopted sons and daughters to use the privileges of their new status to bless all the families of the earth, indeed, to bless the earth itself.

Group Activity: Using Status to Bless Others

A recipient of this mercy (Gal 1:13–16; Eph 3:7–8; 1 Tim 1:12–16), Paul leveraged his education in the Scriptures, his cultural privileges as a "Hebrew of Hebrews" (Phil 3:5), and his status as an apostle of Jesus Christ to advocate for the entrance of the uncircumcised into Christ's social body on the same basis as the circumcised—God's grace through faith in Christ alone. He also took up a collection of funds from predominantly Gentile churches to provide famine relief to predominantly Jewish churches in Palestine. Based on our study of Abraham's story in Genesis, and rereadings with Paul in Galatians 3, and Romans 4, take stock of your 'high' and 'low' status roles and choices; and, your power to participate in and influence each area of image-bearing.

Are you a church leader, a spouse and parent? Are you a teacher or business owner or manager? Are you a government official, on the school board, in the police or military? How do you use your authority to influence social systems? How are you using your status roles to rectify inequities, to identify with the vulnerable, to bless your family, your neighbors, your fellow employees? Describe some of the ways you see others sharing their profits and power with those who helped produce them. Identify one or two ways that each of you will renarrate the way you use your influence to bear witness to God's kingdom in relation to others. How can you use your positions of lower status to imitate Christ? When might it be appropriate to choose a higher status to confront injustice, to rectify an abusive or codependent relationship? Commit to pray for one another as you seek wisdom about the use of your status and undertake small but significant changes.

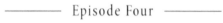

— Episode Four —

Jesus

Turning to Follow the Way of Life

JESUS DID NOT GROW up in a middle-class family. His parents couldn't afford to send him to private school or college. He learned the carpentry trade at home (cf. Matt 13:35; Mark 6:3) and studied the Scriptures at synagogue, but he never owned a house or a business.[1] He never married or became a parent. He didn't speak, write, or read English.

Unless you are a time-traveling, first-century Palestinian Jew, getting to know Jesus of Nazareth is a demanding, cross-cultural experience. Nevertheless, if you have been paying close attention on our journey through the Script, then you have been absorbing the same contours of covenantal thought, attitudes, and practices that shaped Jesus' identity and mission while he was on the earth. Eyewitnesses report that Jesus' life and teachings, death, and resurrection fill up the pattern of covenantal life under God's reign. He is the door that opens Israel's Scriptures and the future of the nations. He defined his vocation as an inaugural expression of God's reign, renewed God's covenant with Israel, and restored them as witnesses of God's reign to the nations of the world.

Much is familiar about Jesus and yet, if we are honest, much is unsettling. As we will see in this chapter, he is the ideal Israelite, "a prophet who

1. *Tektōn*, usually translated "carpenter" (see Matt 13:35; Mark 6:3), could also indicate a "tradesman" who worked with other materials, like stone. Though Jesus' childhood home in Nazareth may well have been owned and transferred to a family member, the New Testament never indicates that Jesus himself laid claim to ownership. In fact, he says, "the Son of Man has no place to lay his head" (cf. Matt 8:20; Luke 9:58).

is mighty in word and deed," and the long-awaited king from David's family line. He calls his followers to study and learn all of his ways. Yet, the path he leads them on is a narrow and difficult road among others who have been marginalized by the world's empire-builders. According to Jesus, to get back into character as humans who bear God's image and reveal God's reign, we must imitate his sacrificial love for God and neighbor. To do so, we, like his first followers, will need the gifts of repentance, purification, and faith to restore us to covenant intimacy with Israel's God, the power and presence of the Holy Spirit, and the encouragement of our fellows who also follow in Jesus' ways. In this chapter, we will look closely at the language of "fulfillment" and "promise" in the Gospels of Luke and Matthew; Israel's need for purification or baptism to restore her to the covenants of promise; and Jesus' preaching and practice of God's reign that enlists forgiven followers to live as its witnesses.

Promises and Patterns

The language of "fulfillment" suggests that something that was partial has now become complete or has been brought to its goal. Throughout the Gospels, Paul's letters, and the writings of second-century Christians, a case is made that Jesus is the fulfillment of Old Testament prophecies. Events recorded first in Israel's Scriptures are redeployed in new contexts to demonstrate the pattern of God's faithfulness to his covenant and people in the gift of their Messiah, who fills up that pattern to overflowing.

For most twenty-first-century readers, the term *prophecy* denotes the idea of prediction. To many, a prophetic word is one that tells what will happen in the future. By this definition, Christians can successfully argue that Jesus fulfilled Old Testament prophecies when the Old Testament language clearly points to something he was (a Nazarene, Matt 2:23), something he did (submitted to his arrest, Matt 26:56), or something he said (his interpretation of Isaiah, Luke 4:18–21).

But when we look more closely at how the New Testament writers use the language of promise and fulfillment, we see that simple prediction is not the whole story—not even most of it. While a few fulfillment texts verify an earlier prediction, most describe how a divine promise has been kept or a covenantal pattern has been actualized in an ideal or intensive manner.[2] In order to understand the way Jesus and his witnesses relate to the language

2. See Moule, "Fulfillment-Words in the New Testament."

of promise and fulfillment, readers of the New Testament must learn to distinguish different aspects of its use.

The Gospel of Luke provides a lesson in this kind of reading through two episodes that bookend its telling of Jesus' story. In each scene, Luke locates Jesus at the center of God's plan for Israel and the world. At the top of Luke's frame, we meet Simeon and Anna, faithful Jews who are looking for "the consolation of Israel" (Luke 2:25, 38). How do they know that Jesus is the one who will fulfill this hope? Simeon and Anna are presented as ideal readers of Israel's Scriptures, members of a faithful remnant of God's people who read the prophets as closely as they follow the Law. Therefore, they were alert to God's action in Jesus when he was presented. They kept watch in prayer, anticipating and asking for God's mighty work in history. Their practice of prayerful reading models a posture of listening to the Spirit, who still speaks through the Scriptures.

At the bottom of Luke's frame, we meet Cleopas and his companion on the road to Emmaus, northwest of Jerusalem. Like Simeon and Anna, these fellow travelers speak of one who will "redeem Israel" (Luke 24:21). Unlike the ideal readers, however, they fail to recognize that the Redeemer himself has joined their journey. Although they had studied the Scriptures in depth and had begun to place their hope in Jesus of Nazareth (v. 21), his condemnation and crucifixion didn't square with their messianic expectations (v. 20), so they assumed they had read the texts and events wrongly. Jesus pointed out, however, that they had not believed "all that the prophets have spoken" (v. 25). This identifies gaps in their reading, gaps that still plague followers of Christ today. In this tantalizing encounter with the risen Jesus, the journeymen are reminded of Jesus' earlier interpretation of his suffering. As they break bread with him, their eyes are opened (Luke 24:30–31).

In both scenes, at the beginning and end of Luke's account of the gospel, Jesus is recognized in relation to Israel's Scriptures and her practices of worship when the Holy Spirit or Jesus himself reveals it. On the road to Emmaus, Jesus not only described himself as the fulfillment of the Law, the prophets, and the Psalms (Luke 24:27, 44–45), he authorized his witnesses and their mission as part of that fulfillment as well. We will return to this point below as we think about how to live out our roles in God's kingdom.

In his own eyewitness account of the gospel, Matthew also describes the events of Jesus' life as the peak or turning point of Israel's story. Twelve times, Matthew punctuates his account with commentary from Israel's Scriptures, using the clear literary marker that these events happened "to fulfill that which was spoken" by Israel's prophets (1:22; 2:5, 15, 17, 23; 4:14; 8:17; 12:17; 13:14, 35; 21:4; 27:9). While one could make a case that the prophet Micah had predicted the Messiah would be born in Bethlehem (Mic 5:2, quoted in Matt 2:6), this would not say enough about this prophecy's fulfillment. Bethlehem is David's city. Thus, Jesus' birth there is best understood as a fulfillment of God's promises to David's house (cf. 2 Sam 7; Isa 9; 11). While the prophecy's predictive element displays the sovereign control of Israel's God over history, the promissory element is interpersonal for David's family. Its fulfillment displays God's faithfulness to Israel.

Moreover, the evangelist Matthew has placed this prophecy in a wider constellation of quotations that trace the biblical pattern of sonship, both Israel's and David's. Jesus fulfills the covenantal requirements of sonship to overflowing. To display his identity and faithfulness as the Son of God, Matthew documents Jesus' genealogy within the promises God made to Abraham and David (Matt 1:1–17). He threads together a series of episodes about sonship from chapters 1–4, against backdrops that are very familiar to his Jewish-Christian readers, the wilderness and the exodus.

To capture the sharp pain of Herod's paranoid slaughter of male infants in Bethlehem, Matthew chose Jeremiah's soundtrack of "Rachel weeping for her children" (Jer 31:15, quoted in Matt 2:18). However, the evangelist balanced this lamenting echo with reverberations of exodus, anticipations of deliverance. Though the holy family must escape to Egypt as refugees from Herod's madness, the Gospel describes their return to Judea with the language of Hosea 11:1: "Out of Egypt I have called my son." This is not a prediction about Jesus. Hosea is speaking of God's deliverance of Israel in the Exodus, but contrasting that event sharply with her plight in his day—she would remain under Assyria's reign (11:5). Like Israel, Jesus is the "firstborn" from God (cf. Ex 4:22; Hos 11:1). Unlike Israel, Jesus passed the test of sonship in the wilderness (Matt 4:1–11) to lead a second exodus through the waters into the kingdom of God.

Luke, Matthew, and the entire New Testament chorus announce good news about the arrival of God's active reign through Jesus and the deliverance of God's people from all other, would-be masters. The way Jesus achieved this deliverance should trouble would-be followers. Instead of leading a violent political uprising like other Messiah-wannabes, Jesus called his witnesses to imitate his self-giving, cross-bearing love of God, neighbor, and enemy. Moreover, Jesus clearly confronted social, religious, and political leaders about the limits and purpose of their power. As Ernest

Shurtleff summarized so well in his hymn, "Lead on, O King Eternal": "Not with swords loud crashing, nor roar of stirring drums, with deeds of love and mercy, the heavenly kingdom comes."[3]

The Pattern of Baptism

The biblical concept of fulfillment can also help us understand the inaugural event of Jesus' ministry, reported in all four Gospels. Why did Jesus choose to be baptized? Even John himself, the prophetic forerunner to Jesus, wasn't sure that Jesus needed this washing (Matt 3:13–15). With biblical patterns backlighting the scenes, however, Jesus' baptism highlights important aspects of his identity and mission. Disturbingly, he said his followers would also drink the cup of his suffering and undergo this baptism (cf. Mark 10:38–39; Rom 6:3–11).

The baptism of Jesus draws on two significant backgrounds: the ritual washings of Israel's Scriptures and the reappropriation of baptism among Jewish sects during the intertestamental period. According to the Mosaic law, washings were required to reconsecrate a covenant member who had become ritually unclean. For instance, ritual washing was required after travel or when reentering the temple for worship after marital relations, a menstrual cycle (Lev 15:16–33), or caring for a sick relative who had died (Num 19:11–22). Of course, washings were required also in connection to sin and guilt offerings (Num 19:1–10). They were both a necessary part of the restoration process for sinners, and a way of consecrating people and things for sacred use. In sum, ritual washings were part of preparing God's people to encounter God's holy, concentrated presence.

From her prophets, Israel understood that the Spirit's return to Israel to renew her covenant life would flow from her repentance and forgiveness, followed by removal of the stain of sins that had led to her exile. Aside from a short period of independence under the Hasmoneans, the Jews had not regained sovereignty over the covenant lands of Israel. In 63 BC, a new overlord, the Roman emperor, took charge of Jerusalem. Though the temple was rebuilt in grand fashion by the puppet king, Herod, the Roman occupation of Judea raised difficult questions about the status of Israel's relationship with God. One faction of Jews, the Essenes, denied the legitimacy of Herod's temple and its priesthood, going so far as to leave Jerusalem to establish a community of study and Torah observance called Qumran, near

---

3. Shurtleff, "Lead on O King Eternal."

the Dead Sea. To join their sect, candidates needed more than their Jewish ethnic identity. For over a year, initiates were catechized in the Law, then baptized to mark their entrance into the new covenant community.

Whether or not he was influenced by the Essenes, John the Baptizer preached repentance and practiced ritual washings at a time when religious and social reforms were being enacted widely. The Pharisees, the party with the broadest influence among the people of the land, popularized an approach to Torah that applied some ritual washings to the people, which had previously only been required of the priests (i.e., Mark 7).

With this background in place, we can say more about why John baptized Jesus. From John's own protest and clear articulation of Jesus' higher status, readers are made aware that his righteousness is greater than John's (Mark 1:7–8; Luke 3:15–16; John 1:29–34). With reference to himself, then, Jesus is baptized as an act of consecration for public ministry, preparing him for endowment with the concentrated presence of the Holy Spirit. For such an intense encounter with the divine, ritual washings pertain. The heavenly voice interrupts the narrative, weaving together two texts, to declare another reason: Jesus is baptized as the leading representative of Israel. Auditors first hear a text from the Davidic covenant identifying the anointed one: "Today, you are my son!" (cf. 2 Sam 7:14; Ps 2:7). Then, immediately a second, interwoven text from the prophet Isaiah, who foresaw a Spirit-anointed servant who would suffer for the people's sins: "With you, I am well-pleased" (cf. Isa 42:1–4, 6; 52:13–53:12; Matt 12:1–21). According to this heavenly voice, Jesus is both the long-awaited, prophetic servant and the Davidic King!

How does anyone leave their old realm and enter into the new age of God's reign? The same way the exodus community entered into the promised land—through the waters of the river Jordan. Jesus came to the lost sheep of the house of Israel as their Davidic king and shepherd to restore them to God's flock (Luke 15:1–7; 19:10; John 10:11–14). He came also as their prophetic servant (Matt 12:15–21) to suffer their baptism (Mark 10:38–40; Luke 12:49–50) for the forgiveness of their sins (Matt 1:21; 26:28). Echoing the prophetic voice, Jesus called Israel to return to the Lord with her whole heart, not merely to renew the old covenant, but to establish a new covenant. Remarkably, this covenant was not mediated through sacrifices in Herod's temple nor by its corrupt priesthood, but on the basis of Jesus' own authority, through his body and blood alone. By following him in baptism, his baptism with the Holy Spirit, a renewed Israel with Messiah-commissioned leaders was sanctified and empowered for its vocation as "the light of the world" (Matt 5:14; cf. John 1:9; 3:19; 8:12; 9:5; 12:46).

Purity, Preaching, Parables, and Practices of God's Kingdom

Tensions rose early in Jesus' ministry when his synagogue sermons, healings, and meals revealed his interest in the unclean, the demon-possessed, and sinners. To follow Jesus meant giving up the status-seeking, segregating purity practices of the temple leaders, scribes, and Pharisees to pursue a thoroughgoing righteousness from the inside out (Matt 15:10–20; Mark 7:14–23). Jesus reversed the direction of cultic contamination. Instead of fearing contamination from the outside, from dirty hands, unclean foods, those with diseases, demons, or even from dead bodies, Jesus approached, engaged, touched, and healed them.

Endowed with the Holy Spirit from his baptism, Jesus did not shrink back from the leper (Matt 8:1–4; Mark 1:40–45; Luke 5:12–14; 17:11–19) or from allowing the sick (Matt 9:20–22; Mark 5:25–34) and sinful (Matt 26:6–13; Luke 7:36–50) to touch him. Contact with impurity could not disqualify Jesus from entering the temple to encounter God's presence. Instead, he filled up the covenantal pattern of righteousness to the point of overflowing on others. As we will see, Jesus' witnesses, his "royal priesthood" (cf. Exod 19:5–6; John 17:19; 1 Pet 2:9), are consecrated, empowered, and commissioned to follow his pattern wherever they are sent. We can look for clues about how to play our role as Jesus' witnesses by studying his preaching, parables, and practices of God's kingdom as they are depicted in the Gospels.

1. Preaching and Practicing Righteousness in His Kingdom

Overlooking the Galilee, in his Sermon on the Mount, Jesus not only called his followers to reform their interpersonal (i.e., anger, lust, divorce; Matt 5:21–32) and religious practices (i.e., prayers, fasting, and almsgiving; Matt 6:1–18), he also commanded them to abandon hatred for their Roman occupiers, to instead love their enemies (Matt 5:38–48). Mimicking rabbinic forms of argument for his Jewish Christian audience, Matthew summarizes Jesus' direct engagement with the Law in a series of antitheses (5:21, 27, 31, 33, 38, 43). For example,

> "You have heard it said, you shall not commit adultery, but I say to you, if a man looks at a woman with lustful intent, he has already committed adultery with her in his heart." (5:27–28)

Jesus' teaching about true righteousness moves from inside the human heart to outer extremities of love for God and neighbor, from heartwork to fieldwork. Consistent with his reversal of cultic contamination, Jesus' ethic probes inwardly to address the true source of defilement for God's image in humankind, the human heart.

> "To eat with unwashed hands does not defile anyone. Whatever goes into the mouth passes into the stomach and is expelled. [Rather,] out of the heart come evil thoughts, murder, adultery and other forms of sexual immorality, theft, false witness and slander. These are what defile a person." (cf. Matt 15:10–20; Mark 7:14–23)

Even as Jesus probed the heart of his listeners, he pointed to the outer extremities of heaven and earthly society—the love of God and neighbor. For example, the objective of marriage is not merely to refrain from adultery. Instead, the aim of a healthy marriage is the extremity of sacrificial love. Accordingly, Jesus confronted the legal maneuvers of the Pharisees (Matt 19:1–12), who tried to trap him in the intricacies of divorce court, debating the legality of Deuteronomy 24:1. Instead, Jesus pointed to the foundational wedding ceremony and its aim, an unbreakable, one-flesh union between husband and wife (cf. Gen 2:24; Matt 19:4–6).[4]

Writing to a wider, ethnically mixed audience, Luke summarized Jesus' social ethic in counterpoint to well-known practices of Roman patronage. Hesiod taught,

> Invite your friend, not your enemy to dine. Be especially cordial to your neighbor . . . [and] measure carefully when you must borrow from your neighbor, then pay back the same or more, if possible . . . Love your friends, visit those who visit you, and give to those who give to you.[5]

According to Jesus, however, the economy of God's kingdom runs more like a household on the largesse of loving provision, not transactional scarcity. In God's household, power and position are used to edify and develop those with needs in the family, not to protect one's power and

---

4. See Wenham, *Torah as Story*, 73–108, where he explores the "ethical gap" between "the floor" of legal requirements and "the ceiling" of the Law's ideals.

5. Quoted in Barclay, *Paul and the Gift*, 25.

position, cultivate dependencies, or flatter others with extravagant gifts. The abundant grace of God's economy does not override justice; it resources it beyond mere retribution to restoration. "Love your enemies; do good to those who hate you; and pray for those who persecute you" (cf. Matt 5:44; Luke 6:27–28) is not possible in an economy of scarcity or a legal system built on retributive justice. These practices only make sense in a kingdom of abundance, under a king whose law of love aims at resurrection.

Jesus made this plain in his debate with the teachers of the law by drawing their attention to Hosea 6:6, a passage he quoted at least twice (Matt 9:13; 12:7). When the Pharisees learn that Jesus had attended a party at Matthew's house, they asked his disciples, "Why does your teacher eat with tax collectors and sinners?" Jesus answered with a proverb: "Those who are well have no need of a physician. Rather, those who are sick need one" (cf. Matt 9:9–12; Mark 2:16–17; Luke 5:30–32). Matthew must have been impressed by Jesus' reference to Hosea 6:6, for he is the only Gospel writer who recorded Jesus' charge to him and his fellow disciples: "Go and learn the meaning of this—'I desire mercy, not sacrifice.' I came not to call the righteous, but sinners" (Matt 9:13).

2. Parables and Practices of the Kingdom

For Jesus, there are "weightier matters of the law" (Matt 23:23), a center of gravity that establishes priorities and cultivates wisdom in the human heart, which, if not directed toward the One who embodies "justice, faithfulness, and mercy" (23:23), is the place from which uncleanness flows. When a Jewish scribe alludes to Hosea 6:6 in response to Jesus' summary of the law in Mark 12:33, Jesus says, "You are not far from the kingdom of God." Both physically in Jesus' presence, and conceptually in his understanding of the Scriptures, the scribe stood at the entrance of God's kingdom. Jesus did not abolish the Law (Matt 5:17–20); rather, he called Israel to adopt his interpretation of the Law, that is, to interpret the Law in relation to him and to engage society with the ethic he himself embodied—justice and faithfulness restored by mercy and love (Matt 7:24–27). Still, Jesus calls his followers to the heartwork and fieldwork of learning his ways from the inside outside to their social embodiment.

The chief priests, Pharisees, and scribes were keepers of the status quo in Israel. However, Jesus acted like things were not the way they were supposed to be. He believed that Judean society was broken. The status quo was compromised with too much disease, demonic activity, extortion, poverty, and social segregation. Like his meals with tax collectors and sinners, Jesus' Sabbath activities restore life. He underscored this point with another proverb, one that exposed the hypocrisy of those who lectured him on Sabbath-keeping: "Which one of you who has a sheep (or ox), if it falls into a pit on the Sabbath, will not take hold of it and lift it out?" (cf. Matt 12:9–14; Mark 3:1–6; Luke 6:6–11; 13:15; 14:5).

Jesus healed, cast out demons, distributed food, and befriended and forgave repentant sinners in order to restore lost lambs to the flock of God. Moreover, he calmed the storm, renewed the created order, even raised the dead, to bring *shalom*. Jesus did not perform miracles primarily to wow the crowds. He did wondrous things to restore the sons and daughters of Abraham to their roles as divine image-bearers—to their proper worship, work, family relationships, and wider social responsibilities, even to their right minds and bodies. Indeed, his parables, which describe what "the kingdom of heaven is like," engage every arena of life on earth.

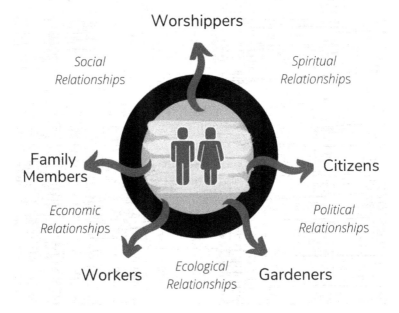

Figure 8—Discipleship Restores Roles of Image-Bearing

Jesus' parables are interpretive exercises in redirecting human attitudes and activities towards life and reincorporating those on the edge of human society into the new covenant community. Engaging familiar scenes from daily life, Israel's teacher *par excellence* led his listeners into surprise endings and moments of decision about their relationship to God's reign in each dimension of human vocation.

Several parables invite audiences to discern kingdom practices in economic relationships involving money and other material goods (the rich fool, the shrewd steward, the lost coin, the talents) or social relationships with the poor (the rich man and Lazarus), the ethnic other (the good Samaritan), or the morally wayward (the lost son). Also, there are parables about spiritual relationships involving prayer (a friend at midnight, the Pharisee and tax collector) and forgiveness (the two debtors, the unforgiving servant) as well as political relationships with an unjust judge and greedy religious leaders (the persistent widow and the tenants). Of course, Jesus' parables often address more than one area, since they are interrelated, and none more fundamentally than parables about physical relationships with the land or created order (the soils and the workers in the field), the basis of all economy and barometer of spiritual life in Israel.

> [Jesus'] announcement of the kingdom was a warning of imminent catastrophe, a summons to an immediate change of heart and direction of life, an invitation to a new way of being Israel and being human.[6]

Jesus called for repentance—turning away from greedy, lustful, death-dealing practices that destroy relationships—and faith—adopting and maturing in practices of practical righteousness, motivated by love and aimed at the hope of resurrected life. He sought those who had wandered away from the covenant, and welcomed those who were strangers, even once enemies, into his company.

Rereading the Script

In a class that I teach called Intercultural City Ministry, my students and I wrestle with Jesus' parables. How? We rewrite them! Of course, I do not advocate changing the script! Rather, I ask them to dig into the original life situation of the story, then translate it into their own

6. Wright, *Jesus and the Victory of God*, 172.

cultural categories. The following week, in groups of two or three, they recite or perform the translated parable before their classmates, who evaluate their production on the basis of two criteria: 1) Is their translation faithful to the script? Are the characters and basic plotline of Jesus' parable recognizable? 2) Is their translation fitting for their local stage? Would their neighbors, fellow students, or colleagues at work see themselves in the story?

Now, it is your turn! Either individually or, preferably, with other members of your group, choose a parable. Choose one you tend to avoid or don't understand so well. Pull out some commentaries. Dig into the story's original life setting, then translate it onto the stage of your neighborhood, workplace, or congregation. How will you transpose its scenes, redraft its characters, and translate its cultural practices? How is Christ calling you to change your own practice to follow the patterns of his kingdom where you live, work, and worship? ___

_____

_____

_____

_____

_____

Fourth Gesture: Turning To Follow the Way of Life

When my family and I moved to Sydney, Australia, from Atlanta, Georgia, our habits, even our attitudes, had to change if we wanted to relate well to our new city and neighbors. Obviously, we had to learn to drive on the opposite side of the road. Unfortunately, I learned this the hard way. We had only lived there about six weeks when I caused a smashup. Approaching a right turn, neural pathways trained to drive in North America told me something that was no longer true. Having noted the vehicle waiting in front of me, I looked over my left shoulder to see if there was any oncoming traffic that would prevent me from merging into the right lane. Seeing none in the near lane, I moved forward, assuming that the driver in front of me had made the same assessment. Colliding with the rear end of his car, I saw that traffic was oncoming in the near lane, a lane we had to cross to turn right Down Under. I wasn't in Georgia anymore.

For members of Christ's body, living in a kingdom that has appeared but is still arriving will lead to some cultural collisions and require many practical changes. Through the gospel, God summons citizens of his new city to turn around or change lanes, redirecting their image-bearing capacities, gifts, and resources towards their original, life-giving, life-sustaining purposes. Luke's Gospel offers Zacchaeus as an example, showing us what this lane change looks like. Wealthy from his extortion of fellow citizens in Jericho under the guise of Roman tax collection, Zacchaeus had made himself a persona non grata, a social pariah. But, like everyone else, when he heard that Jesus was arriving in Jericho, he wanted to get a glimpse of Israel's teacher and wonder-worker.

When he passed under the tree where the diminutive outcast was perched, Jesus declared that he wanted to share a meal with him. Once Jesus arrived at his home, Zacchaeus declared big news: "Lord, half of my goods I am giving to the poor. And, whomever I have defrauded, I am restoring it fourfold" (Luke 19:8). His confession of sin is clear, as is the fruit of repentance that authenticates it. The Law required restitution plus 20 percent for theft (Lev 5:16; Num 5:7); but, reselling stolen property required an additional 5 percent penalty (Exod 22:1; 2 Sam 12:6). Zacchaeus accepted the stiffer fine, and Jesus' evaluation is definitive: "Today, salvation has come to this house!"

Jesus' interpretation of the event reveals the breadth of the biblical vision of salvation. The Son of Man sought out a son of Abraham (Luke 19:9) who had lost his way down crooked lanes, some built by the Romans. In response to the presence of Israel's Messiah, Zacchaeus turned around and followed the way of life. His story reminds us that discipleship is more than mere profession of faith—it is allegiance to the true king and the ways of his kingdom.[7] True repentance bears fruit in repair, restoration, and life-sustaining blessing. Zacchaeus redirected his human capacity into the lanes of Christ's kingdom economy. He was able to do so because the Son of Man did not block him from human fellowship. Instead, He sought him out to reincorporate him. As Lesslie Newbigin summarized well,

> Conversion means being turned around in order to recognize and participate in the dawning reality of God's reign. This turning involves a visible companionship and pattern of conduct.

7. See Bates, *Salvation by Allegiance Alone.*

It involves membership in a new community under the rule of Christ the King.[8]

In his book *Improvisation,* Sam Wells tells the story of a concert pianist surprised by a little girl from the audience. Arriving early, the young concertgoer takes a seat next to her mother in the front row. Just as the house lights go down, she jumps from her seat and climbs the stairs onto the stage. As the renowned pianist emerges into the stage lights, there the child sits at the piano, starting to play her rudimentary lessons. As the one with status and authority, the pianist has several options: 1) he can call security and have her removed or 2) he can remain aloof and let her play alone. Or, there is a third option.

Amused and delighted, the pianist calms and intrigues the audience by sitting down next to the young girl, who had come not merely to hear him, but to meet him as well. Having decided to affirm the girl's interest and initiative, he places his arms and hands around hers on the keys. With each of her notes, he adds color tones, "reincorporating" her efforts, even her errors, into the wider setting of his knowledge and expertise. Together with his presence and engaged play, she begins to follow some of his simpler moves, co-laboring to create beauty and express dignity.[9] This was Jesus' modus operandi with tax collectors, sinners, the outcast, and the sick. To those who climb trees or stages to see him, Jesus' prophetic call sounds like a dinner invitation or a song. But to those who want Jesus only on their own terms or not at all, his prophetic voice sounds like a storm warning, and his prophetic actions look like overturned tables.

Jesus Is the Mediator of God's Kingdom: Prophet, King, and Priest

Israel's prophets often carried out symbolic actions before the people. Hosea's marriage to Gomer and Ezekiel's brick-and-dirt model of Jerusalem (Ezek 4) dramatized the collapses of Israel's covenant with her God. As Israel's prophet *par excellence,* Jesus' symbolic acts depict the climactic turning point in Israel's relationship with the kingdom of God. Many of his living parables are bunched together in the last week of his public ministry—his so-called "triumphal entry" into Jerusalem, his confrontational

8. Newbigin, *Finality of Christ,* 96, as cited in Hunsberger, *Story that Chooses Us,* 15.

9. Wells, *Improvisation,* 131–32.

sayings and actions in the temple precinct, as well as his interpretive foot washing and reinterpretive Passover meal in the upper room.

Lauded by many as "the king" and "the son of David" when he processed into Jerusalem on a colt (Matt 21:1–11; cf. Zech 9:9), Jesus entered the temple precinct and took extraordinary actions that brought the sacrificial system to a temporary standstill. Directly confronting the operating policies of the temple authorities, "gentle and humble" Jesus (Matt 11:29) overturned the tables of the currency exchange and drove the livestock out of the court of the Gentiles (see John 2:13–17). Quoting the prophets, Isaiah and Jeremiah, he asked, "Is it not written, 'My house shall be called a house of prayer for all the nations'? But, you have made it a den of robbers" (Mark 11:17; cf. Isa 56:7; Jer 7:11).

Jesus' words and deeds on the Temple Mount are consistent with his calls to repentance and offers of forgiveness apart from the temple throughout his ministry, beginning with his embrace of John's baptism. His shocking, destabilizing challenge to Israel's central symbol and to its figurehead, the high priest, went beyond "cleansing" or "reform" to anticipate the temple's irrelevance and ultimate destruction when all sacrifices would stop.[10] But, the meaning of Jesus' temple action comes into clear focus only in the wider context of the Messiah's discourse and symbolic actions in the upper room.

According to all four evangelists, and extracanonical sources like Josephus, the city and temple that symbolized Israel's covenant relationship with the Lord had become an unproductive vineyard, an unfruitful fig tree, a den of robbers. Like the prophets of old, Jesus represented the covenant—its blessings and threats, its salvation and judgment—to Israel and her leaders. Like David, his forefather, the Son and Messiah expressed God's reign through his restorative, mighty deeds, including his actions in the temple. Though priestly leaders of the holy place had become a group of status-seeking oppressors who were "devouring widow's houses" (Luke 20:45–47), the rightful, royal priest of Psalm 110 (Matt 22:41–44; Mark 12:35–37; Luke 20:41–43) and servant of the Lord was "numbered among the transgressors" (Luke 22:37; cf. Isa 53:12) to "establish a new covenant with his own blood" (Luke 22:20; cf. Jer 31:31), which he "poured out for many, for the remission of sins" (Matt 26:28; cf. Exod 24:8).

In other words, Jesus, the prophet, king, and priest, filled up the covenantal patterns between Israel and her God, restoring both its familial

---

10. See Wright, *Jesus and the Victory of God*, 413–28.

intimacy and its wider vocation on behalf of all families of the earth (Luke 24:27, 44–47). But, the blessings of the new covenant could only come when the Lord's servant bore the curses of the old. In a borrowed room, Jesus gathered his followers to celebrate the Passover, a reenactment of Israel's deliverance from slavery in Egypt. In the same way that the body and blood of the Passover lamb marked Israel as the firstborn of God for life out of death, Jesus said,

> Whoever eats my flesh and drinks my blood has eternal life, and I will raise him up on the last day. Whoever eats my flesh and drinks my blood remains in me, and I in him. Just as the living Father has sent me and I live because of the Father, so the one who feeds on me will live because of me. (John 6:54–57; cf. Luke 22:14–23)

As prophets of old had enacted living parables before the people, Jesus, the long-awaited prophet like Moses (Acts 3:22; 7:36–37), took the bread and wine of Passover to establish a new table that would be the centerpiece of Christian worship. In the same way that the people of the older covenant had reenacted the central event of their deliverance out of Egypt in the liturgy of their festivals, the people of the new covenant reenact the central event of their deliverance out of the kingdom of darkness into the kingdom of God's Son, the Messiah of Israel. Even as Jesus had offered forgiveness of sins apart from the temple to the paralytic, the demon-possessed, and the blind on the basis of his own authority, he established the basis of forgiveness under the new covenant apart from the temple by the authority His Father had given him over his own house (cf. Matt 21:13; Mark 11:17; Luke 19:46), Jerusalem's temple and the temple of his own body (cf. John 2:21; 10:18). "We have been made holy through the sacrifice of the body of Jesus the Messiah once for all" (Heb 10:10).

Jesus offered one last living parable in the upper room to explain further his authority and its expression in restorative forgiveness.

> Knowing that the Father had put all things under his power, that he had come from God and was returning to God, Jesus got up from the meal, took off his outer clothing and wrapped a towel around his waist. After that, he poured water into a basin and began to wash his disciples' feet, drying them with the towel that was wrapped around him. (John 13:3–5)

As some may have heard, the task of foot washing was a customary act of hospitality, but it was performed by household servants. A later text from the Jerusalem Talmud (*y. Pe'ah* 1.15c.14) puts Peter's shock over Jesus' offer in context. A Jewish mother took her son, Rabbi Ishmael, before the council because he would not allow her to wash his feet. Like Peter, he thought the task too demeaning.[11] For Jesus, the act was necessary. Without it, Peter would have "no part" with the Lord in his kingdom (John 13:8). As we saw in Episode Three, one of the identifying marks of God's ways with his people is the peculiar use of power, authority, or status. "Freely you have received; freely give" (Matt 10:8). Would Peter receive this gift? If not, he has no office, no portion, no place of leadership in the Messiah's kingdom.

This is why a fourth and climactic practice of God's people, now living out this new covenant, is a dramatic turnaround, a lane change, to follow the way, the pattern of life. Imitating Jesus, who took off his outer garments and put on the servant's towel, we take off the self-actualizing narrative of our culture in the West and put on the sacrificial love of the gospel. The gospel cannot be understood as a pronouncement of truth from an un-involved, unimplicated distance; it must be dramatized and witnessed in the living parables of breaking bread, pouring out wine, and washing feet. But, bearing witness to his peculiar kingdom requires a peculiar energy, so though he commissioned his followers to "go and do likewise" (John 13:14–16), Jesus explained in the upper room (John 14:15—15:17; 16:5–16), and again, after his death and resurrection (cf. Matt 28:18–20; Luke 24:48–49), that he would pour out his Holy Spirit to energize their gospel show-and-tell before the nations.

Group Activity: Changing Lanes

As we "go" among all the families or people groups of the world—which includes not only distant travel but also crossing your lawn or office suite to meet your neighbor or crossing campus to meet international students—we are to make disciples by teaching and learning his ways in all five roles of image-bearing (see figure above). As we discussed above, most of Jesus' parables expose "a great chasm" between the status quo and the better practices of God's kingdom, which make for the peace or flourishing of human communities. In order to become and to make disciples of Jesus, we must answer Christ's call to "repent and believe the good news!" This episode of the script has described the central gesture that reveals the people of God—turning around or changing lanes to follow the ways of life!

11. See Bock with Simpson, *Jesus According to the Scriptures*, 615–17, n. 7.

Christ's call summons us to two related actions. First, like me Down Under, we must stop driving the wrong direction in the wrong lane. Sometimes this means turning around in the same lane; other times it means switching lanes altogether. Either way, it involves an immediate second step, getting going in the ways of life, retraining or being discipled in the traffic patterns of God's kingdom. For some followers of Jesus, this change is very dramatic as they are delivered from destructive addictions or other death-dealing habits to turn toward their Savior and sobriety. For others, the change starts, but like my driving Down Under, it requires constant vigilance, asking others to drive, watching and mimicking them, and asking them questions. It's a slow process of forming new driving habits in the traffic patterns of God's kingdom.

Whether dramatic or not, repentance is a change of direction. We each stop going toward self-identified goals and we look to Christ, our King, for command and direction. It is important to realize that we are not turning toward a new lifestyle or religion per se. Rather, we are placing our complete confidence in a person, who is leading the Way, the resurrected Servant King who has overcome the destructive forces of sin and death.

As his disciples, you and I are members of the diplomatic core of Christ's kingdom in our spiritual, physical, family, economic, and political relationships. Using the following diagnostic tool, identify some lane changes in each of your image-bearing roles. In each box, in one sentence, describe an old destination you've forsaken, and the new direction you've set. Be specific. For example, in the worshipper role, under Changing Lanes, I wrote, "With God's help, I have broken my default switch of busy prayerlessness." Under New Direction, I wrote, "I will follow a daily Bible reading plan and take a prayer walk most evenings after dinner." It helps to share these lane changes with your group so they can pray for you, and even join you in some of them.

The world has one king, Jesus. His kingdom is brought in his way, the way of suffering, redemptive love, and life-giving resurrection. After each group member has a chance to share at least one of their lane changes and new traffic patterns, do you notice areas of overlap or repeated emphases? Is Christ drawing your attention as a group to pray for and serve your church, families, neighborhoods, or other people groups in particular ways? Through cruciform service to one another and our neighbors in the Spirit's power, new patterns of life form.

Image-Bearing Role	Changing Lanes	New Direction
Worshipper	With God's help, I am breaking my default switch of busy prayerlessness.	I will follow a daily Bible reading plan and take a prayer walk after dinner most evenings.
Family Member		
Worker		
Citizen		
Gardener		

Figure 9—Turning To Follow the Way of Life

Church

Working Together to Flourish

When we are planning a move to a new neighborhood, we explore its parks, shops, and restaurants. However, before we put down a deposit or a down payment, we also investigate its schools, churches, and real estate values. We get the numbers, including the crime reports. And, we hire a home inspector. We want the whole picture, the beautiful, the good, the bad, and the ugly.

Before we make the move, we need to be able to see ourselves and our family members in that picture. Whether we realize it or not, we are doing an asset inventory and a needs assessment. What's more, we are finding our way in a story that starts long before we arrive in our new neighborhood. We have not been sent so much as we have been brought there by the God who is always the first missionary on the scene.

In her work as a social and cultural entrepreneur in Indianapolis, Joanna Taft has learned that neighborhoods are living stages animated and marked with a history, not blank slates. As founder and director of the Harrison Center for the Arts, Joanna has made a name for herself revitalizing abandoned spaces in the city center. She helped found a nationally ranked high school and a cultural center that connects neighbors through innovative programming like Front Porch Indy.[1] These accomplishments have brought opportunities to work with many leaders of business and

---

1. See Harrison Center, #porchpartyindy.

government who have sought her advice. Like all good teachers, however, Joanna has never stopped learning from her neighbors.

In 2015, the King Park Development Corporation came asking for help to form a revitalization plan and attract investors. But, as Joanna and her team talked to the neighbors, they noticed a lot of fear. These residents weren't against improvement. But they had heard how "improvements" in other neighborhoods had pushed residents out, even erased neighborhood names to start over.

As she listened, Joanna began to reckon with her own role in gentri-fication. Digging into the subject, she identified two forms: 1) economic gentrification, in which a neighborhood's revitalization attracts investors, drives up property values, and pushes out longtime residents who can no longer afford to live there, and 2) cultural gentrification, in which a neigh-borhood's story is forgotten in part or erased completely, such that longtime residents no longer feel at home there or part of its future.[2]

As Joanna and her team cultivated conversations with residents about their life together in King Park, she came up with a way to honor its story. "What if we used theater to reenact the neighborhood's history, like a liv-ing history museum?" As Joanna and her team began gathering memories, photographs, and stories, they realized that the past was riddled with prob-lems and possibilities just like the present. So, a member of Joanna's team suggested a different way to honor the neighborhood's story. "What if we explore our neighbors' hopes as well as their memories? What if we imag-ined a pre-enactment of what the neighborhood could become? We can honor the stories, people, and places of the past, but we can also provide a foretaste of what King Park might become."

In October of 2016, King Park hosted a pre-enactment with the help of former, longtime, and new residents. New business owners in King Park were approached about how they imagined their future there, and how they would pre-enact it for the benefit of their local neighbors. Within the month they responded to say they had adjusted their hiring policies and their pricing to make room for the neighbors, who were making room for them. Together, businesses and nonprofits rented billboards and framed art for the pre-enactment weekend, depicting neighborhood scenes they were imagining together.

The city planned to reopen the Paul Laurence Dunbar Library, closed in 1968, for the pre-enactment to honor former residents and to recall the

2. Joanna Taft, "PreEnactment Theater."

joys and sorrows of their shared history. A neighborhood church invited participants to take a vow of community renewal. Spoken word artist and musician Nabil Ince (stage name Seaux Chill) wrote music and lyrics imagining a "new normal."

> Somehow we've got to find a way to recognize how we got here today.
> In order for us to understand where we ought to go.
> Yes, in order for us to form new realities, to form new normals,
> To help create a neighborhood we've never seen before
> For our children and our children's children.[3]

When Christians move to a new neighborhood to start a new job or school, finding a local church is usually high on the checklist of needs to fill alongside a new grocer, doctor, and dentist. If not, something has gone wrong in their understanding of the character and mission of the church. I say this on the basis of two important modifiers for the word *ecclesia* or *church* in the New Testament.

First, the church is not just any gathering of people. It is the church "of God." "Of God" signifies its primary relationship and its source or origin. The church is God's family, brought about by God's generous, self-giving actions. Therefore, a true church is marked by God's presence, that is to say, by the presence of God's Spirit. Second, phrases like "the church of God in Corinth, Philippi, or Thessalonica" identify a particular locale where members of God's household live, work, and worship. The church is committed to the welfare of a place and the well-being of its citizens. As Mike Goheen has summarized,

> The church is related to God. It exists for God's mission, but it is also related to its place. It exists for Corinth, for Ephesus, for Surrey, for Tempe, and so on. It is of the very essence of the church that it is for that place, for that section of the world for which it has been made responsible.[4]

If the church is to be simultaneously for God and for this place, however, it also must be against indigenous idolatries and injustices that twist the people, the relational and institutional systems of this place away from their original design and direction. In short, by loving both God and

---

3. Nabil Ince's words and music provide the soundtrack for the Harrison Center, "Three Years of PreEnact Indy." Also, see Gornik, *To Live in Peace*, 174, who asks, "What is God's dream for our community?"

4. Goheen, *Church and Its Vocation*, 123.

neighbors well, local churches help reweave a social fabric of redemptive relationships that foster peace. The Holy Spirit's energizing presence in the weave between participants creates a tapestry beautiful enough to fire minds and hearts, and powerful enough to fuel culture-making that produces life instead of death. Of course, even the best efforts of Christians and their neighbors to reform community structures will be partial, in need of constant refinement. The divine-human work of reconciliation and cultivating peace must be passed on to the next generation.

These two edges of the church's mission—against the spirits of the passing age in order to be for the Spirit of the new age—are illustrated in the book of Acts.[5] For example, Paul's proclamation of "the way of salvation" in Philippi liberated a slave girl from a divining spirit that had enabled her fortune-telling. Luke's depiction of a public confrontation with her masters bristles with economic, religious, and political realities: "They seized Paul and Silas and dragged them into the marketplace" and then "before the magistrates" (Acts 16:19). They accuse the missionaries of "disturbing our city" (16:20).

Paul and Silas's message alone would not have disturbed the public square had it concerned merely personal, private beliefs about Jesus. Readers are told, however, that Paul and Silas's "customs . . . are not lawful for us as Romans to accept or practice" (16:21). What customs? Seemingly, Christian proclamation and practices in Philippi were being perceived as an immigrant subculture, a different ethos that challenged the status quo. As C. Kavin Rowe summarizes, "To adopt the *ethe* (customary practices) advocated by these missionaries . . . would thus be to accept and to embody a set of convictions that run counter to the religious life of the city."[6]

Throughout this work I have been arguing that God's people are called to a unique, family identity and character that shows and tells a particular story on each local stage. According to Paul, the church is a new social matrix in which human persons are being formed in the image of God, that is, in the likeness of Christ (Eph 4:24; 5:1). This formative process, which we call discipleship, is slow, personal, interactive, and organic like the *terroir* of wine-making.[7] The vine of the gospel is being planted in the storied soil of people and place.

5. Bonhoeffer describes the life of discipleship as a life of "concrete responsibility to the call of Jesus Christ," which says, "'yes' and 'no' to life in the world" in *Ethics*, 256.

6. Rowe, *World Upside Down*, 26.

7. McGrath, "Cultivation of Theological Vision," 119.

As it is cultivated in the husbandry of discipleship, the gospel vine interacts organically in and through the body of Christ between local people, their cultural practices, and social structures (i.e., families, schools, workplaces, and governments) to produce the wine of peace.[8] But often, this peace does not come without first disturbing the peace or plowing the hard ground of idolatry and injustice. In sum, the planting and watering of the particular grace of the gospel (seed) interacts with the common grace of God in this place, among this people (soil) to produce a more equitable, loving, and life-sustaining social life (cf. Matt 13:1–23; 1 Cor 3:6–9). Such a life together is what Dr. Martin Luther King Jr. described as "the beloved community."

To be sure, local vineyards produce imperfect, bruised grapes, and Christians share wounds with their neighbors. All is not right in us nor in our communities. The church confesses its own brokenness, as well as its faith in the One who laid down his life for us, yet rose to demonstrate his power to bring life out of death. The church is distinguished more by the object of her gaze than the perfection of her vision, by the direction of her journey than the gracefulness of her gait. This is no excuse for her sins. Rather, it is a call for her confession, repentance, and acts of grace. A distinguishing mark, perhaps the distinguishing mark of the church, is the way she shares and invests the benefits of her own salvation in and for the world.[9]

In Episode Three, we reviewed the doctrines of election, justification, and adoption as we reread Abraham's story with Paul. Our rereading revealed the broader, missional purpose of the benefits of our salvation. The narrative aim of election is "blessing all the families of the earth." The purpose of justification is reconciling Jews and the nations together through faith in Christ. Adoption emerged in the Greco-Roman context to indicate how family members invest their household inheritance to advance the interests and honor of their father in society. Paul employed the metaphor of adoption to explain how non-Jews are incorporated into Abraham's family and obliged by this grace to use the benefits of their salvation for God's glory in the world.

In Episode Five, we engage Luke's and Paul's formative descriptions of the church to explore the broader, missional purpose of the church's ongoing sanctification. Why are God's people called to be holy? Does holiness

8. McGrath, "Cultivation of Theological Vision," 120–22.

9. "We are thus given a fuller and sharper understanding of the *nota ecclesia* visible in this context. The true community of Jesus Christ does not rest in itself . . . It exists as it reaches beyond itself into the world." Karl Barth, *Church Dogmatics*, vol. IV, 779.

merely nourish Christ's social body or does it also foster well-being in "that section of the world for which it has been made responsible"?[10] Indeed, "How does our growth in grace contribute to the flourishing of our communities?" To answer these questions, first, we will recall the role of godliness (*eusebia*) or piety (*pietas*) in the civic life of Roman cities in Paul's day. Second, we will trace the pattern of practices that Luke sketched to describe churches that are alive with the Spirit of Pentecost. Third, we will describe how this Pentecostal pattern of new life shapes ensemble performances from Ephesus to Indy to reconsecrate holy people and holy places. Finally, we will describe the fifth gesture of our gospel show-and-tell: working together to cultivate human flourishing for the glory of God (Rom 14:19).

Godliness Is a Civic Duty

It is difficult for Christians in the late modern West to imagine the pervasive presence of "idols" in the cities of early Roman empire. So-called "gods" were everywhere—in households, in professional guilds, in banks and government offices, and in temples that occupied both central avenues and hills that defended the cities. As Larry Hurtado summarizes,

> Members of Roman households, the family and their slaves too, gathered daily to reverence the household *Lares*. Residents of a given city [were] expected to take part in periodic expressions of reverence such as processions and sacrificial offerings to the guardian god or goddess of the city.[11]

Regional games, citywide acclamation assemblies, theater productions, even military victory parades told a cosmic story of how "the gods" had protected and blessed the city and empire through Caesar's household. In short, precisely those activities that were considered "piety" by Roman society were considered idolatrous by Christians. When Christians stopped participating in these pervasive practices, they problematized the piety of their fellow citizens, who then started asking questions and lodging complaints (1 Pet 4:4). Some accused their Christian neighbors of impiety, even atheism, because they refused to attend ritual meals (1 Cor 10:18–22) in their professional guilds or to pour out libations at city council meetings.

10. Goheen, *Church and Its Vocation*, 123.
11. Hurtado, *Destroyer of the gods*, 47.

Given this context, the apostolic call for "godliness" (cf. 1 Tim 2:2; 4:7–8; 6:3; Titus 1:1; 2 Pet 1:3, 5–8) is more, though not less, than a call to a renewed mind (cf. Rom 12:1–2; Eph 4:17–18). More than merely managing one's interior life, godliness is practical righteousness in public life—practicing right social, sexual, economic, and political relations rooted in the fear of the Lord. For Paul and Luke, "the saints" are holy primarily because they have been baptized with the Holy Spirit into the public, social body of Christ (1 Cor 12:7, 13). Holiness characterizes God's covenant people by separating them from practices that honored pagan "spirits" or gods in order to serve the true and living God (1 Thess 1:8–9) as God's image-bearers.

As we saw in the last episode, Jesus embodied holiness.[12] He fulfilled the pattern of covenantal faithfulness articulated in Israel's Scriptures and reversed the direction of sin's contamination, healing and purifying those he touched. Jesus plotted the direction of purification from the inside out. The outer washing—baptism—signifies an inner reconstruction—repentance. While this conversion ignites internally, it burns publicly in a new, "visible companionship and pattern of conduct."[13] While impurity can still pollute, Jesus tipped the scales in the direction of multiplying holy people and holy places. The baptism of Jesus and descent of the Holy Spirit at the beginning of Luke's first volume magnify exponentially at the beginning of Luke's second volume, where 120, then 3,000, are cleansed with the Spirit at Pentecost.

Luke describes this reconstruction of holy space as the spread of God's Word and Spirit in alternative local assemblies that produce a Pentecostal pattern of life.[14] Paul describes the members of these assemblies as "holy ones" who are forming and growing up in Christ's social Body, which is "filling all in all" (cf. Eph 1:23; Col 1:15–20). I am arguing that Luke and Paul's description of Christian witness includes, but goes far beyond, proclamation to redirect cultural practices and repurpose cultural artifacts through local churches and their neighbors. In other words, the Holy Spirit stands at the intersection of common grace and saving grace to create a social experience of "middle grace" through the church.[15]

12. The term is taken from the title of a collection of essays. See Lodahl and Powell, eds., *Embodied Holiness*.

13. Newbigin, *Finality of Christ*, 96.

14. See Perry, "Luke's Narrative Shaping of Early Christian Identity."

15. Leithart, *Did Plato Read Moses?*, as cited by Strange, "Not Ashamed?," 253.

This pre-enactment of social life by local churches in Corinth, St. Louis, Beijing, and more provides a faint echo of the good of Eden and a small foretaste of the new creation. Indeed, because the sanctifying Spirit and interpretive word work together in gospel show-and-tell, the church is called and resourced to cultivate a social experience of peace that bears witness to Christ's claim on this particular people and place. Jesus' once small, culturally Jewish kingdom is expanding exponentially amidst the cultural spaces and peoples of the earth.

A Pentecostal Pattern Marks the Church

Christ commissions witnesses, not mere messengers. These witnesses not only communicate good news—they produce evidence of its power, "firstfruits" of Christ's new order. To do so, the community of witnesses must first receive the life of God's Spirit. So, Jesus tells his first followers to wait in Jerusalem for "power from on high" (Luke 24:49). Luke's description of the first Christian Pentecost depicts "devout Jews from every nation under heaven" (Acts 2:5) gathered to recall "the mighty deeds of God" (2:11). They are startled to hear Israel's covenantal history narrated in their "native tongues" (2:12) and to hear new episodes of God's mighty deeds added beyond the exodus account to include the life, death, and resurrection of Jesus, the Messiah. The voices of women who had visited Jesus' tomb, and diasporan pilgrims with strange accents, are accredited by the Holy Spirit. Indeed, the Spirit fills and overflows each member of restored Israel, regardless of gender, age, or social role, for the benefit of the whole covenant community, as well as for those who are being added.

The festival of firstfruits or Pentecost symbolized Israel's new life in the land of promise (Exod 34:22–26; Deut 26). The firstfruits of flocks and fields were brought as offerings that demonstrated God's faithfulness to his promise to bring them into this new land, to redeem every dimension of their lives from their captivity in Egypt.[16] These offerings not only supported the work of the priests and Levites; they also supported the widows, fatherless, strangers, and sojourners, such that "there would not be any need among you" (cf. Deut 15:4; 26:13; Acts 4:34). Their worship practices resource and anticipate the spread of this Pentecostal pattern of witness among the nations.

16. Wright describes how the exodus sets the pattern for holistic redemption in Scripture in *Mission of God's People,* 96–113.

The Spirit empowered the new covenant community's prophetic proclamation of God's mighty deeds in Christ—its practices of economic interdependence, inclusive hospitality, and advocacy on behalf of the vulnerable. The Spirit guided appropriations of Israel's Scriptures, teaching witnesses what to say even before their powerful persecutors (cf. Luke 12:11-12). Indeed, prophetic speech in the Lord's name signified the Spirit's presence, challenging other "rulers and authorities" (12:11) who claimed ultimacy. So, these signs are words that do things "in the name of Jesus" like heal, pray, baptize, break bread, share necessary goods, exorcise demons, and confront other misuses of power through prayer and service (Acts 2:42-47; 4:32-37; 5:17-42).

Therefore, the summary of practices in Acts 2:42-47 is misunderstood if it is separated from Luke's description of Pentecost. The gift of God's Spirit brings about a renewed society of holistic witness in words and deeds to the reign of Israel's Messiah.[17] Marks of new covenant communities (cf. Luke 22:20; 1 Cor 11:25) extend beyond word (kerygma) and sacrament (leiturgia) in practices of social interdependency (koinonia), neighborly service (diakonia), and justice advocacy (dikaiōma) to cultivate a peace-filled social order.[18] This order is the law of Christ's love (Rom 13:8-10; Gal 5:14); its animating, purifying energy is the Holy Spirit.

The Way of Life Spreads

As Luke described the spread of God's Word and Spirit in the Acts of the Apostles, local, public assemblies of Christ's social body formed and distinguished themselves with this Pentecostal pattern. As synagogues expelled those who worshipped Jesus, these "Christians" (Acts 11:26) congregated in households and created a new economy of goods. The first Christian Pentecost is a defining moment theologically, economically, socially, and culturally. It imprinted a "Way" (9:2; 18:25; 19:9, 23; 22:4; 24:14, 22) or pattern of practices that still mark mature congregations of Jesus' followers today. Paul also picked up this imagery, which originated in the Old Testament

17. See Keener, Acts 1:1–2:47, 991.

18. Though he did not relate them to Pentecost, Conn briefly described five integral practices of Christian witness to God's kingdom in Evangelism, 35–56. Salter's careful exegetical work in Deuteronomy, the Major Prophets (Isaiah, Jeremiah, and Ezekiel), and Luke-Acts supports "a broad, holistic definition of missional ethics." He offers "greater definitional precision" by identifying three primary practices—justice, charity, and worship—that characterize God's people. See Salter, Mission in Action, 227–41.

(cf. Gen 18:19; Exod 18:20; Deut 10:12–13; Ps 35:4–5, Prov 10:29; Isa 35:8; Hos 14:9), to urge congregations to "walk in a manner worthy of the Lord or the gospel" (cf. 1 Thess 2:12; Phil 1:27; Eph 4:1; 5:2; Col 1:10).[19]

Luke and Paul describe mature, not minimal, marks of the church. New covenant communities are people of the Holy Spirit, evidenced by an overarching pattern of holistic witness (cf. Acts 1:8, 21–22; 3:13–15; 1 Cor 4:16–17; 1 Thess 1:6–7). They are people of the Scriptures, as understood and taught by the apostles, who walked with Jesus and received their teaching from him (cf. Luke 24:26–27, 44–48; Acts 2:42; 1 Cor 15:1–4; Eph 2:20). They are people of prayer, guided by "the prayers" of Scripture (cf. Acts 1:14; 2:42; 4:31; Phil 4:6; Eph 6:18; Col 4:2–4). How can they embody the wisdom of heaven without an open, continuous channel of communication with the heavenly council? They are a people of fellowship, not soloists, acting as good-faith partners in the everyday stuff of life, like breaking bread, hosting guests, and sharing other goods (cf. Acts 2:42–46; 4:32–37). As Willie Jennings wrote,

> Luke gives us sight of a holy wind blowing through structured and settled ways of living and possessing and pulling things apart. People caught up in the love of God not only began to give thanks for their daily bread, but daily offered to God whatever they had that might speak that gracious love to others.[20]

Wherever the Spirit goes, it produces "acts of grace" (2 Cor 8:7, 19–20) not greed. This "service" fosters "equity" (2 Cor 8:13–14; 9:1, 12–13), not disproportionate privilege. Leaders in ministry wash the feet of fellow travelers (John 13:1–17). They recognize and rejoice in the gifts of others. They use their status and resources to cultivate the peace or flourishing of their entire community. This gospel show-and-tell results in praise, gladness, and growth for those aimed at peace (cf. Acts 2:46–47; Eph 4:1–16), as well as confrontation, charges of public disturbance, legal challenges, and, sometimes, violent persecution (Acts 5:17–42; 7:54–8:3; 12:1–5; 16:16–40; 19:21–41) from those who serve other gods. As we will see, Paul's confrontation with the risen Christ redefined Paul's understanding of who and

---

19. Guder described the corporate setting and scope of Paul's admonition: "Like John, the missional community testifies to Christ, makes Christ known, anticipates Christ, and rejoices in His truth and presence in their midst. In doing that, it is 'walking worthily of its calling.'" See Guder, "Worthy Walk of the Missional Congregation."

20. Jennings, *Acts*, 40.

what is holy and redirected his life toward "the things that make for peace" (cf. Luke 19:42; Rom 14:19).

Reconstructing Holiness

Saints is an odd word to our late modern ears.[21] Many of us associate saint-hood with the canonization process in the Roman Catholic Church, which gives special recognition to someone like Mother Teresa of Calcutta.[22] We know that her life of sacrificial love and generosity has something to do with holiness. But, in the New Testament, sainthood and holiness are not merely for a class of super-Christians. Indeed, the Apostle Paul used *hagioi*, "holy ones" or "saints," more than any other word to refer to all Christians, includ-ing those who had been pagans![23] How can this be, given the way he initially "persecuted the church" (cf. 8:3; 1 Cor 15:9; Gal 1:13)? How do we account for such a radical restructuring of Paul's understanding of holiness?

Luke's thrice retelling of Paul's encounter with the risen Christ (Acts 9:1–31; 22:3–21; 26:9–23), read alongside Paul's own retellings (1 Cor 15:8–10; Gal 1:11–24; Phil 3:3–11; 1 Tim 1:12–17), reveal a new reference point for holiness in Paul. Ananias proclaims good news to Saul: "the God of our fathers appointed you . . . to see the Righteous One and to hear a voice from his mouth. . . . Get up, be baptized and wash away your sins by calling on his name" (22:14–16). To the Philippian church, Paul wrote about this radical restructuring of righteousness in his understanding and experience:

> I have suffered the loss of all things and count them as human waste, in order that I may gain Christ and be found in him, not having a righteousness of my own that comes from the law, but that which comes through the faithfulness of Christ, the righ-teousness from God that depends on faith. (Phil 3:8–9)

What he once held as the pure standard of measure—his ethnic and tribal identity, his study and practice of Torah—is relativized. Shockingly, he equated that which he once held holy with the impurity of human waste. After his encounter with the righteous one, Paul proclaimed only one

21. See Barton, "Dislocating and Relocating Holiness," 193.

22. Mother Teresa was canonized on September 4, 2016. See https://www.biography.com/people/mother-teresa-9504160.

23. "Paul addresses believers as *hagioi* at the beginning of four letters (Rom 1:1, 7; 1 Cor 1:2; 2 Cor 1:1; Phil 1:1)" and forty more times. See Gorman, "You Shall Be Cruci-form for I am Cruciform," 150n12.

source and standard of righteousness, "the righteousness from God" that comes to sinners by entrusting themselves wholly to the faithful one—Jesus. As John Barclay has noted,

> The "good news" . . . realigns and recalibrates Paul's loyalties: announcing the incongruous gift enacted in Christ, he is at odds with the normative conventions that govern human systems of value. Hence the emphatic statement of Gal 1:11: "I want you to know that the good news announced by me is not in accord with human norms." . . . [This] signals the capacity of the good news to challenge every value-system and every pre-formed tradition, including Paul's own.[24]

This restructuring of righteousness also recategorized those whom Paul had once identified as blasphemers. In the age of the Messiah, the category of holy ones or saints is determined by union with Christ, not tribal or ethnic pedigree, sectarian loyalty, or Torah practice.

In Luke's first account of Saul's conversion, Ananias objected to receiving Saul because of "how much evil he has done to your saints in Jerusalem" (Acts 9:13). By Luke's third account of his encounter with Christ, however, readers hear Paul agreeing with Ananias' assessment of those he had persecuted, saying, "I not only locked up many of the saints in prison . . . I tried to make them blaspheme" (26:10–11). The one who "in raging fury had persecuted them even to foreign cities" (Acts 26:11) was not only stopped, he was transformed into an instrument of "the Righteous One" to bear witness, not only among the Jews, but also among the pagans, "that they may receive forgiveness of sins and a place among those who are sanctified by faith" (26:18).

This was no mere change of mind. Paul completely restructured his relationships with Jews who followed Jesus as Messiah, embracing them as "brothers and sisters." Because of Christ's call, he owed pagans a debt of service. They needed to see and hear the "good news about Christ's kingdom." His sense of ethnic and moral superiority, and violent zeal to impose it on others, was supplanted with a sense of human solidarity in sin, and a shared need for forgiveness. Paul's humbling before the risen Christ humanized him and reintroduced him to the world on equal footing.

The pattern of Paul's encounter with Christ, that is, his experience of God's "incongruous grace" to "the foremost of sinners" (cf. 1 Tim 1:15;

---

24. Barclay, *Paul and the Gift*, 355–56.

Eph 3:8), shapes the church's public witness to Christ.[25] In order to be faithful to this apostolic pattern, the church must identify with sinners as sinners and offer the fruits of its "alien righteousness" in service to its neighbors, even to its enemies. "With deeds of love and mercy, the heavenly kingdom comes."[26]

Therefore, the church must not use its status to justify itself or to set itself over against its neighbors as the standard of righteousness. Christ's righteousness is the standard, not the righteousness of the church. We remain people of the Way, the Lord's Way, a group of Jesus' followers, a group of witnesses, not a group of self-promoters. As Paul put it, "We do not proclaim ourselves, but Jesus Christ as Lord, and ourselves as your servants for Christ's sake" (2 Cor 4:5).

Paul embodied this pattern. Though a Jewish man, he humbled himself to receive financial support from a Greek woman named Phoebe. He not only publicly acknowledged her as his "patron," but called her "my sister." Though an apostle, he recognized her as "a deacon of the church in Cenchreae," and commended her to the church in Rome with his famous letter. As his envoy and letter carrier, Paul knew that Phoebe would serve as his representative. Whether or not she read the letter in church, in all likelihood she answered many questions, making Phoebe the first commentator on Paul's Epistle to the Romans.[27]

On behalf of a runaway slave named Onesimus (see Philemon), who had become a "brother in the Lord," Paul pledged himself and his material goods as a guarantee. These "acts of grace" grow naturally out of "the grace of God" that united Paul to Christ and his social body, the church. Writing from prison, Paul urged the congregations of Ephesus and Asia Minor, "Make every effort to maintain the unity of the Spirit in the bond of peace" (Eph 4:3). This imperative is not theoretical, but rooted in Paul's own strenuous efforts to deliver the collection to the church in Jerusalem at Pentecost, which resulted in his arrest and led, ultimately, to his death. Luke's account of the conversion of Paul's character in Acts is complete: the former persecutor of Christ and his people has become their material witness and leading agent.

---

25. Barclay, *Paul and the Gift*, 355–56.

26. Shurtleff, "Lead on, O King Eternal."

27. For a full discussion of Romans 16:1–2, see Perry, "Phoebe of Cenchreae and 'the Women' of Ephesus."

The Public Purpose of Holiness

"Good works" are life-giving demonstrations of God's character, which bear witness to Christ's righteousness and the restorative purpose of discipleship—the renewal of divine image-bearing in humankind. To "learn Christ" is to be apprenticed in the original design for human beings. According to Paul, "good works" re-employ the gifts and products of human creativity and industry, repurposing them towards their original aim of human flourishing and the glory of God. "Good works" are not primarily religious practices that we perform in worship or in solitude. Rather, the worship of the one true Lord challenges rival lords in our localities as well as the injustices that result from their demands for honor and service. Thus, our culture-making at work and at home, in our churches and in our neighborhoods, does good to all, echoing the "very good" of creation and aiming at the "well done" of the true king.

Several images are important in Paul's description of sanctification, the process of making people and places holy. One all-encompassing metaphor, "walking" (Eph 4:1, 17; 5:2), he borrowed from the Old Testament. In Israel's Scriptures, "walking in the ways of the LORD" (Deut 5:33; 19:9) is a way of practicing all aspects of life in relation to God. "To walk humbly with God" is connected to "loving mercy and doing justice" (Mic 6:8; cf. Gen 18:19). Loving God and neighbor, worship and witness, are integral each to the other. "Walking" is living in covenant relation to God. But, walking also indicates that our destination has yet to be reached, and that our "good works" are incomplete. The church's witness to its neighbors is not "look at how well we're doing" so much as it is "look at who we are following, and join us on our journey into the fullness of his kingdom."

Paul picks up another metaphor from Greco-Roman theater—changing clothes or wardrobes. He urges us to "take off" the old ways of being human and "put on" the practices of the human community that is being renewed in Christ (Eph 4:20–24). This costume change is no mere donning of a new mask or temporary persona. Rather, it is more like putting on the uniform of the king's army.[28] Personal distinctives of gender, ethnicity, social status, even particular gifts of the Spirit remain, but all is put in service to the king and his kingdom.

---

28. The image of putting on a uniform is mentioned in relation to Paul's disrobing and donning metaphor by Tidball, "Holiness," 27.

There is no more all-encompassing aspect of our salvation than this calling to follow or put on Christ. As Bonhoeffer put it,

> The call of Jesus Christ is the call to belong to Christ completely . . . It embraces work with things and with persons . . . . Vocation is responsibility and responsibility is the total response of the whole man [sic] to the whole of reality.[29]

Christ's call recommissions his followers in their original vocation as divine image-bearers, and unites them through baptism to his recasting of that role. To say daily, with Luther, "I am baptized," is to say "I am called *imago Dei* and enabled by union with Christ and his people to bear witness to God's reign in the power of God's Spirit."

This makes the general office of ministry primary for Christian witness and service. As Paul points out, the particular offices of ministry were given "to equip [all] the saints for works of ministry" (Eph 4:12). However, this is no mean task. Though secondary, the particular office of ministry is no less important. As we have seen in Episode Two and learned in the school of life, we humans are susceptible to "every wind of doctrine," "deceitful schemes," (4:14) indeed, we have a habit of "deceiving ourselves" (1 Cor 3:18; Gal 6:3; Jas 1:22, 26; 1 John 1:8). No longer innocent, we humans must relearn our vocation by "learning Christ"—the image of God *par excellence* (cf. Col 1:15; Eph 4:20–24). The knowledge we suppressed and acquired apart from God (Rom 1:21–22, 25, 28) must be remediated (12:1–2; Col 3:10). So, as we will see, Paul disciples the churches of Asia Minor by giving them specific examples of wardrobe changes in every arena of image-bearing. This calling to "mature humanity" (Eph 4:13) is a call to cultivate signs of Christ's peace in every relationship, in every arena and practice of life. The figure below illustrates distinct, but not separate, roles of image-bearing. If "all things hold together in Christ," then we cannot divorce the spiritual, economic, social, political, or physical dimensions of our lives from our role as ambassadors of his kingdom (2 Cor 5:20).

---

29. Bonhoeffer, *Ethics*, 257–58.

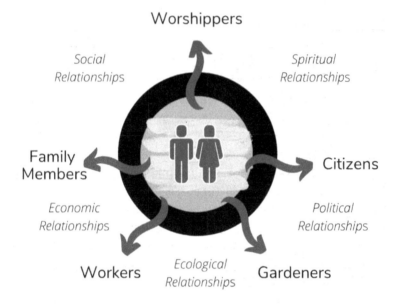

Figure 8—Discipleship Restores Roles of Image-Bearing

The Citizen Role of Practicing the Truth

Paul begins his description of those who have "learned Christ" with "speaking the truth to your neighbor." This is no small matter, because lies characterize "this present evil age," a virtual world of misnomers, false identities, and altered price tags that serve the interests of false gods and their human representatives, "the principalities and powers, the rulers and authorities" (cf. Eph 1:21; 6:12).[30] As commentator Andrew Lincoln states, "the powers and authorities" were associated also with "elemental spirits" (cf. Col 2:8, 10, 15, 20; Eph 1:20–23; 3:10; 6:12) who were thought to control the structures of physical reality and access to God. However, the Gospel declares

---

30. See the description of these "mysterious actors on the stage" by Gombis, *Drama of Ephesians*, 35–58.

that Jesus Christ not only controls access to God; the structures of physical reality themselves "hold together in him" (Col 1:17).[31]

Paul continues: "Do not walk or live" in the futility and ignorance of pagan thinking because it alienates you from God and from one another (4:14, 17–18). All of Paul's exhortations are given in the second person plural, and they all have to do with how we relate to others. Lies fragment reality and destroy the peace of the community. In Christ, Paul says, you have learned the truth, that is, the true way of being human (4:20–21), so "take off this lie and practice speaking the truth with your neighbors, because you are members of each other" (4:25). Of course, practicing the truth (4:15) inside the various virtual realities we create in our local cultures will always attract opposition, because it resists the malformed norms of rival "rulers and authorities" and their injustices. The good news about Christ's kingdom is public truth. The gospel has power to impact the social practices of non-Christians, because it points to a material change in the cosmos effected by the incarnation, death, and resurrection of Christ, the Lord. As Paul wrote to the Colossian Christians, "He [God] disarmed the rulers and authorities and put them to open shame, by triumphing over them in Him [Christ]" (2:15).

History shows that practicing the truth-that-is-in-Jesus mends the social fabric within and beyond the church. Reconciliation or peacemaking is the heart of the gospel—reconciliation between God and humankind, between Jews and the nations, between men and women, between classes or castes. In his physical and social body, Christ has broken the hostility between people, making peace to form one, reconciled humanity (Eph 2:14–16). Social reform movements such as the civil rights protests that grew out of the Black church in America, the Truth and Reconciliation Commission in South Africa, or the post-genocide interventions between Tutsis and Hutus in Rwanda and the Congo share a rationale rooted in gospel-shaped practices of truth-telling, repentance, forgiveness, love for enemies, and restorative justice. As both Old and New Testaments maintain, love for neighbor, immigrants, and enemies is motivated by God's own redemptive acts. "Love the stranger, for you were once slaves in Egypt" (Lev 19:18; Deut 10:19). "Let each of us please his neighbor for his good, to build him up. For Christ did not please himself . . . Therefore, welcome one another as Christ has welcomed you" (Rom 15:2–3, 7). Now that the Word

---

31. See Lincoln, *Ephesians*, 63.

and Light of God has entered the world, so-called "natural law" is being illuminated and redeemed by "the Law of Christ."[32]

As we saw in Episode Two, sin has devastating consequences, not only psychological and physical, but social and legal as well. Local church leaders who do not pursue the truth, report crimes, or adopt policies of due process are creating a culture of deceit and fear, distorting the gospel and misrepresenting a just and holy God. Forgiveness can only be effective if sins and sinners are named. Rachael Denhollander speaks with theological precision when she insists that investigating the facts and pursuing justice in cases of sexual abuse is a gospel matter. It is wicked to use only one aspect of the gospel, forgiveness, to try and silence the victims of sexual assault.[33] The sinner's prayer—"Lord, have mercy on me, the sinner"—underscores the necessity of confession, the need for establishing the truth of the matter publicly. The gospel is about God's restorative justice through Christ's sacrifice for sins. There is no true forgiveness without telling the truth about sin. As we illustrated above in Episode Three, a process of personal and social reconciliation could not begin in South Africa until the truth about apartheid was confessed publicly by those who perpetuated it, in the presence of those who experienced its deadly effects.

While Paul underscores the responsibility of "each" member of Christ's social body to show and tell the truth, truthful living is an ensemble performance, a pre-enactment of "the City of Truth" (cf. Zech 8:3). It is life-giving to deal truthfully with one's "neighbor" (cf. Zech 8:16; Eph 4:25), not just one's fellow church members, because God is "the Father from whom every family in heaven and on earth is named" (3:15).[34] The church's unity is a force for reconciliation and social cohesion between the genders, tribes, and classes, weaving new relationships and mending relations that have been frayed or violently torn. Consider Rose's story.

---

32. See the excellent discussions, "Creation, Redemption, and Moral Law" and "Fate of Natural Law at the Turning of the Ages," by Ziegler in *Militant Grace*, 113–38.

33. Lee, "My Larry Nassar Testimony Went Viral."

34. The word *neighbor* is an intertextual echo of Zechariah 8:16, which describes the final scene of the human story, "the City of Truth" (Zech 8:3). I owe this observation to Arnold, *Ephesians*, 300.

Rose's Witness to the Truth

I met and interviewed Rose Mapendo in the relative safety of her Phoenix, Arizona condo. Though her family's journey there was life-threatening, her journeys back and forth between the US and the Congo are life-giving. Rose is a go-between, a weaver, a lover of enemies. In the region around Lake Kivu between 1996 to 1998, Hutu militias rounded up and killed many Tutsis with the tacit support of the Congolese government. Pregnant with twins, Rose, along with her husband and five other children, were caught in the net and dragged in to a death camp. Rose's husband was executed in front of her.

Offered no provisions, Rose and her kids scrounged for roots and berries on the grounds of the camp to stay alive. As she foraged, she prayed, asking God to let her die. God's answer was not what she wanted to hear. She knew she could not forsake her children, but neither did she believe she could do what God required of her. "Father, forgive them for they don't know what they are doing" (cf. Luke 23:34; Acts 7:60). The words of Jesus and Stephen kept rising in her heart, and sticking in her throat.

Rose told me, "Jesus gives us a choice even in the worst of circumstances. When I chose to forgive those who had treated me and my family as their enemies, it was like a giant stone was lifted off my chest." In the death camp, Rose gave birth to her twins, and named them after the two militia commanders who had executed her husband. Hearing this, they summoned her. "Why have you done this?" They demanded an answer. "I am not your enemy. I am your neighbor, your family member. My children bear your names," Rose explained. Her professed solidarity with her captors and the effects of Rose's faithfulness to Christ on the local network of relationships was immediate. Within a matter of days, the wives of the commanders came with gifts for Rose and the twins out of social obligation. But, the commanders feared Rose and her spiritual power. They ordered that she and her children be placed on a transport to Cameroon, where, eventually, they entered the UN's refugee resettlement process.[35]

Instead of adopting the American story, Rose still chooses the story of Jesus, the one who speaks "good news to the poor," the one who forgives and reconciles enemies. As funds from her foundation allow, Rose returns

35. In 2008, Rose Mapendo was chosen as a CNN Hero and the following year as the United Nations Humanitarian of the Year. See Mapendo, "Rose Mapendo." The story of her work with Tutsi and Hutu women is told in Davenport and Mandel, "Pushing the Elephant," and premiered on the PBS show *Independent Lens*, March 29, 2011.

to the eastern Congo to convene groups of women for conversations about their lives. "One person alone cannot push an elephant. But, many people together can push an elephant."[36] The elephant Rose references is not only the cycle of violence and vengeance between Hutus and Tutsis; it is also the exclusion of women from the discussions and decisions that affect them and their children.

> Women in our society are not involved in politics. They are homemakers. But, the key to change is in their hands. If they are excluded from the men's conference, they must organize their own conference.[37]

Rose knows that the lives of these women will not be understood and considered in relation to others unless they come together and learn to speak with one voice. This is the work of Christian witness, to speak and sing with one voice (Rom 15:5–7) in our communities against the idolatries and injustices that deform human dignity, to push together against the elephant. Because of our solidarity in sin as false image-bearers, we all need the mercy offered by God in the gospel. When we take vengeance and choose bitterness, we bear false witness about our Creator-Redeemer, who is just, but whose justice is restorative. Rose chooses to practice the truer, bigger story of reconciliation between men and women of different tribes, the story of the image-bearer par excellence, Jesus.

The Worker Role in an Economy of Grace

Paul describes this costume and character change further. As we see above in Figure 6.1 and in Rose's story, our role as workers is intertwined with our other image-bearing roles as citizens, family members, gardeners, and worshippers. Going beyond Moses's mere prohibition in the Decalogue (Exod 20:15; Deut 5:19), Paul provides the mirror opposite of theft—philanthropy.[38] "The thief must no longer steal. Instead, he must labor, producing good things with his own hands so that he has something to share with anyone in need" (Eph 4:28). For Paul, the power of the gospel transforms "community destroyers" into community builders through restored image-bearing

---

36. Davenport and Mandel, "Pushing the Elephant."
37. Davenport and Mandel, "Pushing the Elephant."
38. Lincoln, *Ephesians*, 304.

as workers.[39] Whereas theft takes from another for one's own consumption, work for those in Christ not only provides for one's own needs; it also contributes to the needs of others.

Jesus came proclaiming liberty, the year of the Lord's favor, the Jubilee (Luke 4:18–19)! As we saw in the previous episode, this not only restored the economic basis of God's kingdom in Israel under a new or renewed covenant; it now extends the economic policies of Christ's kingdom internationally. As we learned from Luke in the Acts of the Apostles, economic sharing and support is part and parcel of the Pentecostal pattern of life in new covenant communities (Acts 2:44–45; 4:32–37). "Producing good things" participates in the Messiah's kingdom economy, generating surpluses not merely to benefit one's own tribe, but to share as acts of equity and grace (2 Cor 8:6, 7, 13–14, 19) with others, even enemies (Rom 12:20). As Mark Gornik summarized, "a Jubilee-based proposal does not cancel out revenue-generating initiatives, [but] directs them to be recycled back into the community, into empowering families."[40] But what might this look like today?

In their book *Practicing the King's Economy*, Michael Rhodes and Robbie Holt provide several examples of Jubilee-based models, including the story of a family-owned business, Broetje Orchards.[41] The well-being or *shalom* of their workforce, not mere profit for their household, motivated Ralph and Cheryl Broetje. They purchased their first apple orchard in Benton City, Washington, in 1968. Today, their company manages more than 6,000 acres of apple and cherry trees, shipping "nearly 7 million boxes of apples, including their proprietary, non-browning Opal apple."[42] In 1999 the Broetjes created the Vista Hermosa Foundation to support the children of seasonal agricultural workers by creating full-time, year-round employment for their parents, an on-site preschool for their kids, and affordable housing options. These ventures aimed at family stability by putting them to work, nurturing their relationships, capacities, and dreams.[43]

Our image-bearing role as workers is not aimed at self-gratifying consumption. Theft can grab that for us. Rather, it is aimed at a flourishing community that is reconciled to God, between its members, and even

---

39. The phrase "community destroyers" comes from Rhodes and Holt with Fikkert, *Practicing the King's Economy*, 132.

40. Gornik, *To Live in Peace*, 218.

41. Rhodes and Holt with Fikkert, *Practicing the King's Economy*, 146.

42. Mejica, "Sale of Broetje Orchards Creates Firstfruits Farms."

43. Vista Hermosa Foundation, "Theory of Change."

with the earth itself. The practice of Sabbath-keeping brings the integrated character of human identity and our vocation as divine image-bears into clear focus. By refraining from work for one day in seven, both workers and land rest, God is worshiped as the one true sovereign, and family relationships are enjoyed. For those first summoned to Sabbath-keeping, it was a joyful reminder that humans are not meant for slavery. For those in new covenant communities, every Sunday is a sign of resurrection, the first sunrise after Sabbath in the Jubilee Day that will never end. On this "Day of Christ" (cf. 1 Cor 3:13; Phil 1:6, 10; 2:16), his banquet table will be fully furnished with people and cultural goods "from the east and west, from the north and south" (cf. Matt 8:11; Luke 13:29; Rev 21:22–26). Hope in this promise leads us out into the world for six days of "faith working itself out in love" (Gal 5:6). This faith-hope-love invites neighbors to Jesus' table and produces good things to bring with our hunger to his banquet.

Even as the synagogues of the first century served not only as worship centers, but also as local banks, schools, and legal centers, local churches are embassies of God's kingdom and its Jubilee economy in the local communities they are called to serve. As an antidote to the usury of payday loan outlets in north St. Louis, Westside Missionary Baptist Church started its own credit union, which offers an expression of their shared economy of goods and provides banking services to members and their families. Local congregations and faith-based nonprofits find other ways to pool the goods of Christ's kingdom economy to reinvest in their neighborhoods. It is important to understand, however, that this is an act of fellowship and incorporation, not an act of outside intervention. Neighbors pool both their needs and their goods to perform their lives in Christ's kingdom together. Neighbors from other communities are welcome, but they must bring their needs as well as their goods, if they are to become true friends and partners. But, how can Christian leaders foster mutual discipleship and avoid reinforcing false identities of self-sufficiency or dependency?

Co-founded in 1996 by Sammie Morrison and Scott Dimock, the Southeast White House (SEWH) exists in Anacostia as an "incarnate presence" of Christ's kingdom in a community that most Washingtonians avoid.[44] Scott's wife, Marilyn, describes the activities of the house as "answered prayers embodied in action."[45] The SEWH's mission is rooted in John 6 where Jesus asks Philip to feed the 5,000+. To "perform the works of

---

44. McBride, *Church for the World*, 180.

45. McBride, *Church for the World*, 183.

God" (6:28–29), Philip must do several things: 1) an asset inventory reveals five loaves and two fish; 2) a needs assessment reveals that everyone is hungry, including Philip and the boy who shared his lunch. Indeed, there isn't enough to satisfy everyone's needs by mere human planning and effort. 3) Faith in Christ is the necessary "work of God," for only in relation to Christ are needs addressed holistically. So, Marilyn explains,

> Money in and of itself is not the primary need. People . . . and the resources they bring are the need. When someone walks in with a sewing machine . . . we suggest she bring the sewing machine and a friend and that they work together with the neighbors. . . . We want the givers' lives to be affected in the same way as the recipients. . . . People in the community learn how to sew, but [all] are rejoicing in new relationships.[46]

So, we bring our offerings and our lives as firstfruits with which we provide for the needs among us (cf. Deut 15:4, 7–8; Acts 4:35; 6:1–7). The economy of God's kingdom shapes a community that celebrates the gift(s) of life with potluck dinners, where everybody brings their best dish and their hunger to the table.[47] When illness, injustice, or inclement weather strikes the production capacities of image-bearers in this community, its effects are felt, but limited by the community's reinvestment and provision.

The Family Member Role Displays Covenantal Interdependency

By restoring people to their original role as image-bearers, the risen Lord is not only creating new worship spaces, he is reconciling relationships in our homes and workplaces, and renovating neighborhoods. We have begun to see how this takes place through "speaking the truth in love" to fellow believers, neighbors, and enemies, and by "producing good things to share," whether cultivating the earth, creating products, building a business, or starting a school. We continue our investigation of Paul's gospel show-and-tell by exploring our role as family members in his descriptions of the household (Eph 5:22—6:9; Col 3:18—4:1).

Many kitchens and family rooms have a place where parents post a list of expectations or common practices for their home: "laugh a lot, tell the

---

46. McBride, *Church for the World*, 183.

47. Rhodes and Holt with Fikkert, *Practicing the King's Economy*, 86–87.

truth, dance and play, share the household chores, eat well, love fiercely, in everything give thanks!" Peter and Paul are aware that they are not writing household rules for the smooth operation of the Christian nuclear family; instead, they are engaging in social reform by taking up, yet rescripting, a well-developed tradition in Greco-Roman social ethics. As early as Aristotle (335 BC) and as proximate to the apostles as Arius Didymus (70–10 BC), the connection between the household and the city or society was established:

> The household (*oikonomia*) is like a small city (*polis*). . . . Just as the household yields for the city the seeds of its formation, thus also it yields its constitution (*politeia*).[48]

In other words, by writing to members of households—wives and husbands, children and parents, slaves and masters—Paul was presenting a wider social vision for relationships in the household of God, situated among the nations in the overlap of the ages.[49]

As Timothy Gombis understood, the so-called "household code" in Ephesians 5:22–6:9 must be read "as an elaboration of the command in Eph 5:18–21 to 'be filled with the Spirit'—which is a call to embody or actualize the . . . New Humanity, [to be] the dwelling place of God in Christ."[50] Paul's interdependent weave of life in the fullness of the Spirit is also "in fear of Christ" (5:21). Members of this household—remarkably, including its head—yield themselves to the Spirit's influence by subordinating themselves to Christ and to the well-being of other family members, especially those that they govern.

While Paul picks up the familiar tools of Greco-Roman social ethics, his description of household roles is also indebted to the covenantal patterns of Hebrew Scripture and their fulfillment in Christ. "In the fear of Christ" (cf. Eph 5:21; 2 Cor 5:11; 7:1) echoes "in the fear of the Lord," which comes from other household instruction in Proverbs (cf. Ps 33:8–9; Prov 1:7; 2:1–5; 3:1–8) and anticipates "be strong in the Lord" at the end of Paul's letter (6:10). "In the fear of the Messiah" also resonates with Paul's original audience, because emperors from Egypt to Rome depicted themselves as "fathers." Indeed, the Roman *paterfamilias* patterned himself after Caesar. So, the model leadership pattern for the *paterfamilias* was domination, designed to maximize his own well-being, honor, and glory. While the true

---

48. See Gombis, "Radically New Humanity," 321.

49. Gombis, "Radically New Humanity," 322.

50. Gombis, "Radically New Humanity," 323.

Lord, Jesus, is jealous for his own glory, his means of achieving it contrasted starkly with Caesar's. While Caesar risked his life to gain more spoils and slaves of war for his household, Jesus took the form of a household slave, serving the members of his household as their representative, their substitutionary sacrifice—his death for their life.

The apostle insisted that a Christian father use his authority to love his wife, edify and train his children "in the fear of the Lord," and treat his household slaves as someone who is aware of his own submission to a heavenly master. As I have mentioned already, this relationship to slaves is modeled by Paul himself. Specifically, he related as a Christian "father" to Onesimus, "my child" (Philemon 1:10). Moreover, Paul called Philemon to treat Onesimus "no longer as a slave, but as . . . a beloved brother" (1:16). This extraordinary rescripting of the Roman master-slave relation traces the plotline of the gospel. Paul used his resources as "father" to absorb any debts that Onesimus might owe to Philemon (1:18–19). The practices and dispositions that the gospel required of masters and slaves in the first century undermined slavery itself.

In Paul's version of an ancient household code, the relationship of each member of the household to the other is decentered. The central gravitational force in the household is not the marital, parental, or economic relationships. Rather, Christ is the center and Christlikeness is the aim. Each member of the household is called to "submit to one another out of reverence for Christ" (Eph 5:21). Paul's call to mutual submission in the microcosm of both households—the family and the church—is a gospel summons to the law of a different king and kingdom that reverberates throughout the broader community.

Paul's command—"husbands love your wives" (Eph 5:25)—is "completely at odds with contemporary household codes and directly confronts the culture of domination."[51] The husband's headship and love of his wife is evaluated by the pattern of Christ's headship and self-sacrificing love for the church (5:23). Perhaps, having realized this high standard could be hard to grasp, Paul also offered another, nearer, standard—husbands should love their wives the way they care for their own bodies (5:28–30), "just as Christ" washes and nourishes the social body of the church (5:26, 5:29). The aim and emphasis of Paul's teaching is to describe "one flesh" union-in-difference (5:30–31), not distinct gender roles. As Paul reimagines household relationships with reference to Christ, the husband and

---

51. Gombis, "Radically New Humanity," 327.

wife's covenantal interdependence becomes a sign (5:32) of Christ's union-in-difference with his bride, the church. Together, husband and wife bear the image of God, cultivating a place where children are conceived and discipled as image-bearers.

The smaller dramas of marriage, parenting, and administrating the relational and material resources of the household participate in the larger dramas of discipling the nations through the church in Ephesus, Corinth, St. Louis, and Beijing. Both households, family and church, are designed to be reconciled communities of equitable, indeed sacrificial sharing in the gifts of God. Indeed, Christian households and congregations are designed as material expressions of Christ's peace in the world.

How Do People and Places Become Holy?

But what if every member in the familial household has yet to be adopted into God's household? Moreover, how does discipling children work for parents in a religiously mixed marriage or for single parents? In Paul's first letter to the Corinthian Christians, he addressed many issues of calling, including these household roles. Those who are married, even to non-Christians, are called to remain in those relationships, if the unbelieving partner wishes to remain (1 Cor 7:12–16, 20, 27a, 38). Those who are single (7:8, 27b, 38) are called to remain single "for the sake of the kingdom" (cf. Isa 56:4–5; Matt 19:12), unless "they cannot exercise self-control, then they should marry" (1 Cor 7:9) "in the Lord" (7:39).

Note well that the supreme value is not marriage, but the gift and calling of God into the world. Irrespective of gender, ethnicity, marital, social, or economic status, those who are "baptized by the Spirit into the body of Christ" are "members of one another" who make room for, honor, and depend on each other (1 Cor 12:12–26). They each experience "manifestations of the Spirit" and share the gifts they have received for the common good. Sharing their lives in the Holy Spirit, women and men, single and married, slave and free, Jew and Gentile, weave the means of sanctifying grace for their common good and growth—the maturation and extension of Christ's social body in Corinth and also in your city or town.

How do people and places become holy? First, they must be brought into union with the holy one, Jesus, and his Spirit. Then, interactively, interdependently, in and through the Holy Spirit, personal and social bodies take on the dispositions and practices of righteousness. Yet, according to Paul and as borne out by experience, our bodies are contested space. The realms of sin and grace run right through us. To the church in Rome, Paul wrote,

> Do not present your members to sin as *hopla* for unrighteousness, but present yourselves to God as those who have been brought from death to life, and your members to God as *hopla* for righteousness. For sin will have no dominion over you, since you are not under law but under grace. (Rom 6:13–14)

Paul calls members of Christ to submit every part of their body as "weapons for righteousness" in service to their new king. The Greek word *hopla*, often translated "instruments," shares a root with *hoplites*, the word for citizen-soldiers, who fought their battles in close formation. In Romans 6, Paul is describing a war between two kingdoms, the realms of sin and grace. He refers to the same battle in Ephesians 4–6, the battle between the one, true Lord, and the rulers, authorities, and spiritual forces of evil (Eph 6:10–12).

Though the Spirit indwells believers, they are not wholly pure. Though unbelievers are not indwelt by the Holy Spirit, they are not wholly without the Spirit, who animates all life. Remarkably, two works of the Spirit—saving grace and common grace—interact in relationships between believers and unbelievers, between churches and their neighbors. Indeed, these graces interact within believers themselves. The relational, personal, and cultural space of this interaction is the locus of Christian witness. It's where salt and light interact with earth and air, where the gospel vine interacts organically with the soil of reality. Bottom line: This interaction between common grace and saving grace, between general and special revelation, is where the action is! The church's dramatic action, expressed through gestures of gospel show-and-tell on their local stage interacts organically with the local, cultural soils. This is the preferred site of the Spirit's regenerating work.

As we have learned from Paul's description, old clothes are not appropriate for the renewed vocation of divine image-bearing. We must don a new uniform, one fitting for representatives of the kingdom of God. The tools of our trade as emissaries and ambassadors are the proclamations and practices of the king and his kingdom. They take place between and with others. A dynamic field is energized between believers and unbelievers, who live and work in close proximity, a "sphere of sanctification" in which the Spirit of Christ is present and operative.[52] In relation to a believ-

---

52. I owe the phrase "sphere of sanctification" to Johnson, *Holiness and the Missio Dei*, 131.

ing spouse and Christ's social body, an unbelieving spouse is "made holy" (7:14). In relation to a believing parent and Christ's social body, a child is "holy" (7:14). Unbelieving spouses, children, and neighbors are being woven into the social fabric of the church.

As unbelieving family members and neighbors related to the church and its members become entangled with its renewing cultural practices, they become embedded in the Spirit's field of gifts, energy, and fruit-bearing. Many are grafted in with saving grace. Peter Leithart has described this interaction between Christians and non-Christians, between the church and the world, as "middle grace."[53] "Middle grace" stands at the intersection of "saving grace" and "common grace," which is to say that "common grace" is being informed and illuminated, in that moment at that place, by gospel show-and-tell. What Leithart has called "middle grace," I call "illuminating grace." Not only has "the True Light, which gives light to everyone," come into the world (John 1:9; cf. Ps 18:28; John 8:12; 9:5), his written testimony shines like a lamp (Ps 119:105; Prov 6:23), and his social witness serves as "the light of the world" (Matt 5:14).[54] More specifically, Christian bodies—both personal and social—are "grace-with-skin-on." With our words and deeds, we invite fellow actors on the local stage into the king's story and point towards the king's policy aims. In other words, this drama of interpersonal and cultural discipleship is sacramental. "Improving our baptism"[55] makes the presence of Christ's Spirit felt, seen, and heard through our witness. Finally, we turn to our original human calling as royal gardeners and the other tangible sign of Christ's real presence in the world, the church's gathering around the Lord's Table.

Physical Relationships That Extend the Garden of Eden

Gardeners attend the physical, the tangible. They get their hands dirty. As we learned in Episode One, God is the first gardener. From the earth we were made and to the earth we will return. Our bodies are porous, always "doing

---

53. Leithart, *Did Plato Read Moses?*, as cited by Strange, "Not Ashamed?," 253.

54. See Vanhoozer, *Faith Speaking Understanding*, 63, where he describes the role of Scripture not only as a script or transcript, but as "footlights" illuminating the public space or stage. This imagery fits well with Abraham Kuyper's famous imagery of the light of the church's witness shining through its windows illuminating the space outside its walls in the community. See Bratt, ed., *Abraham Kuyper*, 194–95.

55. See The Westminster Larger Catechism, Question and Answer 167, p. 253.

business" with our material world. That "business" is the divinely commissioned work of "keeping" the garden (Gen 2:15). Therefore, we would do "good" to purify and cool the atmosphere we breathe, and the water we need to live. Access to enough clean, drinkable water already has become a contentious issue between states that share rivers and lakes. In some US cities, planting more trees along streets, protecting park space, and encouraging community gardens are helping increase shade to help reduce the amount of heat retained in concrete, as well as to help provide fruits and vegetables in food deserts. Our original human calling to "work and keep" the garden is still operative, because the garden of the earth supports life, our life.

In the sacraments, the gospel is reenacted with physical, tangible elements that signify Christ's human body. In American Protestantism, however, human bodies are often "discerned" as dangerous to the spiritual. Many conflate or confuse what the New Testament says about "the flesh" with what it says about the human "body." If "the Spirit is willing but the flesh is weak" (Matt 26:41), does that mean that the body is also opposed to the work of the Spirit? God forbid! As Paul's words and the Supper itself signify, "your body is a temple of the Holy Spirit, who is in you, whom you have received from God. You are not your own; you were bought at a price! Therefore, glorify God with your bodies!" (1 Cor 6:19–20).

Nevertheless, the practice of communion in much of American Protestantism has been reduced to focus the "mind" of the individual believer on the "soul's" relationship with God. During the COVID-19 pandemic, many churches allowed individual members to serve themselves bread and wine at home, apart from the corporate gathering of the church. Yet, the judgment experienced in the social body of the Corinthian church was physical, a direct consequence of how they arranged or failed to arrange their physical bodies. As we will explain further below, Paul diagnosed compound fractures in the Corinthian body (1 Cor 11:18–19) that had transubstantiated their meals into something damnable, something other than communion.

At one extreme, "one goes hungry." At the other, "another gets drunk" (11:21). Apparently, wealthy, home-owning church members were providing gourmet meals for themselves and their social peers, instead of sharing with the whole church body. They were "going ahead," not "waiting" to eat (11:21) with their "brothers and sisters" (11:33) who worked longer hours as day laborers. When they arrived later, they had to sit in the foyer, not in the dining room. They had to eat leftovers, if they ate anything at all. While this kind of socially stratified, segregated behavior was acceptable social practice at Corinthian dinner parties, Paul rejected it, writing, "This is not the Lord's Supper" (11:20).

Between the springs of 1963 and 1964, white Christian minister and civil rights activist Ed King, and the African American students who joined him on his "church visits," dramatized Paul's practice of "discerning the body" (11:29). They sought entrance to segregated, all-white worship services. Having been turned away repeatedly at First Baptist and First Presbyterian in Jackson, Mississippi, these Black and white Christians surprised ushers at the early communion service of Galloway Memorial Methodist. Hastily forming a human barricade, the ushers blocked entrance to the chapel and to the Lord's able. King and his students began knocking on the closed doors, disrupting the meditative silence of those waiting to partake of one loaf and the common cup.[56]

> The cup of blessing that we bless, is it not a participation in the blood of Christ? The bread that we break is it not a participation in the body of Christ? Because there is one bread, we who are many are one body, for we all partake of one bread. (1 Cor 10:16–17)

The Greek word *koinōnia* repeated in parallel, and translated above as "participation," can also be translated "fellowship." According to Paul, *these* elements—bread and wine—and *this* arrangement of bodies, gendered differently with a variety of skin tones from families of diverse social standing, yet eating and drinking *together* "proclaims the Lord's death until he comes" (11:26). So, what we do with our bodies and the products of our gardening—bread and wine—shows and tells a story. What story are we reenacting? Is it the good news about Christ's kingdom that we have been reconciled to God, to each other, and to the earth? Still, there is more suspicion of human bodies in conservative, American Protestantism to prod. This prodding is necessary, because bodies are vital to Paul's view of the church, its worship and witness.

According to Paul, what we do with our bodies not only reveals how we discern Christ's body, as we have seen above, it also displays our baptism. By taking off the practices of the old humanity in repentance and putting on the ways of the Lord, we are getting into character as his witnesses. Each of us is recognized as Christ's followers both by the scars of what we are dying to and by the longings of what we are living for. Throughout the sacred

---

56. The story of Ed King's "church visits" is told by Marsh, *God's Long Summer*, 131–45.

story, in both the older and newer testaments, chastity is a distinguishing standard of sexual conduct in God's household. Conversely, immorality is a distinguishing characteristic of idolatry for both Israel and the nations.

Chastity is defined as celibacy outside marriage and exclusive sexual faithfulness to one's spouse in marriage. Marriage is defined as the whole life, one flesh union of a male and female. All other forms of sexual expression are illicit in relation to God's law. In Acts 15, when the apostolic conference considered the practices of an intercultural church, they relativized distinctly Jewish cultural markers like circumcision and food use, but underscored the anti-idolatry thread that runs throughout Scripture. The apostolic witness equates the lusts of sexual immorality and greed with idolatry (cf. 1 Cor 6:9–10; Eph 5:5; Col 3:5), so it is no surprise that the apostolic conference explicitly warned against immorality and explicitly called for generosity towards the poor (Acts 11:1–18, 28–29; 15:19–20; 28–29; Gal 2:9–10).

Still, this radical sexual ethic, rooted in the garden of Eden, is not antibody, nor does it prize the spiritual over the material. Outside the one flesh union of husband and wife, yet inside the extended family, nonsexual parental and sibling relations model intimate, loving relations in the church. As we have seen, Paul related to Onesimus as a "father" and to Phoebe as a "brother." When he bid farewell to the elders of the household at Miletus, "they embraced Paul and kissed [him]" (Acts 20:37). Paul avoided characterizing relations within the church with friendship language, because in the Greco-Roman cities to which he wrote such language was freighted with socio-economic expectations weighed in the units of the Roman patronage system. In his mind, however, the debt Paul assumed for Onesimus and the patronage Phoebe offered to Paul were familial gifts of self-giving love, not an exchange of favors.

While Paul avoided the language of friendship, Jesus took it up. Though the language was less freighted in the cultural context of Palestine, still Jesus made it clear to his disciples that he was talking about "laying down your life for your friends" (John 15:13). Jesus' friendship with the Twelve demonstrated a shared economy of goods, time, and space in the shared aims of God's kingdom. They made room for each other, shared their meals, and shouldered their ministry responsibilities together. Though unmarried, Jesus saw and carried himself as part of a family. Though not a parent, he received and blessed children (Matt 19:13–15). Moreover, Jesus described both marriage and celibacy as high callings (19:10–12) and held himself to the standard of his own teaching about sexual expression (Matt 5:27–28). As a celibate man, Jesus welcomed a remarkable amount of physical touch from both women and men, all framed by the interpretive lens of familial love and friendship.

His ease with physical touch attracted comment from Simon, a Pharisee, who was hosting Jesus for a meal: "If this man were a prophet, he would have known who and what sort of woman this is who is touching him, for she is a sinner" (Luke 7:39). Jesus' response to Simon exposed Simon's lack of love and hospitality in comparison to the "sinful woman." Instead of shrinking from the woman's touch, including her kisses, Jesus celebrated them:

> Do you see this woman? I entered your house and you gave me no water for my feet. Yet, she has wet my feet with her tears and wiped them with her hair. You gave me no kiss, but from the time I came in, she has not ceased to kiss my feet. You did not anoint my head with oil, but she has anointed my feet with ointment. (7:44–46)

By welcoming her public display of affection and interpreting it within the frame of hospitality, Jesus authenticated her touch as pure, and exposed how little Simon loved. The love he withheld revealed how little he had sought forgiveness, though he too was "a sinner" whose sins were "many" (7:47).

The Spiritual Power of Friendship

Jesus remains "the friend of sinners" (7:34). He not only allowed himself to be touched. He washed the feet of his friends (John 13:1–15). He even washed the feet of his betrayer and enemy. "The disciple, whom Jesus loved" described the scene, as an eyewitness, whose vantage point was intimate, reclining against the chest of his friend and Savior (13:23, 25). This feeding and washing of bodies at the Lord's Table and in baptism affirms and redirects our bodies, repurposing bread, wine, and water to their original *telos*: communion with God and each other in dignifying, familial love. But, how do friends and followers of Jesus demonstrate and describe this love in Western cultures whose worship of romantic love devalues and undermines friendship?

As we have seen, the physical space between believer and nonbeliever, between local churches and their neighbors, is the field of God's mission to restore his image-bearers. It is a place of finding true peace and disturbing false peace, a place of spiritual friendship that echoes our original identity as the beloved of God. The Spirit bears witness: "We are God's children!" That is the essence of Christian witness, the call back to the one who is love. Jesus' meals with sinners anticipated his supper with the disciples he loved. Jesus' pattern of loving-neighbors-into-friends-into-family is the pattern of faithful witness. But, it is not comfortable for the family system, as Simon's confrontation with Jesus dramatized. A closed system seems much more stable. However, when any family stops adopting new members, it dies. Remarkably, Jesus ate, drank, and celebrated with new family members. He established public ceremonies of adoption called baptism, and regular family feasts that anticipate the banquet he will host in the new world.

The Fifth Gesture: Working Together to Flourish

Paul did not write to individual congregations. Instead, he addressed the church in a particular place, including all the congregations there. By addressing them together, he expected them to be recognizable to their neighbors as one social body of Christ in that place. First and foremost, he addressed them as "holy ones," and as family members, "brothers and sisters." He accepted their gifts from the Holy Spirit, and called each to share their gifts in corporate worship (1 Cor 14:26), and to pool their material gifts for corporate "acts of grace" in witness (cf. 2 Cor 8–9; Rom 12:13, 20–21; 15:26–27). He prayed with thanksgiving for the grace and love they had received from Christ, and for the faith, hope, and love they were expressing together in Christ. Yet, ever the theological realist, Paul named the broken places in himself and in those he taught, lamenting the ways sin was fragmenting their social body. Is Christ's body discernible as one body in your community? Jesus prayed for such unity, because there are ways of showing Christ's love and addressing local needs only when congregations work together.

For example, in 2012, the State of Arizona faced a crisis in their foster care system. Local pastors in Phoenix initiated a conversation with government leaders to ask how their churches could help. The answer was simple but not easy: "These kids need foster families and foster families need a community of support." From this conversation, the Arizona 1:27 Network was born. Rooted in James 1:27, the churches of the 1:27 Network promote training for volunteer families to be certified to receive foster children. The goal is to provide a stable home of love and provision whether temporarily or more permanently. Either way, these foster families need and benefit from the support of a network of churches in their community.

The "indescribable gift" of Christ (2 Cor 9:5) and the Holy Spirit of Pentecost form the capital resources of a new economy that extends "surpassing grace" (9:14) to such an extent that every adopted member of the household can act as a benefactor in their families, schools, workplaces, churches, and neighborhoods. Each represents the true head of the new household of Christ. Within this sphere of sanctification, the Holy Spirit is reordering human loves and reanimating human powers as image-bearers fill the space to weave the graces, common and salvific.

In this episode, we have seen how the interdependent giving and receiving of grace in and through Christ's social body continues to sanctify its members, extended family members, even neighbors, as surpassing grace flows through them into the wider community. As we have engaged examples from both script and stage, we have noticed that the costume change of sanctification casts off social practices that destroy human trust and interdependency, to take on social practices that strengthen Christ's social body, and perform a pre-enactment of the new city.

Group Activity

As a group, plan and host a cookout, potluck block party, ice cream social, or holiday celebration (perhaps around Thanksgiving, Christmas, or Easter). Invite your neighbors, parents and kids who are connected to your local schools, or colleagues and their families from work. Within budgetary and space limitations, make an invitation list that is diverse by age, ethnicity, gender, educational level, etc., and incorporate different cultural traditions in your themes, music, games, and food choices. Potluck-style, invite all to share a dish, or to share some music for the playlist, a game or dance from their heritage, or artwork to decorate the space.

When you gather, offer a brief prayer of thanksgiving for friendship and for food to share. Start a conversation and/or play a game that explores the following questions: 1) What is one thing you love about living here? 2) If we could put our resources together, like we did for this potluck, what kind of "new normal" could we build in our community? After the event, discuss what you learned about your neighbors, your community, and how you and your church might contribute to the potluck of a "new normal." What are some natural connection points with your neighbors that provide opportunities to keep this conversation going?

New Creation

Celebrating Little Restorations

WE HAD JUST ARRIVED in Sydney and were starting the process of unpacking our boxes when my phone rang. The principal of Christ College was on the other end of the line inviting my family to a picnic. The event, designed to welcome us to the community, would be held the following Saturday at one of Sydney's many parks. When Saturday came, we piled into the car to find our way in a new city, and stopped to buy a Sydney city map along with our fuel at the petrol station. Given my earlier description of vertigo Down Under, you may be guessing what happened next—not another fender bender, but a misadventure to the wrong park with a similar sounding name in a car full of kids who were hungry for lunch. You guessed it—we arrived late to our own party!

In those days, when GPS devices were still emerging, printed Sydney maps were divided into sections and gathered in a book-sized anthology of neighborhoods. Large citywide maps were glued to the front and back panels, with numbered subsections referring you to neighborhood maps in the middle. The trick for using them well was turning back and forth between the wide-angle and telephoto perspectives to identify your route. As we have seen in our journey through the script, biblical authors did something similar to reorient God's people to general covenantal patterns for particular, faithful choices in each generation and geography. They reference "the big picture" of God's kingdom and covenant promises, then zoom in to show how their small piece of redemptive history-making and culture-making fits and fills out that picture.

In Episode Four, we saw Jesus do this repeatedly with his parables. First, he set the wide frame by saying, "the kingdom of God is like . . ." then he "zeroed in" on a specific life situation, whether it was how citizens of his kingdom use their money, relate to their neighbors, or how they pray. In Episode Five, we heard Paul describe local churches as a new body politic whose members are reweaving particular threads of their social fabric in relation to Jesus and in accord with the interdependent, covenantal pattern of his kingdom.

In this, our final episode, I will say more about this pattern and goal of our journey—a resurrected life on the new earth. First, however, we will examine some of the popular stories that we are telling ourselves in North America about the end, and how they frame human identity and purpose. Then, we will read together from the authoritative, apostolic version of the script's ending—John's Apocalypse of Jesus the King. Our engagement with John's vision will reveal how Jesus' witnesses are formed for the challenges of kingdom living in the streets by the focus of their corporate worship in the sanctuary. Finally, we will participate in the sixth gesture of our witness, mini-celebrations of the future in the present around appetizing anticipations of the Messiah's victory banquet in the new world.

Stories about the End and Beyond

As we have seen, endings are important. Like destinations, they keep us moving forward despite the cost of the journey, including its detours and setbacks. Endings help us understand the meaning of the whole story, especially those parts in which we have suffered or lost our way. Moreover, endings are important because they fire our imagination and action towards a "new normal" beyond our present circumstances.

Stories about the end have never been more popular—whether onscreen or in a book, speculations about world-ending scenarios are all around us. Yet, these stories have taken a decidedly dark turn. As Robert Joustra and Alissa Wilkinson summarize in *How to Survive the Apocalypse,*

> Like apocalypse, tales of neo-apocalypse involve the collapse of the social order, punishing human sin and error. Like apocalypse, neo-apocalypse is pessimistic about humanity's capacity to rehabilitate itself. But unlike apocalypse, neo-apocalypse doesn't

restrain that pessimism. There is no *Deus ex machina*, no hope for the renovation of humankind.[1]

As Joustra and Wilkinson clearly illustrate with their interpretation of various television series, contemporary stories are haunted by the end of our material environment as we know it. They are post-apocalypses about human identity and development amidst or beyond the ruins. For example, in the reboot of *Battlestar Galactica* (BSG), after 9/11, "The Cylons were created by Man. They evolved. They rebelled . . . And, they have a plan."[2] At first glance, this sounds like a typical "man-versus-machine" story. But, this simplistic summary doesn't capture the central question put before us in BSG. The question isn't "Will humankind be destroyed?" Rather, it's "Are the Cylons really alive? Can robots gain personhood?" The Cylons' evolving plan, though it includes patricide, is to use humans, even mate with us, in order to become more like us. There is no end in sight.

The only hope BSG offers is a continual process of Cylon self-actualization and the ironic plot twist that we provide the pattern of the self they mimic. So, what are Cylons becoming? Who are we? This journey toward a self-authored identity has only one compass, what theologians call a consequentialist ethic. This way of thinking judges every choice according to how "good" it is for my own development. "What's 'right' is what produces in and for me, my own unique way of being human."[3] These individual, often immediate goods not only undermine a sense of the common good. My good, my truth, my justice collides in the courts, in the media, and in very partisan politics with your good, your truth, and your justice. If the highest good is self-actualization, and we each get to write our own endings to the story, then, when our story lines cross, and they inevitably will, whoever exercises the most force wins. Indeed, as Stansa Stark proclaims in *Game of Thrones* (GOT), "There are no heroes. In this life, the monsters win."

Do we all live in Westeros, the mythical continent where GOT is set? Is every agenda, every angle we work, a will to power? Is that what it means to be human, to be alive? As Jorgen and Wilkinson argue, even Westeros cannot operate consistently in this manner. As those who have watched the series will know, whether the Mother of Dragons marches or flies, her lust for the Iron Throne gets the best of her in the end. Moreover, the oft-repeated phrase, "Winter is coming," reminds GOT viewers that pieces of the

1. Joustra and Wilkinson, *How to Survive the Apocalypse*, 58–59.

2. Joustra and Wilkinson, *How to Survive the Apocalypse*, 62.

3. Joustra and Wilkinson, *How to Survive the Apocalypse*, 121.

puzzle are set within a bigger picture, an epic story. In his famous speech of the final episode, the character Tyrion Lannister asks,

> What unites people? Armies? Gold? Flags? Stories. There's nothing in the world more powerful than a good story. Nothing can stop it. No enemy can defeat it.
>
> And who has a better story than Bran the Broken? The boy who fell from a high tower and lived . . . He is our memory. The keeper of all our stories. The wars, weddings, births, massacres, famines, our triumphs, our defeats, our past. Who better to lead us into the future?[4]

As we noted in the introduction to our *Drama*, "We enter upon a stage that we did not design and find ourselves part of an action that was not of our own making."[5] Followers of Jesus, the Word who made this world, are broken keepers of the truest, deepest story, the story authored by the Creator who chose to place human partners in every chapter, on every page. Before we look at the big reveal of our place at the end of the story, let's turn back to the panels of the map to regain our sense of the whole plot, and its major twists and turns.

The Direction of Salvation Runs from God to Us, from Heaven to Earth

Israel's script testifies that God's speech-acts, divine words and deeds, shape the world and its purpose. The Lord made the earth to give and sustain life. The Lord came to the earth to plant a royal garden, to form man from the soil and woman from man's flesh and bone, and to give them breath, that they might bear the divine image together. To be like God is to act with God's Breath to make good things out of the "very good" world. Called to mirror God's character, capacities, relatedness, and rule, we are, at best, micro-authors within tiny episodes of a macro-script primarily authored by God's Spirit. As Paul reminded the Athenians, God "determined allotted periods and the boundaries" of our dwelling place (Acts 17:26). Indeed, "in God we live and move and have our being" (17:28). Though micro-authors and improv actors have creative agency within the greater story they enact, they are responsible both to its author and to the other actors on their stage.

---

4. Gallo, "Best Speech In The 'Game of Thrones' Finale."
5. MacIntyre, *After Virtue*, 199.

But, by determining good and evil for themselves, our original parents deformed the image and departed from the plotline of the script to manufacture their own virtual worlds. These self-made worlds are animated with breath from a different source than the life-giver. They are electrified with demons. Because these virtual worlds and their maleficent forces exist in, indeed depend on, the life force and goods of the original world, many have described salvation as escape to a different world. But, the Creator did not give up so easily on the good world he made or the life it produces. "For God so loved the world that He sent His One and Only Son into the world" to renovate and redeem it, not to foreclose and condemn it (John 3:16–18). The pattern of salvation in the Old and New Testaments is God's entrance into the world and presence with his people. His very names tell the story. They set the trajectory towards new life in a new land, not a disembodied existence. "I AM present and I AM powerful on your behalf" tells the story of the exodus. "Immanuel" or "God-with-us" tells us the gospel!

When "the Word became flesh and dwelt among us" (John 1:14), the kingdom of God and its king arrived (cf. Matt 4:17, 23; Mark 1:14)! The physical, material presence of God's Word entered God's world to recapitulate the role of humankind, indeed, to renew all things. To follow Jesus is to return to our original role in the script as divine image-bearers, who not only make good things out of the good world, but also overcome evil with good. The light of God's glory is set on "lampstands" (Rev 1:20), local congregations of kingdom witnesses, who "shine as lights in the world, holding forth the world of life" (Phil 2:15–16) amidst many rival kingdoms. We turn now to the last scene of the script and the last battle between kingdoms. What is the goal of the story? Which king will overcome all others? Which kingdom will stand?

John's Vision of the Goal of All Things

There are many scenes in Scripture that teach us about the "end of all things." But, the most poignant and misunderstood is the last episode of the script, John's Revelation of Jesus Christ. This apocalypse rips open the scenery of the world stage, unveiling the goal of the script all along: "the kingdom of this world has become the kingdom of our God and of His Christ" (Rev 11:15). Clearly, however, this goal of reconciliation comes only at great cost. The king on the throne of the universe is a slaughtered lamb, who laid down his life and took it up again to overcome the demonic power of death. As Dennae Pierre reminded us with a quote from Howard Thurman during protests in response to George Floyd's murder,

> There is a veil of hate that separates us from one another—black and white, rich and poor. Because we cannot see, our imaginations run wild . . .
>
> But, every now and then, there is a crack and blood seeps through . . .
>
> But rarely is there—broken surrender, hearts cracked open, pockets emptied, falling prostrate to the ground, asking to do whatever can be done to bring down the veil.[6]

A work like the final episode of the script—a prophetic, apostolic apocalypse—rips open the veil, focuses the mind, and cracks open hearts. John's visionary writing reviews the script and displays its goal. As the credits roll over the last scenes of the Bible, some of its first scenes reappear. The river of life (Gen 1:9; 2:10) flows (Rev 22:1–2), the way to the tree of life (22:2) stands open, and the heavenly city, the new Jerusalem, descends to the earth renewed in righteousness (21:2). This is the proper answer to all our prayers and longings for more justice, more beauty, more goodness and love in this world: "Thy Kingdom come, thy will be done on earth as it is in heaven" (Matt 6:10). The plot line of the biblical story runs from heaven to earth. As the final scene of John's vision shows, the end of the story takes place on the earth. We do not ascend; the heavenly city and its King descends. "Joy to the world, the Lord has come. Let earth receive her king!" Isaac Watts was writing about Christ's second advent not merely his first.

Awaiting the Return of the King

However, many well-meaning pastors and teachers, not to mention fiction writers, envision a very different ending for the human story—escape from the body, not the body's resurrection, a flight of souls from "this evil world," not this world's renewal. The Greeks perfected this telling of the story's end through a dualistic worldview that dignified the spiritual and demeaned the material. But that is not the way that Jesus or his apostolic witnesses depict the *denoument* of the biblical script. First, in Jesus' teaching about "the end" (Matt 24:14) on the Mount of Olives, he says, "the coming of the Son of Man"

---

6. Pierre, "Untitled."

will be like the days of Noah (v. 37).[7] What does this mean? One way to discover this is to notice how Jesus set his illustration of "the two men in the field" and "the two women at the mill" (24:40–41) in relation to "the days of Noah." Jesus established an important context within which we must interpret what it means to be "taken" or "left." Who was taken away in the days of Noah? Those who refused to repent and enter the safety of the ark were swept away by the waters. Likewise, at the coming of the Son of Man, the man and woman who are taken away are those who refuse to repent and respond with faith to Jesus the Messiah and the arrival of his kingdom. Those who remain in the land are like Noah and his family. They remain under the king's protection and will be saved through the experience of judgment.

Jesus' parables of warning and judgment in Matthew 25 work the same way. They follow the direction of the drama from heaven to earth. The bridegroom, the property owner, and the king, who have been away, return to their land. On the one hand, those who are sent away in these parables are those who are under judgment, like Adam and Eve who were sent away from the garden, and Israel when she was taken away into exile. On the other hand, those who "stay awake" (24:42) and remain as "wise" and "faithful stewards" of God's land and household (24:45; 25:1–13) will go out to meet (*apantēsis*; 25:6) the Bridegroom and King, when he arrives (*parousia*; 24:3, 27, 37, 39) at home in his kingdom.

Paul's encouragement to the church in Thessalonica follows the same direction, but his imagery utilizes a protocol for welcoming returning kings or visiting dignitaries, a protocol that was well-known in the Roman world of the first century. Two words, and their use in Paul's day, are vital to our understanding of the protocol—*parousia* and *apantēsis* (1 Thess 4:15, 17, respectively). As F. F. Bruce noted,

> When a dignitary paid an official visit (*parousia*) to a city in Hellenistic times, the action of the leading citizens in going out to meet him and escort him back on the final stage of his journey was called the *apantēsis*.[8]

Indeed, we sometimes see a contemporary version of this custom on our television or computer screens. When the American president travels abroad or foreign heads of state visit the US, an official welcoming party is

---

7. I follow the traditional reading of "the coming of the Son of Man" (cf. Mark 8:38; 13:26) as referring to Jesus' *parousia* or second advent. Most recently, see Stein, *Jesus, the Temple and the Coming of the Son of Man*, 103–20.

8. Bruce, *1 and 2 Thessalonians*, 102.

sent to the airport to meet them. The host country's leader does not wait for the visitors to come to their official residence. Instead, he or she goes out to meet them, to extend their nation's welcome! The same was true in the days of Jesus and Paul.

As Cicero wrote about Julius Caesar's journey through Italy in 49 BC: "Just imagine what *apantēseis* he is receiving from the towns, what honors are paid to him!" (Ad Att. 8.16.2). According to Luke, an eyewitness, Paul's delegation received the same kind of welcome when they arrived at Rome (Acts 28:14b–15):

> And so we came to Rome. When the brothers and sisters from there heard about us, they came out as far as the Forum of Appius and the Three Taverns to meet us (*apantēsin*). When Paul saw them, he gave thanks to God and took courage.

So also, Paul honored Christians who had died as leading citizens of the assembly at Thessalonica. On the Day of Christ, they will rise first to lead the welcome party who go out to meet the arriving King (1 Thess 4:15–17)! The Lord's *parousia* is wrapped in royal glory with warrior angels and battle trumpets: "The Lord himself will descend from heaven" and "God will bring with him those who have fallen asleep" (4:14, 16).

Peter's description of "the Day of the Lord" (2 Pet 3:10) draws the same comparison to Noah's flood that Jesus had drawn on the Mount of Olives. Peter wrote,

> The earth was formed out of water by the word of God, and . . . the world that then existed was deluged with water and perished. But, by the same word the heavens and earth that now exist are stored up for fire, being kept until the day of judgment and destruction of the ungodly. (3:5–7)

In the same way, by the same word, the earth will be purified, not destroyed. As the waters cleansed the earth of violence, the refiner's fire will remove the dross. Like "the days of Noah," "the day of judgment" will destroy the wicked and reveal "a new earth in which righteousness dwells" (3:13). According to Jesus, Paul, John, and Peter, the goal or end of the story is not heaven in and of itself. It is, however, heaven and its King coming down to renew the earth!

The Seer, John, and His Lens—the
Apocalypse of Jesus the King

John, the seer and prophet, offered seven representative churches a dramatic retelling of their lived experience in relation to their true Lord. Though his hearers were suffering and sorely tempted at the hands of faux lords, John's "word of prophecy" offered them the resources they needed to "overcome" the idolatrous matrix of Roman economic, political, and religious claims to superpower status. John's Apocalypse unlocks our imaginations to envision the vast wonder of the real world, to break free from the propaganda and iconography of small, relatively brief, rival kingdoms.

In 1998, a movie called *The Truman Show* told the story of an infant who was adopted by a corporation and born into a reality TV show.[9] Every person who related to Truman Burbank was part of a cast with scripted lines. Product placements and ads were posted everywhere. Truman did not realize he was living on a soundstage until things began to happen to raise suspicions that there was a bigger reality beyond what he could see. The question posed by writer Andrew Niccol and director Peter Weir is really for us, those who viewed the viewers of *The Truman Show*. Are we trapped in our own voyeurism? Can we regain our agency as actors in a bigger story, or are we experiencing much smaller stories that others want to sell us?

In a similar way, John's vivid Apocalypse raised suspicions about the bigger story. It poked a hole in the background horizon of the Pax Romana. Behind the so-called "Peace of Rome" lay a story of conquest, of lands stolen and people enslaved. John's prophetic letter fed underground gossip that a new kingdom was growing amidst the towns and cities of an empire that was only apparently, not actually, much stronger, much larger in scope. Tim Keller has often told the story of G. Campbell Morgan's visit to a Rome cemetery to illustrate of how the Pax Christi broke through to overgrow the Pax Romana. On a morning stroll, while visiting Rome, Dr. Morgan was stunned by the site of an oak tree growing up out of a marble sarcophagus. How did this happen? The only thing he could surmise was that an acorn or acorns must have fallen into the ground before the sarcophagus was built over it. Unseen at first, it sprouted within the grave. At first, the stalk could not possibly move the weight of the marble, but as it wound round within, it grew strong. Eventually, the growth and mass pushed the marble slab to create an

---

9. Weir, dir., *Truman Show.*

opening where the lid met the wall of the sarcophagus. Over time, the tree grew up and out, splitting the marble slab and destroying the grave.[10]

John's vision authenticated human longings for greater justice and a more perfect love as longings for a real kingdom, the city of God. John the Seer wrote,

> On the Lord's Day, I was in the Spirit, and I heard behind me a loud voice like a trumpet, which said: "Write on a scroll what you see and send it to the seven churches—to Ephesus, Smyrna, Thyatira, Sardis, Philadelphia and Laodicea. (Rev 1:10–11)

Each of the seven receives a direct message from "the Living One," who knows their words and deeds, the one who "was dead, but is now alive forever and ever" (1:18). Each congregation overhears the messages to the others contained in John's one letter. Each message is spoken by the prophetic Spirit in and by whom John sees, hears, and writes. "He who has an ear, let him hear what the Spirit says to the churches" (2:7, 11, 17, 28; 3:6, 13, 22). Just as you were called to consider your own lane changes in Episode Four, for these seven representative churches hearing and heeding the Spirit involved changing directions in some of their ways. Only the church at Philadelphia is told: "Hold on to what you have, so that no one will take your crown" (3:11). They are on course for the final destination, "the new Jerusalem, which is coming down out of heaven" (3:12).

This reference to a crown isn't just a generic crown, but would have brought to mind certain images and events for the original hearers of John's Apocalypse. Who usually received such crowns in the cities of Roman Asia Minor in the first century? In exchange for their support of Caesar's house and ways, city elders and benefactors received acclaim, rule, and the best seats, thrones even, at the local amphitheater. There, onstage, scripted stories dramatized how local deities were thought to protect and bless the city through Caesar and his household. Shouts of acclaim were raised: "Hail, Caesar! You are worthy to receive glory and honor and power! Great is Artemis of the Ephesians!" (Acts 19:28, 34). In Ephesus, the capital city of Roman Asia Minor, Paul had challenged the order of things. He had poked a hole in the way the Ephesians explained their good fortune, saying that "man-made gods are no gods at all" (19:26) and proclaiming, "Jesus is Lord!" (cf. 19:10; Eph 1:15, 17, 19b–23). Needless to say, this caused a disturbance, a riot.

---

10. I heard this illustration in a sermon delivered by Tim Keller, who also referenced by Richard Smith III, "Can a Person's Life Be Truly Transformed?"

So, writing from political exile on the island of Patmos, John the Seer knew the stakes were high. He knew that his call to be "faithful witness[es]" (cf Rev 1:2, 5; 3:14) to the world's one, true Lord would cause quite the stir. As Richard Bauckham summarized,

> Revelation advances a thorough-going prophetic critique of Roman power. [It is] the most powerful piece of political resistance literature from the period of the early Empire. It is not simply because Rome persecutes Christians that Christians must oppose Rome. Rather, it is because Christians must disassociate themselves from the evil of the Roman system that they are likely to suffer persecution.[11]

Immediately after he had heard the voice from behind him . . . "in the Spirit," that same voice and same Spirit ushered John through a door standing open in heaven, a door into the King's throne room (cf. 1:10; 4:1–2). By this same voice, same Spirit, and "seven lamps," the worship in the seven churches on earth is coordinated with the worship before the throne in heaven. Like the acclamation ceremonies in the local amphitheaters, the oral performance of John's letter in the churches told a cosmic story about how heaven and earth relate.[12] Who is the true king? Who is/are the god(s), who guide or produce what is happening on our local stage? How are heaven and earth interrelated?

Worshipping the Living Lamb, Who Was Slain, Shapes Faithful Witness

John not only draws together what is happening on earth with what is happening in heaven: he draws together the two central figures in the throne room, "the Lord God" (4:8, 11) and "the Lamb" (5:6, 12, 13). In addition to the correlation of the seven lampstands on earth (1:20) and the seven blazing lamps in heaven (4:5), "four living creatures" and "elders" surround what is clearly the same "throne" in chapters 4 and 5. This scene not only echoes scenes of the heavenly council in Daniel 7, Ezekiel 1, and Isaiah 6; it also lampoons the acclamation ceremonies, which were performed regularly in local Roman amphitheaters.

---

11. Bauckham, *Theology of the Book of Revelation*, 38.
12. Bauckham, *Theology of the Book of Revelation*, 4.

Who is "worthy to receive glory, honor, and power"? Who is "the Lord"? These are not abstract, academic questions. How John's hearers answered these questions was a matter of life and death, of heaven or hell. In addition to Yahweh, Israel's Lord and God, John described "a Lamb, looking as if it had been slaughtered, standing in the center of the throne, encircled by the four living creatures and the elders" (Rev 5:6)!

> The visions unmask the illusory power of "realistic" politics and disclose God's truth about human historical experience. For those who have eyes to see, the present order of the earthly city, built upon exploitation and violence, is a foul demonic parody of the city of God.[13]

Like "the One who sits on the Throne" (4:2, 3, 10), "the Slaughtered Lamb" (5:6) is deemed "worthy" "to receive glory, honor and praise" (4:11; 5:12). Indeed, John "heard every creature in heaven and on earth and under the earth and on the sea, and all that is in them, singing "To the One who sits on the Throne *and* to the Lamb!" (5:13). Those who joined this chorus in the house churches that gathered throughout the seven cities and beyond joined the bigger, better story being told in the heavenly council. But not without cost. To acclaim "Worthy is the Lamb!" in the new city is not to acclaim "Hail, Caesar" in the old. To drink the wine of the new covenant at the Lord's banquet table is not to partake of the wines of Dionysius. To share in the first fruits of the Lord's Day is not to rely on the gods of the guilds for your income. No one can serve two masters.

With particular reference to John's Apocalypse, let us briefly review how rehearsing the drama of redemption in worship shapes us for gospel witness to Christ's reign in all of life.

---

13. Hays, *Moral Vision of the New Testament*, 173.

GOSPEL SHOW-AND-TELL

Worship Gesture	Biblical Episode	Witness Gesture
Praise/Thanksgiving	1. Creation	Accepting the Gifts
Confession/Lament	2. Rebellion	Naming the Broken Places
Benediction & Commission	3. Israel	Using Status to Bless
Gospel Proclamation in Word & Sacrament	4. Jesus	Redirecting the Gifts
Offer/Exercise Gifts	5. Church	Working Together
Assurance of Pardon/Testimonies/ Passing the Peace	6. Restoration	Celebrating Little Restorations

G. R. PERRY   C2022

Figure 2–Gestures of Worship and Witness in the Drama of Discipleship

1. Praise and Thanksgiving—Creation—Accept the Gifts

As we have seen, acclamation or praise belongs only to the true and living God and his Son, Jesus the Messiah. They are the true source of life and peace, not Caesar nor any other tiny, rival lord. If we "supersize" one man or woman beyond their creaturely limits, attributing godlike powers to them, we necessarily diminish others who are not like them. Because the "supersized" are not gods, they can only produce a small story, a small peace. They can only manage a small world that cannot possibly include everyone. Thus, as they attain the acclaim of an idol, they must leave out justice and dignity for all.

But if, instead, we give proper thanks to our Creator, who built every stage—sky, sea, land—and filled each with living things, including all people, who he made, male and female, in his image, we begin to see and celebrate the good in every place and people. We accept the large, life-giving definition of the "good," shaped by the living one, the slaughtered lamb, who laid down his life to redeem every people and every place. Through the lens of John's vision, we remember how the stories of smaller gods ended in floods, plagues, wars and death, not the lasting city of the King of kings, where the gates stand open to the goods of all nations.

2. Confession & Lament—Rebellion—Naming the Broken Places

As the blood of the slaughtered lamb attests, his reign is challenged by the dragon (12:3–4), that serpent which stands behind and within all beasts, who lust for power. This great dragon is a great liar, for he must puff up himself and slander others. He is the accuser of the sons and daughters of God. His lusts and lies cause extensive damage. And so, the witnesses to the truth, the characters of the truer bigger story (6:9), cry out, "How long, Sovereign Lord, holy and true, until you judge the inhabitants of the earth, and avenge our blood?" (6:10).

Though these witnesses have endured great hardship, having suffered much for the name and word of God, they, too, must repent from seeking the comfort of food offered to idols and return to the feast of their first love. So, we join them to name the broken places in ourselves and in our communities. We take up the psalms of lament, the slave spirituals, the songs of protest against dehumanizing injustices. We sing in hope against our own sins and the ways we have been sinned against. We sing to the one who saves:

> Never again will they hunger; never again will they thirst.
> The sun will not beat upon them, nor any scorching heat.
> For the Lamb at the center of the throne will be their shepherd;
> He will lead them to the springs of living water.

And, God will wipe away every tear from their eyes (7:16–17; cf. 21:4).

As Brian Blount writes, "Like the spirituals, Revelation never gives up hope. Its liturgical hymns witness to the promise that God is relieving Rome of its historical command. Right now."[14]

3. Benediction & Commission—Israel— Using Status to Bless Others

We come again to the use of power and resources in the gospel script. The blessings of the covenant are given to renew our capacities as image-bearers and to propagate that pattern of renewal with our neighbors. Worship models not only the proper place of authority and power, but its proper use to "set right" or reconcile, to share our gifts for the common good. As Paul wrote, "Each one has a hymn, a lesson, a language and an interpretation."

---

14. Blount, *Can I Get a Witness?*, loc. 1930.

Each gift offered to the whole for building up the body (1 Cor 14:26). The slaughtered lamb, the one who had the power of the Almighty, did not grasp it, but shared its life-giving energy. So, we sing, forming habits with another ancient hymn:

> He emptied himself, taking the form of a slave.
> Being born in human likeness
> Being found in human form
> He humbled himself, becoming obedient to the point of death
> Even death on a cross.
> Therefore, God has highly exalted him . . . (Phil 2:7–9)

As Richard Hays summarizes,

> The church follows Jesus by bearing prophetic witness against the violence, immorality, and injustice of an earthly empire that claims authority that belongs rightly to God . . . . By excluding themselves from the "normal" activities of the [imperial] economic system (13:16–17; 14:6–11), they refuse to succumb to the illusion that power equals truth.[15]

The purpose of power rooted properly in the character of Israel's God and slain-but-risen Messiah is to "set right" what has swerved from the plotline of the script and its movement towards life. It is a different sort of "might making right" through the overwhelming force of redemptive love, instead of violence.

4. Gospel Proclamation—Jesus—Turning
To Follow the Way of Life

This covenantal pattern—using the blessings we enjoy to bless others and sacrificing benefits we could enjoy to avoid harming others—is fulfilled in Christ and his gospel. Throughout this drama we have seen how reducing the gospel to its personal benefits is a perversion of the bigger story. The source and subject of the good news is the one who has been given "all authority in heaven and on earth" (Matt 28:18). The horizon of this good news is "all nations" (28:19) and "all things" (Col 1:20), not my life, nor my little church or theological heritage. So, rather than blocking others in the mode of cancel culture, we can redirect the drama in our hearts and on our local stage toward the life-cultivating purposes of human vocation. With

---

15. Hays, *Moral Vision of the New Testament*, 176.

appetizing anticipation, having tasted of the firstfruits, we are inviting our neighbors to a banquet (Rev 19:7–9).

> If the shedding of Jesus' blood effectively unleashed the kingdom, ensuring our transfer from one sphere of existence to another, then the recapitulation of the same moment every time we take the Lord's Supper brings home that transference on a conscious and subconscious level . . . . Only as the community of believers comes to terms with this deliverance [will we] realize our destiny as mediators between God and the world.[16]

We live in the overlap of the ages, the time between the times. We gather every week in worship around the Lord's Table to taste and see that the Lord is good in anticipation of the wedding feast of the Lamb. Who gathers around his table with us? Are there people from every tribe, language, and nation? Are there people like Lazarus who are sick and poor? Are there people like Zacchaeus or Peter who once betrayed us, who have now experienced the same forgiveness? As we go out from the Lord's Table into his world, what sort of materials are we using to build our lives, precious materials that will survive the purifying day of Christ or materials that will burn up? Does our life together signify his peaceable kingdom, the presence of his life-giving Spirit?

5. Offering Our Gifts—The Church— Working Together to Flourish

Even as the Festival of Firstfruits shaped the worshipping community of Israel to remember that God had brought them out of slavery and death in Egypt into a good land that produced crops and sustained life, Jesus is described as "the first fruits of those who have fallen asleep" (1 Cor 15:20, 23). His way of life and crucified-yet-risen body establishes the pattern for the new creation that he launched amidst the old, the pattern that now shapes the new covenant community in its worship and witness. As we saw illustrated repeatedly in the last episode, this pattern—from death to new life—marks the bodies, products, and relationships of those who have been baptized with the Holy Spirit and with fire. Members of Christ's social body not only have "the first fruits of the Spirit" (Rom 8:23), they are "the first fruits of those who are being saved" (2 Thess 2:13).

---

16. Perrin, *Kingdom of God*, 181–82.

As we gather for worship each week, we each bring a song, a word of encouragement, a material offering from the work of our hands for our shared task of reweaving, repair, and restoration in the world. Because Jesus' life, death, and resurrection launched the new creation, changing the structure of the cosmos itself, to produce the firstfruit of a new world, what we do together in the world can also effect change, can also heal, can also produce firstfruits.

What is done in the present affects the future (Matt 25:31–46), not only in terms of reward but in terms of ongoing responsibilities! Do you manage properties and cultivate their produce? Do you run or own a business that makes things people need and provides jobs for families to feed and raise their children? Do you paint, sculpt, dance, sing, play an instrument, act, write, or make films? Does your art display the beauty, joy, goodness, and truth of life? Does it expose injustice? These activities are all aspects of bearing the image of God, of being human. Though Jesus told the Sadducees that we would no longer give and receive in marriage (Matt 22:30), he also said that in his kingdom the one who stewarded his talents well would be given more to oversee (25:14–30).

As John's vision in Revelation describes, there is continuity between the vocation of God's people now and their role in the new heavens and the new earth: "You made them a kingdom and priests to our God, and they shall reign on the earth" (Rev 5:10; cf. Exod 19:4–6; 1 Pet 2:9). So, Jesus' resurrected life and our life in the Spirit provide a pattern for life in the new heavens and the new earth, and they guarantee that the Lord's full harvest will surely be gathered. The martyrs, "who were slain for the word of God and the testimony they maintained" (Rev 6:9), look like their Savior in both their suffering and their glory. Like the one who now reigns, "they come alive and reign with him for a thousand years" (Rev 20:4).

Remarkably, the New Testament insists that Jesus remains fully human, that he has and is a body, a once-crucified-now-resurrected body. The body that died is the body that has risen. As the two men in the garden told the women who came to administer spices to his corpse, "He is not here! He has been risen!" (Luke 24:5–6). The risen Jesus is not a ghost. He ate bread and fish with his disciples. His body still interacts with the dimensions of the physical world in ways similar to the ways he did before his death and resurrection, but something is different. His interaction with the spiritual dimension is more apparent. As Paul writes, the body that is raised is imperishable, glorious, powerful, and spiritual (1 Cor 15:42–44).

To describe resurrected bodies as spiritual is not to say they are immaterial. Rather, it is to make clear that these resurrected bodies are animated and controlled by the Holy Spirit. So then, as "the first fruits of those who have fallen asleep" Jesus sets the pattern that the resurrected life of believers will be human, corporeal, and also incorruptible. The incorruptibility of the resurrected life is rooted in the Spirit's present work in the church. Because believers have "the first fruits of the Spirit" they bear "the fruit of the Spirit" in marked distinction from "the works of the flesh" (Gal 5:16–26). Indeed, when Paul writes of life in the Spirit or walking in the Spirit, he is not only speaking of a manner of life, but also of a realm of life, life in the new age.

6. Passing the Peace—New Creation— Celebrating Little Restorations

In the last episode, we saw how the author of the script is placing new public assemblies in neighborhoods as embassies of God's kingdom. The fact that these local churches are reconstruction sites is clear in their corporate confessions of sin and faith. Though its members carry scars from self-inflicted wounds and have borne the impact of many sins against them, the church's foundation is sure and its role as a hub of development for a new city is clear. At least it should be, for, as we have read now backwards and forwards, the script describes the church's mission holistically. In space, each church is a temple that mediates God's holy love in a particular place, the church of God in Orlando, Jakarta, Sydney, or Tehran. In time, local churches are "people of the eighth day." Sundays are a symbol of new creation launched in the midst of the old age. "Jubilee," "freedom," "release" is proclaimed!

> The church, if it is true to its guidelines, must preach the acceptable year of the Lord. It is an acceptable year to God because it fulfills the demands of His kingdom . . . The acceptable year of the Lord is that year when people in Alabama stop killing civil rights workers and people who are simply engaged in the process of seeking their constitutional rights. . . . [It is] that year when men learn to live together as brothers. The acceptable year of the Lord is that year when men keep their theology abreast with their technology . . . that year when men beat their swords into plowshares, and their spears into pruning hooks. The acceptable year of the Lord is that

year when we send to Congress and to state houses men who will do justly, who will love mercy, who will walk humbly with God.[17]

If Jesus came into this world, took on flesh, and lived among us fully as a man, and if "all things are created by him and for him, both visible and invisible" (Col 1:16; cf. John 1:3, 10–11), then Jesus has the decisive stake in the future of humankind and "all things." He is the pattern of our hope and future. Even as he proclaimed and practiced "the year of the Lord's favor" (cf. Isa 61:2; Luke 4:19), that same season of Jubilee continues in the wake of the complete atonement which secured and paid for it.

And so, as these firstfruits, signs of new creation emerge, we celebrate! We tell of God's wondrous deeds of restoration. Luke renarrated three stories that Jesus told about the celebrations that happen in heaven over one who changes addresses, changes lanes, changes destinations, and heads towards the new city. Of course, there is that famous story of the prodigal son who had squandered his father's inheritance, lost his sense of his true self, and yet returned home. The reunion was exquisite; the celebration was lavish. But there was also a lost sheep. Unlike the father, who waited for his son to return, the shepherd went after this lamb and found it. Finally, a woman had lost a coin, which meant she could not use it to buy needed food and supplies for her family. When she found it, she did just what the father and shepherd had done—she told everyone, inviting her friends and family to share in her joy.

What do we celebrate in our churches around the Lord's Table? What do we celebrate in our homes around the dinner table with our neighbors? We celebrate the "little restorations"! When an underemployed or unemployed family member gets that new job; when a marriage that has been struggling through a season of separation is reengaged; when a friend who is fighting addiction stays sober for another year; and, yes, when an inquirer and seeker becomes a brother or sister by professing their faith and entering the waters of baptism—we hear their testimonies! We retell their stories! We celebrate the firstfruits of the new creation! These incomplete, imperfect, small, appetizing bites of healing help us keep going. They reassure us that our longings for more justice, more love, more beauty, more peace are longings for a city whose foundations were designed and built by God (Heb 11:10; 13:14).

Our destination affects our direction and manner of travel. It affects every single thing about the way we live—the big and the small, the lesser and the great. Like my misadventure in the early days of my sojourn in

17. Carson and Holloran, eds., *Knock at Midnight*, 112–13.

Sydney, many disciples have the wrong destination in view. Many of us believe that heaven is the goal. To be sure, heaven, that is, a new heaven, is part of our destination, just like the park that I had aimed for was part of Sydney. But so was that other park, the actual place where we gathered for the picnic. Likewise, the new heavens and new earth is the place where a much greater celebration of welcome is planned, the Messiah's feast. What an over-the-top celebration that will be! And, part of the good news is, we can start celebrating in small ways even now.

Group Activity

In Revelation 21:24–27, John describes a city of light into which the nations and their kings carry their goods, their glory, to honor "the Lord God, the Almighty." The echoes of Isaiah 60 are unmistakable. Into the great city of God, once devastated because of Israel's sins, her sons and daughters return in droves. The wealth of the nations streams through gates that never close. Kings process into the city with the cultural products of their kingdom—their great flocks, fabrics, spices, foods, jewelry, dancers, and more. The people's works of justice and righteousness are recognized. All of these glorious cultural products are brought before the Lord as a reflection of his glory and "everlasting light" (Isaiah 60:19–22).

During the COVID-19 pandemic of 2020, actor and director John Krasinski decided that he had had enough of all the bad news. So, he started a new show that he shared with everyone on YouTube called *Some Good News*, or SGN.[18] In each episode, he captured the stories of people who were being good neighbors, people who were serving the community, people who were using their talents, treasure, and influence to make good things happen, not just for themselves, but for others. In his first episode, he thanked all the health care workers who were on the front lines every day risking their health to heal others. When the pandemic extended through the spring and swallowed up proms and graduation ceremonies, John recruited top musicians and singers to lead parties all over the US by connecting them online with "live" performances.

Your discipleship activity for Episode Six is to capture the stories of "little restorations" that are already happening all around you. Plan a video online and/or make a paper scrapbook that celebrates "the mighty deeds of the Lord" in your household, church, workplace, and neighborhood. Who

18. Krasinski, "Some Good News."

are the friends you've made, the children you've tutored or mentored, the people you've served? Who has started a new job or created jobs for others? Who welcomed new neighbors, planted new gardens, planted new churches? What are the songs of your soundtrack, the Scriptures on your mirrors and walls, the favorite dishes you've shared, or that have been shared with you? Who are the missionaries and ministries you've prayed for and supported? The Spirit of God is at work through his image-bearers reweaving relationships, advocating for their neighbors, and cultivating the common good by proclaiming and practicing the good news. Tell those stories and make your physical or digital scrapbook shareable! As appropriate, reach out to the individuals and groups that you are celebrating, and let them know that you recognize the good work they have accomplished!

Closing Notes and Additional Tools for Stage Directors in the Drama

As ANYONE WHO HAS participated in a school play will remember, each rehearsal ends with a recap and the director giving "stage notes." Some notes are given to the group as a whole, while others are delivered in smaller groups or individually. But, these notes (no matter how they are given) are aimed at amplifying the power of the drama through the cast's dialogue and actions. How can members of the ensemble access the emotional and material resources they need to do the heartwork and fieldwork the script requires? What changes does the group need to make to inhabit the meaning and direction of the story more truly? How can each member honor the unique role of "others" as agents of the same story? What are ways this group can break through "the fourth wall" to include its audiences in showing and telling the story of which we all are a part?

To be sure, the Holy Spirit directs this drama of discipleship, but local elders and deacons serve as assistant directors and stage managers. The pastoral and diaconal offices support and resource the gospel show-and-tell of the whole body of Christ. As we will see below, elders and deacons are charged with cultivating the local ensemble's connection between the script and their local stage in both word and dead, dialogue and gesture. Staging "gospel theater"[1] surely involves more but not less than three fundamental

---

1. Kevin Vanhoozer first described the gospel as "theodrama" and local church ministry as "gospel theater" in *Drama of Doctrine*, 37–56; 399–457; and developed the metaphors in *Faith Speaking Understanding*, 73–110; 139–206.

activities, hinted at in the questions above: 1) *the interpreting task*—Elders or pastors lead the cast in regular rereadings of the script.[2] Deacons develop the choreography, the bodily movements and material interactions, which dramatize the redemptive story. Both rereadings and choreography, dialogue and gestures, are vital to the storytelling. 2) *the connecting task*—Elders and deacons are both "go-betweens" cultivating connections between the scriptwriter and the cast, between each cast member, between the ensemble and the audience, and between neighbors and their material environment.[3] The words *minister* and *deacon* are different translations of the same underlying Greek word, *diakonos*. Its most basic meaning is "go-between." The role of these authorized agents is to weave loose ends together, to make connections. And, 3) *the extending task*—According to Lesslie Newbigin,

> The task of ministry is to lead the congregation as a whole in a mission to the community as a whole, to claim its whole public life, as well as the personal lives of all its people, for God's rule.[4]

From the beginning of the script, the human calling has been to extend the royal garden, to subdue the earth. Many religious zealots, including Saul the Pharisee, have sought to impose God's rule coercively. As he did with Saul, the true Adam, Jesus of Nazareth, confronts and forbids such violence. The task of extending the kingdom is an act of diplomacy. King Jesus sends ambassadors with his message of reconciliation (2 Cor 5:16–21). Outreach from Christ's local embassies acknowledges the shared dignity of image-bearers, and fosters dialogue about and participation in various forms of neighbor-love. As "ministers of reconciliation," followers of Christ are go-betweens, the Holy Spirit's local weavers of the fabric of peace.

As we have seen in our journey through the script, the redemptive drama is enacted in at least two interdependent, mutually informing spaces—in the sanctuary and on the streets. Local ensembles of gospel theater offer two different types of performances: 1) More traditional recitations

2. My description of these activities of church leadership is indebted to Branson and Martinez, *Churches, Cultures & Leadership*, 54–57, 210–31. However, my emphasis in the third area is on extension, instead of implementation.

3. See Keller, *Center Church*, 293, on "connecting" the "four ministry fronts." See also Fikkert and Corbet, *When Helping Hurts*, 56–62, and Myers, *Walking with the Poor*, 64–69 on how sin/fall alienates humans from their constitutive relationships with God, self, others, and the earth.

4. Newbigin, *Gospel in a Pluralist Society*, 238.

and reenactments of the script are rehearsed in the sanctuary. These gospel performances are more attuned to the transgenerational, catholic character of Christ's social body. They draw not only on the script itself but on master readings and performances that have proven meaningful in many cultural moments and localities. And, 2) adaptations of the script are improvised in workplaces, schools, and on the streets. This gospel show-and-tell, like Jesus' spoken parables and parabolic actions, are more attuned to particular locations, cultural categories, rhythms of speech and relationships, and the ways in which local stories harmonize with or challenge the redemptive drama. Together, elders and deacons "give notes" to the local ensemble which help them interpret the script, connect to each other and their audiences, and extend the drama of discipleship to every corner of the stage.

The Interpreting Task: Renarrating Our Lives

Our episodic reading of the script has revealed identifying gestures for a Christian congregation's local gospel theater. These gestures express and nurture the character of Christ's social body, which, out of love for both God and neighbor, take on different tones, cultural hues, emphases, and levels of formality in different locales. Yet, we have not only been rereading the script together, we have been rehearsing our role in the drama in our small groups and in our neighborhoods. We have been doing the heartwork and fieldwork that the script and its author require of understudies to act in character as the body of Christ.

In Episode One we praised the goodness and covenant faithfulness of the triune Creator in worship and accepted the gifts on our stage—both the Spirit's gifts in our groups, and the common graces in our communities. Our heartwork of gratitude animated and energized our fieldwork of taking an asset inventory. The blessings we counted and the field notes we recorded provide vital resources for our mission together as church.

Though there is much to celebrate, the cracks in our own character are as obvious as the broken windows and boarded-up buildings of our cities. Thus, in Episode Two, we began with the heartwork of confessing our own sins and lamenting the ways that we and our neighbors have been sinned against. The script provides psalms of lament, which connect our sin, sorrow, and grief to God, who is present, though sometimes shrouded in darkness and silence. In our fieldwork, we took a needs assessment, naming the broken places in the physical and relational space of our communities, in our schools and workplaces, in our economies and public policies, and in our relationships with our neighbors. Field notes from our asset inventory and needs assessment provide vital coordinates for staging our gospel show-and-tell. Both the delight we experience in our enjoyment of all that is good about our communities, and the pain we experience in the absence and depravation of good reveals a longing for Eden and its re-creation.

As we saw in Episode Three, God's people have roles as fellow travelers and trail guides in our journey together towards new creation. We continue to learn as we lead, because, we lead as followers of the way of Christ, picking up the cues of others, who have passed this way before us. Our ensemble's use of status and resources is framed by our Servant-King and his gospel script. We accept the gifts on the stage and receive the blessings of restored relationships not to hoard them, nor to spend them on ourselves only, but to share them with the nations in our midst (cf. Gen 12:3; 17:5; Rom 4:16–17).

This "priesthood of all believers" or general office of ministry is supported, resourced, and modeled by the particular offices of ministry, the elders and the deacons. They help direct the drama of discipleship in local congregations by example, and by providing encouragement, resources, equipping, and stage notes. They provide this "service" as a group, not as solo directors, because they too are actors in the redemptive drama. They need the same encouragement, resources, equipping, and stage notes. Though this is not the place for a full theology of church office or government, I want to throw a spotlight on their core responsibilities, and how they embody the third distinguishing gesture of Christ's body in their use of status, authority, and influence. In contrast to prevalent power dynamics on the local stage, they lead well by following well, they exercise their influence by loving sacrificially.

Character Profiles for Jesus' Leading Followers

According to eyewitnesses, Jesus and his followers were in Jerusalem during the week of Passover for the feast. While they were sharing the meal, a dispute broke out about "which of them was to be regarded as the greatest" (Luke 22:24). This dispute continues today, every day, on Twitter and You-Tube: Who is an influencer? Who can attract donors, sponsors, and clicks? Jesus interjects:

> The kings of the pagan nations exercise lordship over them, and those who are in authority over them are called benefactors. But, not so with you. (Luke 22:25–26)

As in our day, there was a lot of talk about greatness and influence during Jesus' earthly ministry, the greatness of nations and the influence of leading men. Jesus said plainly to his followers, "Not so with you." In the wake of this and many other encounters, those who "had been with Jesus" (Acts 4:13) studiously avoided the primary words that were being used in their moment on their stage to identify leaders. Instead of "rulers," "ruling priests," "authorities," or "masters," the apostolic script describes leaders among Jesus' followers as "shepherds," "elders," "servants," "stewards," and "witnesses."

With both words and deeds, Jesus upended the operative definition of greatness and strategies to build influence. At the Passover meal, he told them, "Let the greatest among you become as the youngest" (Luke 22:26a). Quite possibly, he was recalling that day when the disciples were keeping mothers and their children away from Jesus, only to hear him say, "let the little children come to me, for to such belongs the kingdom of heaven" (Matt 19:14). The Lord of all asked, "who is greater, one who reclines at table or one who serves?" Before his disciples could answer, he reminded them, "I am among you as one who serves" (Luke 22:27).

In both narrative and letter form, the script describes the work of God's Spirit in the church to align its words and deeds in worship and witness. The hard work of elders and deacons is to cultivate our integrity so that we act in character as Christ's body, so that our "word(s) of grace" (Acts 20:32) are confirmed by our "act[s] of grace" (2 Cor 8:7); and, our "acts of grace" are interpreted by our "words of grace." To be sure, this integral mission requires competence, and charisms, but it demands character most of all. The work of Jesus' leading followers is hard, because of our ongoing struggle with sin, but also because the drama of discipleship is necessarily intercultural, transgenerational, and holistic. Jesus said, "Go apprentice all ethnic groups in all of my ways, initiating and teaching them"—not just to grasp the information of his teachings with our heads, but to obey them from our hearts, mimicking him with our hands and feet. Following Jesus requires both heartwork and fieldwork.

In his second volume, Luke describes the stage direction the apostles gave the church in Jerusalem when a legitimate complaint arose from members who were on the edge of the community culturally and socially:

> In those days when the number of disciples was increasing, the
> Grecian Jews among them complained against the Hebraic Jews,
> because their widows were being overlooked in the daily distribu-
> tion. So, the Twelve gathered all the disciples and said to them, "It
> would not be right for us to neglect the ministry of the word of
> God to serve tables. Brothers and sisters, choose seven men from
> among you who are known to be full of the Spirit and wisdom. We
> will turn this responsibility over to them and give our attention to
> prayer and the ministry of the word." (Acts 6:1–4)

Remarkably, Luke describes "this responsibility" of "serving tables" as
"ministry." Whether due to administrative incapacity, cultural bias, or both,
Greek-speaking widows in the church at Jerusalem "were being neglected
in the daily distribution" (6:1). The word, translated "distribution" in Acts
6:1 is the same word that Luke uses in 6:4 to describe the "ministry" of the
word. Distributing both material necessities and spiritual necessities are
"ministry." Both gospel-show and gospel-tell require the Holy Spirit, faith,
prayer, love, and wisdom. One cannot do one without the other in a true
witness to God's reign.

The Aramaic-speaking apostles trusted the Spirit's presence and work
among the Greek-speaking members of their ensemble, and asked them to
discern the Spirit's work in their midst by choosing seven of their brothers
(6:3). This power-sharing, ministry improvisation was not limited to the
Jerusalem stage or to male actors. Paul asked the gospel ensemble at Ephesus to test men and women in their midst, "then, if they prove blameless,
let them serve as deacons" (1 Tim 3:10–11). Why are the same character
qualifications required of both elders and deacons? Why must both be "full
of the Holy Spirit" and of good reputation, even with "outsiders"? Because
they share the same mission, and the same tasks of interpreting the script,
connecting the players, and extending the production of gospel theater.
Though they share this ministry and these tasks, they do so with different
roles and responsibilities.

As we have already seen in Luke's account, both the apostles and the
seven carry out a "ministry." As Peter puts it in his first letter to the churches
dispersed throughout Asia Minor, they are stewards of "God's varied grace"
(1 Pet 4:10). Each member of the troupe has a bundle of gifts from the Spirit
(cf. 1 Cor 12:7–11; Rom 12:6–8; 1 Pet 4:10). As Peter's description suggests,

however, the Spirit's gifts can be categorized broadly as gifts of speaking or serving (1 Pet 4:10–11).[5]

Gifts of Speaking	*Gifts of Serving*
a word of wisdom	healing
a word of knowledge	miracles
prophecy	helping
various languages/tongues	administrating
interpreting tongues	service
teaching	acts of mercy
exhortation	giving
evangelism	faith

Gifts of the Spirit

Gospel preaching and teaching interpret the script for action on the local stage. Bodily movements and the use of material goods display the grace, mercy, faithfulness, and love that is being declared. By directing the drama of discipleship together, elders and deacons ensure that the dialogue and gestures of gospel show-and-tell align and the church acts in character as Christ's social body. Now, some of you are wondering, "What about pastors? What is their role?" The word *pastor* (*poimēn*) means "shepherd." Peter makes the connection explicit in his first letter that pastors are elders: "To the elders among you, I appeal to you as a fellow elder and a witness of Christ's sufferings . . . Be shepherds of God's flock" (1 Pet 5:1–2). The leadership model in the New Testament is communal and familial. Peter writes to "fellow elders." Paul writes to "co-laborers." "Paul and Barnabas appointed elders for them in each church" (Acts 14:23). Solo performances as leaders are not warranted by the New Testament. Pastors are elders and,

5. I understand the various New Testament lists of "spiritual gifts" (cf. 1 Cor 12–14; Rom 12; Eph 4; 1 Pet 4) as representative, not exhaustive.

together with the deacons, they equip the ensemble to proclaim and practice the grace of God.

In 1 Timothy 3:2, Paul notes that elders or pastors must be equipped with a particular skill that is not required of deacons. Elders must be "able to teach" (*didaktikon*). They are the script supervisors and the dialogue coaches. But, there is a second skill that is also required of elders or pastors—hospitality (*philoxenon*; 3:2). This word, translated literally, means "loving strangers." As we saw in Episode Four, this practice was integral to Jesus' *diakonia* or ministry. Meals are where strangers become friends, and friends become family. With this requirement it becomes clear why elders must possess "a good reputation with outsiders" (3:7), and why elders need their partnership with deacons.

Even a cursory reference to the Greek New Testament reveals the verb *diakoneitōsan* in 1 Timothy 3:10 shares the same root as the noun *diakonous* or "deacons" in 1 Timothy 3:8 and 12. "Let them serve as deacons" is redundant in order to be emphatic! Deacons are the stage managers, choreographers, and banquet planners in the drama of discipleship. They focus on the use of material resources and bodily movements on the local stage. While deacons oversee ministries of service, elders oversee ministries of speech. Their roles are distinct, but overlapping, integral and interdependent. In order to stage gospel theater with integrity, in which "words of grace" and "acts of grace" cohere, elders and deacons must work together.

The Climax of the Interpretive Task

In Episode Four, we focused on Jesus Christ, the climactic turning point, and only hero of the script. Jesus is "the Word who dwelt among us" (John 1:14) as "the One who serves" (Luke 22:27). Word and deed are integrated aspects of gospel ministry because they are integrated in Christ, the Good Shepherd (cf. John 10:11; 1 Pet 5:3) and Deacon (Rom 15:8-9). He lives not only as the true Israelite, fulfilling the patterns and promises of Israel's covenant, but also as the true human person, the very image of God (Col 1:15). In every arena of image-bearing, Jesus offered parabolic stories and actions to illustrate the ways of his kingdom. "A prophet mighty in word and deed" (Luke 24:19), "a high priest who sympathizes with our weaknesses" (Heb 4:15), a king who "came not to be served but to serve" (Mark 10:45), Jesus' life tells the story of God's love for the world in all the roles he plays. He is the Shepherd and Servant, the Elder and Deacon, who shows us the way of life.

His luminous life however, cannot be captured nor mimicked by one person. Rather, Paul describes the network of house churches in each local area as that mime—the body of Christ. Described vividly in Paul's circular letter to the Asian churches, local congregations display "the manifold wisdom of God" to local rulers and authorities (Eph 3:10). This "manifold wisdom" is kaleidoscopic, reflecting and refracting the light of Christ in a collage of images that display an outline of the suffering Servant King through the local colors, languages, and cultural patterns of his worldwide kingdom. As we have said, this body suffers from its own failures to mimic Christ and it suffers from those who oppose Christ. As we have seen throughout the script, the hero chooses the weak and sinful far more often than the strong and noble to display the magnitude of his grace.

Discipleship Restores Image-Bearing Roles

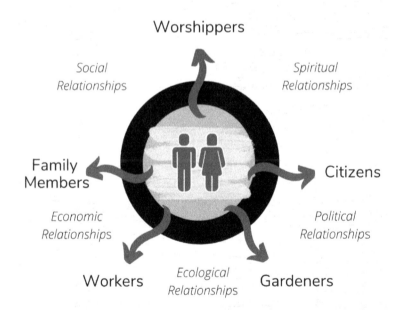

Figure 8 —Discipleship Restores Roles of Image-Bearing

By engaging familiar scenes from each dimension of our human calling, Rabbi Jesus leads learners to turning points, personal and practical opportunities, to realign our lives with the policies of God's kingdom. In parables unique to Luke's account, Jesus takes a robust interest in our relation to money, work, the poor, and the ethnically "other." In parables unique to Matthew's account, Jesus, no less interested in our stewardship of wealth and relations with the poor, illustrates the growth of his kingdom with salt, light, leaven, fishing nets, and a wedding banquet. We, too, are agents of God's kingdom, fishing for people, illuminating places, fertilizing situations so they may one day produce fruit. Jesus dramatizes the value of his kingdom with pearls and hidden treasure, which can only be purchased when its citizens exchange all other currencies.

John Mark, the first to record Jesus' parables, describes their twofold purpose to reveal and to obscure the kingdom, depending on the posture of those who hear them. This is the gospel about God's kingdom: Jesus of Nazareth is the King of kings and Lord of lords, who summons you, me, and all nations to worship and follow him as witnesses of his reign over life and death as he reconciles all things to God. The gospel is no mere proposition, it is news about who Jesus of Nazareth is, what he has accomplished, and how his life, death, and resurrection changes everything. The gospel is about a new state of affairs on the ground, a victorious king who calls people to restructure their lives in accord with his reign.

Though John did not record Jesus' spoken parables like the other evangelists, he paired his unique "I-am sayings" with "signs." John describes Jesus' living parables in which he reenacts scenes from Israel's script, and improvises them in gospel show-and-tell. For example, John dramatizes the saying, "I am the bread of life" with Jesus' "sign" of feeding more than five thousand people on their way to Passover. Like the Lord who provided manna in the wilderness for those whose houses were passed over, Jesus provided his body and blood as "the bread of life" and Passover sacrifice for all who will give him their full allegiance. The call of Jesus in the Gospels declares "follow me" in every arena of life. His promise to those who follow is, "I will be with you always, even to the end of the age."

The Connecting Task: Redirecting Our Words and Deeds Towards Life

If, as we have been describing, the gospel is an ongoing, life-encompassing story about Christ's reign, being actualized among his followers, then how might we show and tell it in our various roles? The following diagnostic questions arise from each episode of the script (E1–E6) and invite appropriation in each role that we play as divine image-bearers. Image-bearing and its central activities—multiplying other image-bearers, and extending the boundaries of the royal garden—require two or more, who gather and scatter in God's name. The following questions are designed for use in small groups, whose members are committed to challenging, encouraging, and serving each other in the heartwork and fieldwork of holistic disciple-making.

Depending on the size of your group, you may only get through three questions per gathering in order to allow enough time for each member to share their answers. So, you may want to take two weeks to give focused attention to each of the five roles. This dramatic process will generate stage notes for each member and action items for both heartwork and fieldwork. Let's start with our role as worshippers, a role that Jesus resourced with parables about prayer (cf. Luke 11:1–13; 18:9–14).

Our Role as Worshippers

E1 (Creation): What and who are we thankful for in our church, in our neighborhood? Why? Count the blessings! Tell the stories with gratitude. *(Accepting Our Gifts)*

E2 (Rebellion): What are we confessing and asking God to change in ourselves? In our church? What are we lamenting with our neighbors? *(Naming Our Broken Places)*

E3 (Israel): What are our spiritual gifts, ministry roles, and avenues of influence? How are we stewarding these resources to build up our congregation, our neighborhood, and the global church? *(Using Our Status to Bless Others)*

E4 (Jesus): Which religious practices do we need to forsake or redirect? Are we using activities intended for service to God and others to build our own platform and reputation? If so, how do we repent and redirect these activities? *(Turning To Follow the Way of Life)*

E5 (Church): How are we relating in the church? How is our church partnering with other churches and non-profits? Can we strengthen our collaboration? (*Working Together to Flourish*)

E6 (New Creation): What is one change you have seen in your sister or brother this past year that you want to recount and celebrate? (*Celebrating Little Restorations*)

We come now to our economic relationships and our role as workers. As we saw in Episode Four, Jesus' visit to Zacchaeus's house radically reordered his relations with God, his neighbors, money, and his work (Luke 19:1–10). Many parables address the use of wealth in the kingdom of God (Matt 13:44–46; 20:1–16; 25:14–30; Luke 14:12–24; 16:1–15, 19–31; 19:11–27). In Episode Five, we learned how the earliest synagogues and churches functioned as an alternative "household" or "economy of goods," supplying the material necessities of its members and neighbors, when they were lacking. Consider the following questions, arising from each episode of the script. How do they connect with what's happening on your local stage?

Our Role as Workers

E1 (Creation): What do we love about our work? (*Accepting the Gifts*)

E2 (Rebellion): What isn't going well? Who's getting left out? Are resources being underutilized or misappropriated? Is anyone we know out of work? (*Naming the Broken Places*)

E3 (Israel): Are we using our wisdom, time, skills, resources, and decision-making authority to bless others? Are we advocating for and mentoring others? (*Using Status to Bless Others*)

E4 (Jesus): What changes are needed in ourselves and our organizations in order to serve our teams and customers better? Where do we need to redirect our gifts at work? Should you or I consider a change of job or career path? (*Turning To Follow the Way of Life*)

E5 (Church): How well are our teams working together? Are new investors, partnerships, supply chains, contractors, or distributors needed? (*Working Together to Flourish*)

E6 (New Creation): How do you and I celebrate people and their achievements? How do you and I recharge? Are we keeping the Sabbath and observing sabbatical rhythms? (*Celebrating Little Restorations*)

It is hard to overestimate the importance of families as cultures of discipleship. But households in the Mediterranean basin of the first century should not be confused with the modern, nuclear family. As some of you will re-member from the 2002 romantic comedy *My Big Fat Greek Wedding*, fami-lies from the Mediterranean are large, loud, and involved in each other's lives.[6] Most of the movie is a culture clash between Ian Miller, Toula's non-Greek suitor, and the Portokalos family, including Toula, who is struggling to find her voice and to redefine her sense of herself. The conflict of Toula's story provides a fitting metaphor for the drama of discipleship. Each of us is born into a system of relationships that shape our sense of the world and ourselves. But, Christ, our betrothed, who awaits his bride at the wedding feast of the lamb, pursues and calls us to himself, with whom, it turns out, we are discovering a fuller sense of our true selves.

As we saw in Episode Five in our description of households in Christ's kingdom, those who are united to Christ must re-center their domestic relationships around Christ. This new allegiance takes precedence. A new, widely extending family becomes our place of belonging and identity for-mation. In the bosom of the church, we are being nurtured in the ways of Christ and his worldwide, intercultural kingdom. Give your attention now to questions which ask you and your group members to reconsider your image-bearing role as members of a new kind of household.

Our Role as Family Members

E1 (Creation): What are some of the good things we've learned from our families of origin? Who mentored you, whether a family member or someone who has become "like family" to you? *(Accepting the Gifts)*

E2 (Rebellion): Can you and I ask for help when we need it? Can you and I apologize and ask for forgiveness? How well do we speak the truth in love? What are the broken places in our extended families, in our households? *(Naming the Broken Places)*

E3 (Israel): How are we using our resources and influence in our extended families? Are we advocating for one another as Paul did for his "sister" Phoebe, and as she did for her brother? Are we investing our time and material resources in fellow members of Christ's body? *(Using Status to Bless Others)*

6. Zwick, dir., *My Big Fat Greek Wedding.*

E4 (Jesus): Are we reconciling our disputes with humility, patience, godly sorrow, repentance, and forgiveness? How are we applying grace in the wounds of our households? (*Turning To Follow the Way of Life*)

E5 (Church): How are we serving together as a household? Are we taking the initiative to show hospitality? How are we receiving the invitations of others? (*Working Together to Flourish*)

E6 (New Creation): How are we celebrating birthdays, anniversaries, and the interests, growth, and achievements of household members? (*Celebrating Little Restorations*)

In his book *The Four Loves,* C. S. Lewis distinguished between a demonic and healthy patriotism. What's the difference? In the former, one's love for country is greater than one's love for goodness, truth, and beauty, one's love for God. Thus, patriotism becomes an idol, rooted in a false sense of national and/or ethnic supremacy. The latter, however, is a truer patriotism, a truer love, for it reads and researches the history of a nation in the illuminating, sometimes searing light of greater loves. As Lewis reminded us, "The actual history of every country is full of shabby, even shameful doings."[7]

And yet, as we have seen, every city, every country, every culture also shines with the good work of those who are created in the image of God. Thus, a "healthy patriotism" discovers and documents a full national history—the truth of the bad with the good. This true and tough love of country not only celebrates the achievements of its body politic, it also faces the ways in which that body carries diseases that need remedies which strengthen its capacity to provide liberty and justice for all its citizens, and in its relation to other nations.

Like leaven in a lump of dough or salt fertilizing the soil, citizens of Christ's kingdom form a new "assembly" (*ekklesia*) within the local "assembly," a new social body within the local body politic. Indeed, Paul called the church in Philippi to "live as citizens" in a manner worthy of the gospel (Phil 1:27). In January 27 BC, Philippi was named *Colonia Augusta Iulia Philippensis* as a colony of the city of Rome. Its citizens enjoyed the same rights as Roman citizens and were expected to foster its civic values. By urging the Philippian Christians to shape their public life around the gospel of Jesus, Paul provided a different standard for image-bearers in their role as citizens and ambassadors of God's kingdom.

7. Lewis, *Four Loves*, 32.

E1 *(Creation)*: Do we know our neighbors' names? Are we welcoming them with hospitality and willing to receive their invitations? Which neighbors or community leaders do we need to thank and, for whom, give thanks to God? *(Accepting the Gifts)*

E2 *(Rebellion)*: How are we addressing the inequities in our community? Are we speaking and writing about our political views and religious commitments in ways that respect the dignity of neighbors who hold different views? *(Naming the Broken Places)*

E3 *(Israel)*: Are we participating in our neighborhood associations, local government, or nonprofit advocacy organizations? Are we using our influence and resources to foster justice and equal opportunity? Do we support sound journalism and seek information from multiple, reliable news sources? Do we vote? (*Using Status to Bless Others*)

E4 *(Jesus)*: Do we love our enemies and work to live at peace with our neighbors, especially with those who have different views? Do we pray for and seek to work with our leaders, even those who are members of other political parties? (*Turning To Follow the Way of Life*)

E5 *(Church)*: Are we known for building bridges? Do we cross party lines to work together for the common good? (*Working Together to Flourish*)

E6 *(New Creation)*: How do we celebrate good citizenship? Are there festivals, parades, public forums, and educational events we can attend to celebrate improvements in our community? (*Celebrating Little Restorations*)

Many of Jesus' parables are rooted in the agrarian economy of first-century Palestine. God's gift of land and blessing on flocks and fields were a barometer of the state of Israel's covenant relationship with the Lord. Sabbath rest, gleaning laws, and the year of Jubilee underscored God's ownership of the land and punctuated its economy of grace both to Israel and even to the stranger and alien. As we saw in Episode Five, the Festival of Firstfruits, fulfilled on the Day of Pentecost, celebrates God's gift of life, embodied in the resurrection of Jesus and the new patterns of life among those who have been baptized with the Holy Spirit. The sacramental elements of water, wine, and bread symbolize the way in which Christ is redeeming all things to himself, redirecting bodies and the cultural products they produce towards life and "very good(ness)" under God's reign.

The pouring of wine and breaking of the bread with thanksgiving in the name of Jesus Christ are emblematic expressions of what we were called to in the garden, and are renewed to as disciples who extend his grace to the ends of the earth—the fashioning and use of the material of creation to support, sustain, and give life. Thus, what we rehearse around the Lord's Table of blessing, we are called to extend around tables of hospitality in our communities. Elders are to be exemplary in "hospitality" (1 Tim 3:2), and deacons in "serving tables" (Acts 6:2). At the Lord's Table, word takes on flesh. How are we cultivating the natural resources and material goods of our communities and regions? Do we offer a cup of cold water to the thirsty? Do we break bread with the lonely? Do we advocate for those who have no place at the table?

Our Role as Gardeners

E1 (Creation): How do we celebrate God's beauty, goodness, and glory in our food, art, parks, and other natural resources? What are the physical, material blessings of our city and region? (*Accepting the Gifts*)

E2 (Rebellion): Where is land being underutilized, food and water wasted or access to them hindered? What are the greatest health threats in our community? Who needs our hospitality or a place at the table? (*Naming Broken Places*)

E3 (Israel): How are we using land, food, water, energy, natural, and financial resources to support the flourishing of all who live in our region? How are we using our personal resources to invest in our community and demonstrate hospitality? (*Using Status to Bless Others*)

E4 (Jesus): Are there habits we need to break and other practices we need to adopt in order to live more sustainably? Are we "remembering the poor"? Are there people we need to repay? Are there systems of supply and delivery we need to repair, to make more equitable? (*Turning To Follow the Way of Life*)

E5 (Church): How are we working with our neighbors to cultivate equity in our community in relation to material resources like housing, food security, access to health care, and education? (*Working Together to Flourish*)

E6 *(New Creation)*: What food festivals, markets, or events celebrate local products and goods? What fitness goals have you reached? What renovation projects have you completed? (*Celebrating Little Restorations*)

Doing the Fieldwork: Engaging and Extending the Drama on Your Local Stage

How is the drama of redemption playing out on your local stage? Remarkably, Jesus did most of his gospel show-and-tell out and about, among the people. Of course, he went with them "up to the temple," or "into the synagogue" but most gospel scenes play out in people's homes, on the roads, beside wells, around tables, on hillsides, or in fishing boats. The drama of discipleship is experienced, and our missionary God is more deeply known, in the covenantal interplay between the Spirit who speaks through the script and the Spirit who works in the lives of the people onstage.

In addition to their interpreting task, and connecting task, the third and final task of elders and deacons is to equip their local ensemble to extend their performance of gospel show-and-tell both locally and globally. This extending task requires us to get to know neighbors, who share our local stage, even to get to the know the stage itself. A neighborhood survey is a good place to start. You'll be glad to know your fieldwork is already well under way.

Remember when you and your group were "walking the stage" in Episode One to do an asset inventory? What did you discover? Return to your field notes to review what you recorded. Perhaps some members of your church work or volunteer inside one of the assets you placed on your map—a local school, business, or nonprofit organization. Where do your fellow members live in the neighborhood? Where are the places where a representative cross section of the neighborhood gathers? A local coffeehouse, diner, YMCA, community center, or park?

Your field notes should also contain a community needs assessment and prayers of lament from your group activity in Episode Two. Remember not to overlook the broken places in yourself and in your church. What are the pressure points in your community? What are the broken places that you and your group have named in yourselves and in your city? How does your church pray about these things? How do you intercede together spiritually and materially as "go-betweens"? Sometimes Community

Assets and Needs Maps mark routes to local schools, clinics, and other nonprofits where volunteers from your church can serve. Other times the asset inventories and needs assessments reveal gaps where new structures or organizations may need to be built in order to support growth in your neighborhood.

Having reviewed your field notes and group activities from each episode, consider two remaining, yet vital tools for your ministry's missionary fieldwork: still photos and video, that is to say, demographic and ethnographic research, respectively. The classroom was filled with anxious energy and lots of questions. Most of the graduate students, who were preparing for church leadership, had never done missionary field research. Many had been on a short-term mission trip or participated in a service project, but they had followed someone else's plan. A cross-cultural missionary or project manager had mapped the assets, assessed the needs, and lined up the logistics in partnership with national or community leaders. To address their fear of the unknown, I held up a familiar object—my iPhone.

With their enthusiastic permission, I took a selfie of me and the class and flashed it up on the screen. The still photo documented who was on the stage, the *dramatis personae*. "Demographic research," I explained, "is like this still photo." It tells us who lives in this neighborhood or zip code. It shows us a picture of who is onstage with us. How old are they? What is their ethnicity? What is the taxable value of their home? What percentage rent? What percentage own? People who want to start a business, plant a church, or even buy a home know this information is an important starting point for getting to know a place. What is your theology of place? We will return to this question in a moment.

Still shots are only a starting point. Turning to the picture on the screen, I said, "demographics can tell you who and what is in the picture, but they can't tell you why." To answer that question, we need moving pictures, dynamic dialogue. I swiped my iPhone camera over from its photo to video setting, and walked over to a student in the front row. "Is it okay if I record?" I asked, and he nodded. "What is your favorite park in St. Louis?" Without hesitation he identified, "Tower Grove." Exploring, I observed, "Most people choose Forest Park. What do you like about Tower Grove?" Again, without hesitation, he said, "I live near the park, so my family and I use it all the time. I jog there. We play soccer and walk our dogs there. And at least one Thursday night a month, when the weather's good, my wife and I get a babysitter, then take our lawn chairs, blankets, and cooler out to the park to enjoy the live music and food trucks with our neighbors." "Is Tower Grove part of the reason why you and your family don't live on campus?" I asked. He continued, "We started out in student housing, but as we got to know St. Louis, we found a church in South City and the restaurants on South Grand. So, last summer, we made our move." I pushed pause on my camera. He had given a short, but significant asset inventory. More importantly, he had revealed some of his heart, he had narrated a love story about a place.

We need both still photos and video to really get to know a people in a place. If demographic research is akin to still photos, then ethnographic research is akin to video. Many people have reviewed the still photos of their neighborhood; they've studied the census data. Nevertheless, set aside some time to visit the Census Bureau's website and learn your way around its album of photos (https://www.census.gov/quickfacts/fact/table/US/PST045219). Put your city and state or your church's zip code in the search bar at the top left corner. Use the "select a fact" drop-down menu to explore information about the ethnic, generational, and economic composition of your region. Most municipalities offer access to more detailed information about local neighborhoods. Many neighborhoods now have their own websites and social media. Start following.

For most of the students in the orientation that day and for most leaders in your church, ethnographic fieldwork requires some practice, some role playing. But, the most important skill of an ethnographer and being a good neighbor is the same. In *Life Together*, Dietrich Bonhoeffer reminded us that listening is the first service we owe to our neighbors.[8] If ever there were an apostolic word for our cultural moment, James has it: "My dear brothers and sisters take note of this: You must all be quick to listen, slow to speak, and slow to get angry" (Jas 1:19). By undertaking a neighborhood survey, you and your ministry leaders will not only discover how the story of redemption is already playing out on your local stage, you will hone your skills for civil discourse, starting and continuing gospel conversations. Instead of walking around with clipboards, however, I recommend setting up brief conversations in a third space, like a local coffee shop, community center, or food court.

---

8. Bonhoeffer, *Life Together*, 97–99.

Conducting a Neighborhood Survey

Start by introducing yourself. "Hi, I'm Greg! I'm glad the coffee is good here, because my wife and I like to support local businesses. We moved here not too long ago, and we'd love to learn more about the community. I've seen you in here pretty regularly. When you have a few minutes for a conversation over coffee, I have a few questions that I'd like to ask you. If now isn't good for you, I'm in here most Tuesdays and Thursdays. Does next Tuesday work?" I continued the orientation by dividing the room into conversation partners and had each pair practice their introduction.

To get a good cross section of neighbors and perspectives, you'll need to branch out from the coffee shop to interview different stakeholders in various institutional spaces. The goal is to gather information from community members from the standpoint of each of the five areas of image-bearing. Once you've interviewed workers and managers in local businesses like the coffee shop, reach out to local clergy. How are worship leaders and worshippers in local mosques, synagogues, or churches engaging life on the local stage? You may be thinking to yourself, "What questions should I ask?" I'm not sure where to start. I will offer specific questions below, but first we need to complete the list of interviewees. Citizens and civil servants in local or state government provide an important perspective on the quality of life in a place. Reach out to your alderman or councilwoman to meet locally. Often, school leaders have their fingers on the pulse of how family members are doing in the community. Your school principal knows the stats and stories. She knows both what percentage of her students enjoy strong support at home and what kinds of discipline, mental health, and learning issues her school population experiences. Finally, as gardeners, we bear God's image in our physical, bodily life and how we interact with the material world. Health care workers, YMCA and other gym managers, community gardeners, and local farmers' markets (or the lack thereof) can provide insight on how the community values and manages its physical well-being. If you send people out two by two, and have each pair interview at least ten people, then a trained group of two dozen church members can start 240 neighborly gospel conversations.

Notice how the following questions follow the story, providing a lens to see how the missionary God is present and active on your local stage in the drama of redemption.

1. Tell me some of the things you love most about living / working here? What's good, even very good about [name of community]? Follow up: "Tell me more about . . ."

2. What are some of the needs that you see in our community? Where do we have room for improvement? Follow up: Who are our most vulnerable neighbors?

3. Who are the long-term leaders and new influencers in our community? Describe some of the ways they are using their status and resources to make things better? Follow up: Who else needs to find their voice, step up, and use their influence?

4. How can churches and other faith-based organizations be better neighbors? What changes can they make to put feet to their faith? Follow up: Where are churches and nonprofits doing good, helpful work?

5. How do you see neighbors working together? Follow up: What partnerships need to be explored? Which partnerships need to be adjusted?

6. What are some ways our community celebrates? Do we have regular festivals, parades? Follow up: How do we recognize citizens and organizations who are making a difference?

Summarize Your Findings and Put Them to Good Use on Your Local Stage

After the students had practiced their interview questions in pairs, I offered the following stage notes on how to analyze and use the still photos and video from their fieldwork.

1. Make sure to file your notes from your field visits and your interviews into one Google doc or Dropbox file. Staying organized will make it easier for your group to summarize its findings and make meaningful recommendations to your ministry team leaders, elders, and deacons.

2. When local stakeholders have been interviewed, read through the interview files together, and identify common themes that emerge in each question area. Also, take note of comments from neighbors who have specialized training or long-term experience in the community. Do their comments need extra weight?

3. Once you've listed your observations in bullet points, stop and pray for your neighborhood and for your local ensemble's service to your neighbors.

Now, you are ready to write a final summary of your findings. What have you learned about this place from your demographic research and ethnographic interviews? Who is the cast of neighbors on the stage? How have they summarized the stories of this place? What is "very good" about this place and its people? Where are the points of dramatic conflict?

It is vital to take one final step. The findings from this neighborhood survey provide you and your ministry team with an opportunity to assess how well your production of gospel theater is connecting with each episode of the biblical script and the people on your local stage. Each question of this survey explores how each respective episode of the Spirit's script is interacting with the characters, props, and scenery onstage. What are you learning about that interaction and the ways in which your gospel summaries and embodiments of grace are communicating? Where are your church's outreach efforts simultaneously faithful to the script and fitting for the stage? How can you extend and strengthen those activities? What aspects of your service to God and neighbor is not faithful to the script, nor fitting for your particular stage?

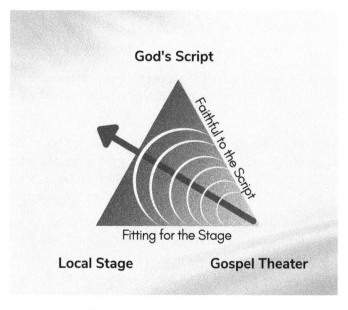

Figure 1—Gospel Theater Is Faithful to the Script and Fitting for the Stage

Your findings from the neighborhood survey will confirm where your performance is connecting, and offer guidance for adjustments that are needed to strengthen your storytelling. Your findings will provide key points for your stage notes.

Much more could be said about the extending task of building structures of outreach in the community to support the production of gospel theater in every arena of image-bearing. As we have mentioned above, some churches have started schools in partnership with families both in the church and out in the community. Some churches have started job programs, budgeting classes, even credit unions to equip workers. Other churches have hosted town hall meetings or co-sponsored teach-ins to explore the role of faith in practices of restorative justice. While some churches have chosen to provide these programs as in-house ministries under the oversight of their elders and deacons, other churches have chosen to partner with separate nonprofit organizations or to start one.

As we have seen throughout this *Drama*, holistic disciple-making requires leaders who will take up the necessary tasks of interpreting the script; connecting the members of the ensemble with the author, each other, and their audience; and, extending the drama of redemption into every arena of human vocation. To close, I return to the question I asked my students, the question we have been answering all along: "what is your theology of how the gospel takes root in a particular place?"

What is Your Theology of How the Gospel Takes Root in a Particular Place?

As we learned from Paul's missionary approach to planting and watering the gospel vine in particular places, different climates require different cultivation practices to produce good fruit. The characteristics of wine produced in a particular *terroir* are not only a factor of the vine and type of grape, but shaped also by the minerals and other nutrients in the soil, the pollens and moisture in the air, the elevation, access to water, exposure to sunlight, and the practices of cultivation that have been passed down in that region.[9]

A master interpreter, connector, and extender, the apostle Paul knew that he had to study not only the characteristics of the vine, but also the ground in places he had been sent to cultivate its fruit. Soil and water samples needed to be taken, sunlight patterns studied, plots plowed and

9. See McGrath, "Cultivation of Theological Vision," esp. 119–22.

terraced, trellises and irrigation ditches built, before the planting could begin in earnest. In most cases, his research started before he arrived on the field. He read their poets, their philosophers, their historians. He corresponded with people who lived and loved there. Still, when he did arrive on the scene, he walked the stage. He carefully observed. He not only visited synagogues, he was also out and about in the marketplace and around tables listening to the topics of conversation.

Then, he spoke their language(s) in the register of their institutions, weaving intertexts from the Spirit's script, and pointing clearly to Jesus, the true human being. Local people responded with questions and with faith. When they started to gather as the "assembly" of God in that place, as the social body of Christ, Paul did not ship in foreign leaders, but appointed local elders and deacons (Phil 1:1) to extend the trellises, to build the wine vats and to bring the firstfruits of the vine, at last, to the Lord's Table.

In this concluding chapter, we have reviewed the drama of discipleship by exploring the elements of ensemble productions of gospel theater on local stages. Like Pauline preparation, planting, cultivation, and harvest, producing gospel theater requires a thorough knowledge of both the script (vine) and the local stage (*terroir*). As Timothy Gorringe reminded us,

> In Scripture there is no timeless space but also there is no spaceless time. There is, rather, storied place. . . . People en-story and en-soul their places and then, in the course of the dialectic of material life, their places en-soul them.[10]

So, as you have walked your stage and conversed around tables, what have you learned about the stories that live in your church, in your extended family, in your workplace, and in your neighborhood? Stories that have staying power mark memories of rich blessings or deep wounds, special places on your local stage that are hallowed or haunted. Looking through the lens of the script, some of the storied action on your stage harmonizes with the drama of redemption. Some of the dialogue and gestures compete and clash with the script, signaling false narratives that crack and break the covenantal shape of reality. But, as Gorringe confesses, "all space is potentially sacred, waiting for the moment of encounter in which it mediates God."[11]

---

10. Gorringe, *Theology of the Built Environment*, 38.
11. Gorringe, *Theology of the Built Environment*, 40.

As we have reviewed the script and walked our local stages (fieldwork), we have reoriented ourselves to our role as the social body of Christ (heart-work). We have sought to answer our casting call to bear God's image and imitate Christ together in every square inch of God's world. For that role, we have sought to recover our agency as covenantal partners, our place on local stages, and our role as "go-betweens" (*diakonoi*). We have sought to reimagine our world as God's. Indeed, in our fieldwork we have seen the missionary God already present and working in our communities. Father-Son-and-Holy-Spirit are reconstructing holy space in every neighborhood among every ethnic group. Oddly, mysteriously, their plan is to build local temples out of "living stones" (1 Pet 2:5), to display God's grace with skin on in a drama of discipleship that is "filling all in all" (Eph 1:22–23).

Bibliography

Allen, John. *Rabble-Rouser for Peace: The Authorized Biography of Desmond Tutu*. New York: Free Press, 2006.

Arizona 1.27. A Movement of Arizona Churches. https://az127.org.

Arnold, Bill T. *Genesis*. The New Cambridge Bible Commentary. Edited by Ben Witherington III. New York: Cambridge University Press, 2009.

Arnold, Clinton. *Ephesians*. ECNT. Grand Rapids: Zondervan, 2010.

Augustine. *Confessions*. Translated with Introduction and Notes by Henry Chadwick. Oxford: Oxford University Press, 1992.

Balthasar, Hans Urs von. *Theodrama: Theological Dramatic Theory*. 3 Dramatis Personae: Persons in Christ. San Francisco: Ignatius, 1993.

Barclay, John M. G. *Paul and the Gift*. Grand Rapids: Eerdmans, 2015.

Barth, Karl. *Church Dogmatics* IV: *The Doctrine of Reconciliation*. Parts 1–3. Edited by G. W. Bromiley and T. F. Torrance. Edinburgh: T&T Clark, 1956.

Bartholomew, Craig, and Michael Goheen. *The Drama of Scripture: Finding Our Place in the Biblical Story*. Grand Rapids: Baker Academic, 2004.

Barton, Stephen. "Dislocating and Relocating Holiness: A New Testament Study." In *Holiness: Past and Present*, edited by Stephen Barton, 193–216. Edinburgh: T. &T. Clark, 2002.

Bates, Matthew W. *Salvation by Allegiance Alone*. Grand Rapids: Baker, 2017.

Bauckham, Richard. *The Theology of the Book of Revelation*. New Testament Theology. Cambridge: Cambridge University Press, 1993.

Beale, Gregory K. *The Temple and the Church's Mission: A Biblical Theology of the Dwelling Place of God*. Downers Grove, IL: InterVarsity, 2004.

Bediako, Kwame. *Jesus in African Culture: A Ghanaian Perspective*. Accra: Asempa, 1990.

———. "Scripture as the Hermeneutic of Culture and Tradition." *Journal of African Christian Thought* 4.1 (June 2001) 2–11.

Berkouwer, G. C. *Man: The Image of God*. Studies in Dogmatics 10. Grand Rapids: Eerdmans, 1952.

———. *The Providence of God*. Studies in Dogmatics 2. Grand Rapids: Eerdmans, 1952.

Blocher, Henri. *In the Beginning: The Opening Chapters of Genesis*. Translated by David Preston. Downers Grove, IL: InterVarsity, 1984.

Blount, Brian K. *Can I Get a Witness? Reading Revelation Through African American Culture*. Louisville: Westminster John Knox, 2005.

Bock, Darrell L., with Benjamin I. Simpson. *Jesus According to the Scriptures: Restoring the Portrait from the Gospels.* 2nd ed. Grand Rapids: Baker Academic, 2017.

Bonhoeffer, Dietrich. *Creation and Fall, Temptation: Two Biblical Studies.* New York: Simon & Schuster, 1997.

———. *Ethics.* Translated by Neville Horton Smith. Edited by Eberhard Bethge. London: Macmillan, 1955.

———. *Letters and Papers from Prison.* Dietrich Bonhoeffer Works 8. Edited by John W. de Gruchy. Translated by I. Best, L. E. Dahill, R. Krauss, and N. Lukens. Minneapolis: Fortress, 2009.

———. *Life Together.* Translated by John W. Doberstein. New York: Harper & Row, 1954.

———. "Report on the Mass Deportation of Jewish Citizens." In *Conspiracy and Imprisonment 1940–1945,* edited by Mark Brocker and Lisa E. Dahill, 225–29. Dietrich Bonhoeffer Works 16. Minneapolis: Fortress, 2006.

Book, Stephen. *Book on Acting: Improvisation Technique for the Professional Actor in Film, Theater & Television.* Los Angeles: Silman-James, 2002.

Branson, Mark Lau, and Juan F. Martinez. *Churches, Cultures & Leadership: A Practical Theology of Congregations and Ethnicities.* Downers Grove, IL: IVP Academic, 2011.

Bratt, James D., ed. *Abraham Kuyper: A Centennial Reader.* Grand Rapids: Eerdmans, 1998.

Brooks, David. *The Road to Character.* New York: Random House, 2015.

Brown, Francis, S. Driver, C. Briggs, eds. *The Brown-Driver-Briggs Hebrew and English Lexicon.* Peabody, MA: Hendrickson, 1994.

Bruce, F. F. *1 and 2 Thessalonians.* WBC 45. Dallas: Word, 1982.

Brueggemann, Walter. *Genesis.* Interpretation Series. Louisville: Westminster John Knox, 1982.

Calvin, John. *The Institutes of the Christian Religion.* Translated by Floyd Lewis Battles. Edited by John T. McNeill. Philadelphia: Westminster, 1960.

Carson, Clayborne, and Peter Holloran, eds. *A Knock at Midnight: Inspiration from the Great Sermons of Reverend Martin Luther King, Jr.* New York: Warner, 1998.

Carson, D. A. *How Long, O Lord?: Reflections on Suffering and Evil.* Grand Rapids: Baker, 1990.

Collins, C. John. *Genesis 1–4: A Linguistic, Literary and Theological Commentary.* Phillipsburg, NJ: P&R, 2006.

Conn, Harvey. *Evangelism: Doing Justice and Preaching Grace.* Phillipsburg, NJ: P&R, 1982.

Cross, Terry L. *The People of God's Presence: An Introduction to Ecclesiology.* Grand Rapids: Baker Academic, 2019.

Davenport, Beth, and Elizabeth Mandel. "Pushing the Elephant." *Independent Lens.* PBS. Premiered March 29, 2011. https://www.pbs.org/independentlens/documentaries/pushing-the-elephant.

Davis, Ellen. *Scripture, Culture, Agriculture: An Agrarian Reading of the Bible.* New York: Cambridge University Press, 2008.

Dumbrell, William J. *Covenant and Creation: A Theology of Old Testament Covenants.* Eugene, OR: Wipf and Stock, 2009.

Eastwood, Clint, dir. *Invictus.* Burbank, CA: Warner Brothers, 2009.

Fikkert, Brian, and Steve Corbet. *When Helping Hurts: How to Alleviate Poverty Without Hurting the Poor and Yourself.* Chicago: Moody, 2009.

Bibliography

Frame, John. *The Doctrine of the Christian Life*. Phillipsburg, NJ: P&R, 2008.

Gallo, Carmine. "The Best Speech In The 'Game of Thrones' Finale And Why It Matters To Today's Leaders." *Forbes*, May 22, 2019. https://www.forbes.com/sites/carminegallo/2019/05/22/the-best-speech-in-the-game-of-thrones-finale-and-why-it-matters-to-todays-leaders/#1150ffb072d6.

Glancy, Jennifer A. *Slavery in Early Christianity*. Minneapolis: Fortress, 2006.

Goheen, Michael W. *The Church and Its Vocation: Lesslie Newbigin's Missionary Ecclesiology*. Grand Rapids: Baker Academic, 2018.

Gombis, Timothy G. *The Drama of Ephesians: Participating in the Triumph of God*. Downers Grove, IL: InterVarsity, 2010.

———. "A Radically New Humanity: The Function of the *Haustafel* in Ephesians." *JETS* 48.2 (June 2005) 317–30.

Gorman, Michael J. *Apostle of the Crucified Lord. A Theological Introduction to Paul and His Letters*. 2nd ed. Grand Rapids: Eerdmans, 2017.

———. "You Shall Be Cruciform for I am Cruciform: Paul's Trinitarian Reconstruction of Holiness." In *Holiness and Ecclesiology in the New Testament*, edited by Ken Brower and Andy Johnson, 148–66. Grand Rapids: Eerdmans, 2007.

Gornik, Mark R. *To Live in Peace. Biblical Faith and the Changing Inner City*. Grand Rapids: Eerdmans, 2002.

Gorringe, T. J. *A Theology of the Built Environment: Justice, Empowerment, Redemption*. Cambridge: Cambridge University Press, 2002.

Green, Joel. *Body, Soul, and Human Life: The Nature of Humanity in the Bible*. Grand Rapids: Baker Academic, 2008.

———. "The Problem of a Beginning: Israel's Scriptures in Luke 1–2." *Bulletin for Biblical Research* 4 (1994) 61–85.

Guder, Darrell. "The Worthy Walk of the Missional Congregation." Payton Lectures, Fuller Theological Seminary, 2007. https://podcasts.apple.com/us/podcast/missional-leadership-after-christendom-2007-payton/id380159850.

Hall, Douglas John. *Imaging God: Dominion as Stewardship*. Grand Rapids: Eerdmans, 1986.

Harrison Center. #porchpartyindy. https://www.harrisoncenter.org/porch.

———. "Three Years of PreEnact Indy." https://www.harrisoncenter.org/preenact-indy.

Hart, Ian. "Genesis 1:1–2:3 as a Prologue to the Book of Genesis." *Tyndale Bulletin* 46.2 (1995) 315–336.

Hauerwas, Stanley. *Performing the Faith: Bonhoeffer and the Practice of Nonviolence*. Grand Rapids: Brazos, 2004.

Hays, Richard B. *The Moral Vision of the New Testament: A Contemporary Introduction to New Testament Ethics*. New York: Harper Collins, 1996.

Heim, Erin M. *Adoption in Galatians and Romans: Contemporary Metaphor Theories and the Pauline* huiouthesia *Metaphors*. Biblical Interpretation Series. Leiden: Brill, 2017.

Hoekema, Anthony A. *Created in God's Image*. Grand Rapids: Eerdmans, 1986.

Hunsberger, George R. *The Story that Chooses Us: A Tapestry of Missional Vision*. The Gospel and Our Culture. Grand Rapids: Eerdmans, 2015.

Hurtado, Larry W. *Destroyer of the gods: Early Christian Distinctiveness in the Roman World*. Waco, TX: Baylor University Press, 2016.

Ince, Nabil (stage name Seaux Chill). Words and Music, "New Normal," Used with permission. https://harrisoncenter.org/preenact-indy.

Jennings, Willie James. *Acts*. Belief: A Theological Commentary on the Bible. Louisville: Westminster John Knox, 2017.

Johnson, Andy. *Holiness and the Missio Dei*. Eugene, OR: Cascade, 2016.

Jones, Sam. *The Off/Camera Show*. Interview with Keegan-Michael Key, The Off Camera Show YouTube Channel. https://www.youtube.com/watch?v=coZARWbdNls.

Joustra, Robert, and Alissa Wilkinson. *How to Survive the Apocalypse: Zombies, Cylons, Faith, and Politics at the End of the World*. Grand Rapids: Eerdmans, 2016.

Keener, Craig S. *The Gospel of John: A Commentary, Volume 1*. Peabody: Hendrickson, 2003.

———. *Acts 1:1–2:47*. Grand Rapids: Baker, 2012.

Keller, Timothy. "Can a Person's Life Be Truly Transformed?" https://thecenterbham. org/2017/07/21/can-a-persons-life-truly-be-transformed/.

———. *Center Church: Doing Balanced Gospel-Centered Ministry in Your City*. Grand Rapids: Zondervan, 2012.

King, Martin Luther, Jr. *Stride Toward Freedom: The Montgomery Story*. New York: Harper & Brothers, 1958.

Krasinski, John. *Some Good News*. SomeGoodNews YouTube Channel. Premiered March 29, 2020. https://www.youtube.com/channel/UCOe_y6KKvS3PdIfb9q9pGug.

Lartney, Jamiles, Jan Diehm, and Aliza Aufrichtig. "Grasping for Change on America's Most Violent Streets: 'We Must Stop Killing.'" *The Guardian*, January 17, 2017. https://www.theguardian.com/world/ng-interactive/2017/jan/10/st-louis-gun-crime-missouri-natural-bridge-avenue.

Lee, Morgan. "My Larry Nassar Testimony Went Viral. But There's More to the Gospel Than Forgiveness." Interview in *Christianity Today*, January 31, 2018. https://www. christianitytoday.com/ct/2018/january-web-only-rachael-denhollander-larry-nassar-forgiveness-gospel.html.

Leithart, Peter. *Did Plato Read Moses? Middle Grace and Moral Consensus*. Biblical Horizons Occasional Paper 23, 1995.

Lewis, C. S. *The Four Loves*. New York: Harper One, 1960.

Lewis, Robert Brian. *Paul's "Spirit of Adoption" in its Roman Imperial Context*. LNTS 545. London: Bloomsbury, 2016.

Lincoln, Andrew T. *Ephesians*. WBC 42. Edited by Bruce M. Metzger, David A. Hubbard, and Glenn W. Barker. Grand Rapids: Zondervan, 1990.

Lodahl, Michael E., and Samuel M. Powell, eds. *Embodied Holiness: Toward a Corporate Theology of Spiritual Growth*. Downers Grove, IL: InterVarsity, 1999.

Lucas, George, dir. *Star Wars: Episode IV—A New Hope*. Lucasfilm, Twentieth Century Fox, 1977.

MacIntyre, Alasdair. *After Virtue: A Study in Moral Theory*. 3rd ed. Notre Dame, IN: University of Notre Dame Press, 2007.

Mandela, Nelson. *Long Walk to Freedom: The Autobiography of Nelson Mandela*. New York: Little, Brown and Company, 1994.

Mapendo, Ruth. "Rose Mapendo." https://en.wikipedia.org/wiki/Rose_Mapendo.

Marsh, Charles. *God's Long Summer: Stories of Faith and Civil Rights*. Princeton, NJ: Princeton University Press, 1997.

———. "What is a Lived Theology?" https://www.livedtheology.org/resources/papers.

Marsh, Charles, Peter Slade, and Sarah Azaransky, eds. *Lived Theology: New Perspectives on Method, Style and Pedagogy*. Oxford: Oxford University Press, 2016.

McBride, Jennifer M. *The Church for the World: A Theology of Public Witness*. New York: Oxford University Press, 2012.

Bibliography

McGrath, Alister. "The Cultivation of Theological Vision: Theological Attentiveness and the Practice of Ministry." In *Perspectives on Ecclesiology and Ethnography*, edited by Peter Ward, 107–23. Grand Rapids: Eerdmans, 2012.

McKinley, John E. "Necessary Allies: God as *ezer*, Woman as *ezer*." Unpublished paper presented at the Evangelical Theological Society 67, Atlanta, 2015.

Mejica, Jonelle. "Sale of Broetje Orchards Creates Firstfruits Farms." *Goodfruit Grower*, February 27, 2019. www.goodfruit.com/sale-of-broetje-orchards-creates-firstfruits-farms/.

Middleton, J. Richard. *The Liberating Image: The Imago Dei in Genesis 1*. Grand Rapids: Brazos, 2005.

Moule, C. F. D. "Fulfillment-Words in the New Testament: Use and Abuse." *NTS* 14 (1967–68) 293–320.

Murray, John. *Principles of Conduct: Aspects of Biblical Ethics*. Grand Rapids: Eerdmans, 1991.

Myers, Bryant L. *Walking with the Poor: Principles and Practices of Transformational Development*. Rev. ed. Maryknoll, NY: Orbis, 2011.

National Conference of Catholic Bishops. *Economic Justice for All: Pastoral Letter on Catholic Social Teaching and the U. S. Economy*. 2nd ed. US Catholic Conference, 1986.

Neely, Alan. "Funeral for Noriko-San." In *Christian Mission: A Case Study Approach*, 51–65. Maryknoll: Orbis, 1995.

Newbigin, Lesslie. *The Finality of Christ*. Richmond, VA: John Knox, 1969.

———. *The Gospel in a Pluralist Society*. Grand Rapids: Eerdmans, 1989.

Perrin, Nicholas. *Jesus the Temple*. Grand Rapids: Baker Academic, 2011.

———. *The Kingdom of God: A Biblical Theology*. Grand Rapids: Zondervan, 2019.

Perry, Gregory R. "Luke's Narrative Shaping of Early Christian Identity." PhD diss., Union Presbyterian Seminary, 2008.

———. "Phoebe of Cenchreae and 'the Women' of Ephesus: Deacons in the Earliest Churche." *Presbyterion* 36.1 (Spring 2010) 9–36.

Pierre, Dennae. "Untitled." Instagram, May 31, 2020. https://www.instagram.com/p/CA1yqW9gVNP/.

Pius XI. *Quadragesimo anno: On Reconstruction of the Social Order* (1931). St. Athanasius, 2016. https://www.vatican.va/content/pius-xi/en/encyclicals/documents/hf_p-xi_enc_19310515_quadragesimo-anno.html.

Plantinga, Cornelius, Jr. *Not the Way It's Supposed to Be: A Breviary of Sin*. Grand Rapids: Eerdmans, 1995.

Pratt, Richard L., Jr. *He Gave Us Stories: The Bible Student's Guide to Interpreting Old Testament Narratives*. Phillipsburg, NJ: P&R, 1993.

———. *Pray with Your Eyes Open: Looking at God, Ourselves, and Our Prayers*. Phillipsburg, NJ: P&R, 1987.

Presbyterian Church (U. S. A.). The Westminster Larger Catechism. In *The Constitution of the Presbyterian Curch (U. S. A.)*, 223–78. Louisville: The Office of the General Assembly, 2016.

Pritchard, James B., ed. *Ancient Near Eastern Texts Relating to the Old Testament with Supplements*. 3rd ed. Princeton, NJ: Princeton University Press, 1969.

———. *The Ancient Near East: An Anthology of Texts and Pictures*. Princeton, NJ: Princeton University Press, 2011.

Rhodes, Michael, and Robbie Holt, with Brian Fikkert. *Practicing the King's Economy: Honoring Jesus in How We Work, Earn, Spend, Save, and Give*. Grand Rapids: Baker, 2018.

Richter, Sandra L. *The Epic of Eden: A Christian Entry into the Old Testament*. Downers Grove, IL: InterVarsity, 2008.

Rowe, C. Kavin. *World Upside Down: Reading Acts in the Graeco-Roman Age*. New York: Oxford University Press, 2009.

Salter, Martin C. *Mission in Action: A Biblical Description of Missional Ethics*. London: Apollos, 2019.

Sayers, Dorothy. *Creed or Chaos?* New York: Harcourt, Brace, and Co., 1949.

Scharen, Christian. *Fieldwork in Theology: Exploring the Social Context of God's Work in the World*. The Church and Postmodern Culture. Edited by James K. A. Smith. Grand Rapids: Baker, 2015.

Shurtleff, Ernest W. "Lead on, O King Eternal." In *The Trinity Hymnal*, 580. Rev. ed. Suwanee, GA: Great Commission Publications, 1990.

Stein, Robert H. *Jesus, the Temple and the Coming of the Son of Man: A Commentary on Mark 13*. Downers Grove, IL: InterVarsity, 2014.

Strange, Daniel. "Not Ashamed? The Sufficiency of Scripture for Public Theology." *Themelios* 36.2 (2011) 238–60.

Taft, Joanna. "PreEnactment Theatre: Fighting Cultural Gentrification." TedX Wabash College. TedX Talks YouTube Channel. https://www.youtube.com/watch?v=nZ-SF0d3du4.

Tidball, Derek. "Holiness: Restoring God's Image (Colossians 3:5–17)." In *Sanctification: Explorations in Theology and Practice*, edited by Kelly Kapic, 256–386. Downers Grove, IL: InterVarsity, 2014.

Vanhoozer, Kevin. *The Drama of Doctrine: A Canonical-Linguistic Approach to Christian Theology*. Louisville: Westminster John Knox, 2005.

———. "A Drama of Redemption Model: Always Performing?" In *Four Views On Moving Beyond the Bible to Theology*, edited by Stanley N. Gundry and Gary T. Meadors, 151–99. Grand Rapids: Zondervan, 2009.

———. *Faith Speaking Understanding: Performing the Drama of Doctrine*. Louisville: Westminster John Knox, 2014.

Vista Hermosa Foundation. "Theory of Change." www.vistahermosafoundation.org/theoryofchange/.

The Wachowskis, dirs. *The Matrix*. Burbank, CA: Warner Brothers, 1999.

Weir, Peter, dir. *The Truman Show*. Los Angeles: Paramount Pictures, 1998.

Wells, Samuel. *Improvisation: The Drama of Christian Ethics*. Grand Rapids: Brazos, 2004.

Wenham, Gordon. *Torah as Story: Reading Old Testament Narrative Ethically*. Grand Rapids: Baker, 2004.

The Westminster Larger Catechism.

Wolterstorff, Nicholas. *Hearing the Call: Liturgy, Justice, Church, and World*. Edited by Mark R. Gornik and Gregory Thompson. Grand Rapids: Eerdmans, 2011.

Wright, Christopher J. H. *The Mission of God. Unlocking the Bible's Grand Narrative*. Downers Grove, IL: IVP Academic, 2006.

———. *The Mission of God's People: A Biblical Theology of the Church's Mission*. Biblical Theology for Life. Edited by Jonathan Lunde. Grand Rapids: Zondervan, 2010.

Wright, N. T. "How Can the Bible Be Authoritative?" *Vox Evangelica* 21 (1991) 7–32.

Bibliography

————. *Jesus and the Victory of God. Christian Origins and the Question of God* 2. Minneapolis: Fortress, 1996.

Ziegenhals, Gretchen E. "Living Out of Abundance." *Faith & Leadership*, November 4, 2014. https://www.faithandleadership.com/living-out-abundance.

Ziegler, Phillip G. *Militant Grace: The Apocalyptic Turn and the Future of Christian Theology*. Grand Rapids: Baker Academic, 2018.

Zwick, Joel, dir. *My Big Fat Greek Wedding*. Santa Monica: CA: Gold Circle Films and Playtone, 2002.

CPSIA information can be obtained
at www.ICGtesting.com
Printed in the USA
JSHW022122040522
25590JS00003B/16